The South
COAST PATH

2010 GUIDE

THE COMPLETE GUIDE
TO THE LONGEST NATIONAL TRAIL
BY THE
SOUTH WEST COAST PATH
ASSOCIATION

(FORMERLY THE SOUTH WEST WAY ASSOCIATION)

South West
Coast Path
Association

 Printed on Recycled Evolution Text Paper with Eco Select Vegetable Oil Based Inks

THE SOUTH WEST COAST PATH ASSOCIATION

Registered as a charity (No. 266754)

*The Association formed to promote the interest of users of the
South West Coast Path*

**South West Coast Path Association
Bowker House
Lee Mill Bridge
Ivybridge, Devon, PL21 9EF
Tel: 01752 896237
Fax: 01752 893654
E-mail: info@swcp.org.uk**

Visit our Website at www.southwestcoastpath.org.uk

CHAIRMAN
Bryan Cath
Harwill House, Victoria Street, Combe Martin, EX34 0JS
Tel: 01271 883487
E-mail: bryan@combewalks.com

TREASURER
Neil Williams
Bowker House
see above
E-mail: neil.williams8@btconnect.com

SECRETARY
Eric Wallis MBE
'Windlestraw', Penquit, Ermington, Devon, PL21 0LU
Tel/Fax: 01752 698048
E-mail: info@swcp.org.uk

ADMINISTRATOR
Liz Wallis
Bowker House
see above

Published by:
The South West Coast Path Association

Trade Sales and Distribution:
Halsgrove,Ryelands Industrial Estate,
Bagley Road, Wellington, TA21 9PZ
Contact: Marie Lewis 01823 653777

Printed in England by Advent, Andover

ISBN 978-0-907055-15-0

Jacket photograph:
Gwynver Beach, West Cornwall, by Bryan Cath

CONTENTS

THE SOUTH WEST COAST PATH

The South West Coast Path National Trail is a 630-mile adventure around the coastline of the south-west peninsula. From Minehead on the edge of the Exmoor National Park all the way to the shores of Poole Harbour, it is simply the best way to enjoy the scenery, wildlife and heritage of this wonderful coastline.

The Coast Path is enjoyed by millions of residents and visitors to the South West every year. The sheer variety means that there are plenty of gentle stretches as well as dramatic headlands and steep coastal valleys where the going can be strenuous and demanding. Relaxation, challenge, tranquillity or inspiration – the choice is yours!

National Trails are walking or riding routes through the country's finest scenery and heritage. They are created and mainly funded by Natural England and managed by Highway Authorities and the National Trust. They receive a high standard of care and are the flagships of the rights of way network. No one in England and Wales lives more than 50 miles from a National Trail.

As a result of the 1999/2000 survey of the full length of the Coast Path using a global positioning system, we now have access to very precise distances – the Coast Path is 630 miles (1014 km) long. The survey carried out by the South West Coast Path Team included the Isle of Portland.

During a 3 year walk of the entire Coast Path, an Association member used a sophisticated altimeter to calculate that the walker who has completed the whole Coast Path will have climbed 115000 feet (35030 m), which is just a little short of walking the height of Mount Everest from sea level four times!

The path passes along some of the finest coastal scenery anywhere, and with its enormous variety and contrast between bustling resort and quiet cove, is a never-ceasing source of delight. This path is the longest National Trail in the country. We think it is the finest, and hope you will too. We certainly know of no other that has as much contrast and variety as ours; try it!

Members receive an Annual Guide as part of their membership plus two Newsletters a year, with up-to-date information on the state of the path.

So here it is - Britain's longest and most beautiful walking trail - read about it, then go for it!

THE SOUTH WEST COAST PATH ASSOCIATION

Dedicated to helping everyone enjoy the path

Thirty-seven years ago the Association was formed by a group of enthusiasts to encourage the development and improvement of the South West Coast Path. This is still one of the main aims of the Association, and it works closely with Natural England, local authorities and other more general user groups such as the Ramblers' Association and the Long Distance Walkers' Association.

Over those thirty-seven years the Association has continuously campaigned for maintenance, signing and alignment improvements. Of primary importance is to have the Coast Path removed from roads. There have been many improvements as long-standing members know, and we like to think we have strongly influenced the implementation of these.

Today one of the Association's functions is to assist and advise all those who wish to walk along this wonderful coastline - whether in short, relaxing strolls around a headland, or by more demanding long distance walks lasting several days, or by heroic attempts at covering the whole length of 630 miles (1014 km) in one go!

The aims and objectives of the South West Coast Path Association

1)   To secure the protection, improvement and preservation of an acceptable South West Coast Path and public access thereto in order to improve the conditions of life of the users of the South West Coast Path.

2)   To educate users of the South West Coast Path to a greater knowledge of, respect and care for the coast and the countryside.

To this end we aim:

1)   To provide advice and information for all who want to walk all or parts of this National Trail known as the South West Coast Path. As the user group it has, and continues to do so, lobbied Highway Authorities to properly maintain and improve it so as to provide the best coastal experiences for all.

2)   To encourage all to take on healthy outdoor walking.

3)   To be committed to help part fund re-alignments of the Coast Path off dangerous roads or to improve views.

4)   To provide advice and information to other charities who use the Coast Path for fundraising walks.

MEMBERSHIP

Subscriptions: Single: £12.50; Joint: £14.00; Associations & Local Authorities: £21.00;

Life Membership: £190.00; Joint Life Membership: £210.00; Non-UK Membership: £19.00.

Payment may be made using a cheque or postal order made payable to the South West Coast Path Association. We can accept the credit/debit cards shown below, providing we have the following information:

Card Number - Start Date - Expiry Date
Full name as it appears on the card
Issue Number (Switch Cards Only)
Last 3 digits on the reverse of the card

A WORD TO BEGINNERS

Long Distance Path Walking

These words are not for those hardy veterans who have all the gear, have done several paths already, and know all about it. We will only say to them at least read the second paragraph of 'Grading' near the beginning of the 'Trail Description' section. However, we do get a number of letters each year from those who have not ventured before on long distance paths and need some advice. This we are pleased to try and provide and we do hope those who read this will find it helpful. However, it is easy to miss out things that folk wish to know, so if you who are new read this, and are still baffled, please contact us and we will try to provide the answers. As well as perhaps helping you, it will enable us to improve this section for another year and so be of help to more people.

Newcomers to the Coast Path

To get the feel of the Coast Path you are advised to take some day walks along it - there are some very good ones on the coast. Better still, look for the sections marked 'Easy' - start at one end and stop and turn back before you have half had enough. We say before half because it is always better to do a bit less and really enjoy it.

You can soon progress to setting out to walk a whole section either by using two cars or using public transport. One point here - if possible use the public transport to go out and walk back to your car or base; this means that you do not get yourself in a position of having to race the clock if you should take a bit more time than you thought.

If you are walking on your own, do please take additional care, for as you will appreciate, if you fall or twist an ankle there can be problems. If you are on your own therefore, you should leave a note with someone to make sure that you arrive at your destination. Not everyone is happy walking on their own and can feel lonely. There is also an added problem that you may try to do too much, so please bear this in mind.

There is no need to buy expensive equipment for the easy sections at the start; a pair of stout shoes and a rainproof jacket is all you need. As you progress, a small rucksack for 'eats' will be needed next.

Obviously if you can join a walking club and go out with them you will collect lots of friendly advice on all sorts of gear you may care to purchase as you become more serious about walking. Maps, guides, etc., are all listed in their appropriate sections.

For Those Who Have Walked, But Not On Long Distance Trails

Day walking on long distance trails is really no different from any other kind of day walking. It is only when you contemplate several days' continuous walking that other considerations arise and there are some pitfalls which even quite experienced day walkers often overlook.

Do not be too ambitious in the distance you plan. Do not carry too much weight of gear.

Having stated the two big points, we will elaborate. You will not be able to accomplish in daily distance the same amount you normally cover in a day walk; you will have to settle for less. The first reason is that you will be carrying more equipment; you must for instance, have a complete change of clothing and footwear, possibly nightwear and toilet kit. For this you need a bigger rucksack so you will be carrying quite a bit more weight than you normally do. Secondly, there is what we call the 'wear' factor. For the first few days until you are really fit, it is just simply more tiring having to walk each day. The last point could be called the 'interest' factor. Usually, if you are walking a long distance path, you are further from your home base, in fresh fields and pastures new; there is more to see so you will need more time to look around.

If you usually accomplish 15 miles (24 km) a day, aim, say, for 12 miles (19 km). This is particularly important if you are booking ahead. You can find yourself tied to a treadmill which you cannot get off. Booking ahead has the advantage that you know there is a bed ahead. On the other hand, it does mean even if you are tired, have developed blisters, and the weather is diabolical, you have to go on. Be guided too by our `Trail Description' section and the terrain you are tackling. 6 miles (10 km), say, of a `Severe' section can equal in effort 10-12 miles (16-19 km) of an 'Easy' one.

We have stated you must carry more gear and this is true. Having said that, think long and hard about every item you imagine you may need. You will be surprised - you may find you will not want it at all. Watch particularly those extras such as cameras and binoculars - they are often a source of considerable weight. One little additional point, many rucksacks, even modern ones, are not as waterproof as you think. A plastic liner, which can be obtained quite cheaply from rambling shops, etc., as an additional inner layer, may save you that most unpleasant discovery after a long day spent in the rain that your only change of clothing is no longer dry. We would also recommend that in addition to this liner, your dry clothing should then be enclosed in further plastic bags to ensure dryness. Trainer shoes are useful for wearing at the end of the day and can be worn on some parts of the path.

A sensible idea before undertaking a long walking holiday is to take, say, a weekend of two or three days first, walking continuously as a practice.

Another point to watch especially on our Coast Path is the availability of refreshment. At main holiday times, you will get it nearly everywhere, except for the few places we especially mention in our 'Trail Description' section. Out of season, you will find it in surprisingly few places on long stretches of coast. The usual remarks about carrying stand-by supplies, therefore, certainly apply; better to carry an extra couple of bars of chocolate than to go hungry.

Walking Alone

The Association has a scheme that enables single female members who are a little nervous about walking alone to team up with other single female members. Contact the Administrator for information.

Easing The Load

On long trips it is a good idea to:

a)   Send guides, maps etc. ahead to larger post offices Poste Restante. The only snag is if you arrive on a Saturday evening.

b)   Start out with a few map-sized envelopes and the smallest available roll of sellotape so that you can despatch finished guides, maps, books etc. home.

c)   Many of our B & B proprietors will transfer your kit to your next destination (see p105).

SOUTH WEST COAST PATH ASSOCIATION PUBLICATIONS

PATH DESCRIPTIONS

Path Descriptions written by our Association are detailed accounts on all aspects of short sections of the Coast Path and include maps and illustrations. They cover in great detail what cannot be included in our Annual Guide book.

Minehead to Porlock Weir (9.5 miles/15.3 km)
Porlock Weir to Lynmouth (12.3 miles/19.8 km)
Lynmouth to Ilfracombe (18 miles/30 km)
Ilfracombe to Croyde Bay (13.6 miles/21.9 km)
Croyde Bay to Barnstaple (14.4 miles/23.1 km)
Barnstaple to Westward Ho! (19.1 miles/30.7 km)
Westward Ho! to Clovelly (11.2 miles/18 km)
Clovelly to Hartland Quay (10.3 miles/16.6 km)
Hartland Quay to Bude (15.4 miles/24.8 km)
Bude to Crackington Haven (10.2 miles/16.4 km)
Crackington Haven to Tintagel (12 miles/20 km)
Tintagel to Port Isaac (8 miles/13 km)
Port Isaac to Padstow (11.7 miles/18.9 km)
Padstow to Porthcothan (13.6 miles/21.8 km)
Porthcothan to Newquay (11.1 miles/17.9 km)
Newquay to Perranporth (10.8 miles/17.5 km)
Perranporth to Portreath (12.2 miles/19.7km)
Portreath to Hayle (12.4 miles/19.9 km)
Hayle to Pendeen Watch (19.5 miles/31.3 km)
Pendeen Watch to Porthcurno (15.6 miles/25.2 km)
Porthcurno to Penzance (11.5 miles/18.5 km)
Penzance to Porthleven (14 miles/22.5 km)
Porthleven to The Lizard (13.9 miles/22.3 km)
The Lizard to Coverack (10.6 miles/17.1 km)
Coverack to Helford (13.1 miles/21.1 km)
Helford to Falmouth (10 miles/16.1 km)
Falmouth to Portloe (13.7 miles/22 km)

Portloe to Mevagissey (12.3 miles/19.8 km)
Mevagissey to Charlestown (7.2 miles/11.6 km)
Charlestown to Fowey (10.3 miles/16.6 km)
Fowey to Polperro (7.1 miles/11.5 km)
Polperro to Looe (5.0 miles/8.0 km)
Looe to Portwrinkle (7.6 miles/12.2 km)
Portwrinkle to Plymouth (13.3 miles/21.4 km)
Plymouth (River Tamar) to Wembury (River Yealm) (14.8 miles/23.8 km)
Wembury (Warren Point) to Bigbury-on-Sea (13.5 miles/21.8 km)
Bigbury to Salcombe (13 miles/21 km)
Salcombe to Torcross (12.9 miles/20.8 km)
Torcross to Dartmouth (10 miles/16 km)
Dartmouth to Brixham (10.8 miles/17.3 km)
Brixham to Torquay (8.4 miles/13.5 km)
Torquay to Shaldon (10.8 miles/17.3 km)
Shaldon to Exmouth (7.9 miles/12.7 km)
Exmouth to Sidmouth (13.1 miles/21 km)
Sidmouth to Lyme Regis (17 miles/27 km)
Lyme Regis to West Bay (9.7 miles/15.6 km)
West Bay to Abbotsbury (9.4 miles/15.2 km)
Abbotsbury to Ferry Bridge (10.9 miles/17.5 km)
Isle of Portland (13.2 miles/21.3 km)
Ferry Bridge to Lulworth Cove (13.2 miles/21.3 km)
Lulworth to Kimmeridge, Lulworth Range (7 miles/11 km)
Kimmeridge to South Haven Point, Poole Harbour (20.9 miles/33.6 km)
Alternative Inland Route, West Bexington to
Osmington Mills (18 miles/28 km)

These Path Descriptions are all priced at £1.00 including UK postage. All are available from the Administrator (see page 2).

(Please note that as each Path Description is revised, we shall be using the new accurate distances accordingly)

A History of the South West Coast Path and the Association

Philip Carter has written a history of the origins of the Coast Path and the Association. It is a fully illustrated hardback book with over 100 black and white photographs, maps and drawings, and also a colour plate section.

Price £19.99 including postage – please add £5.00 for surface mail for non-UK or £9.00 for airmail.

Exploring The South West Coast Path

An illusltrated celebration of the Coast Path with superb aerial photographs by Jason Hawkes and text by Philip Carter. The price includes UK postage. Non-UK postage is extra.

Price £17.49 including postage

The Reverse Guide

The Association has written a description of the Trail for those walking in the Poole to Minehead direction. It deals only with the path so this Annual Guide will be necessary for all the other information. Our Reverse Guide supplement was comprehensively revised in 2008.

Price £3.50 including postage for members of our Association (£4.50 for non-members).

THE ASSOCIATION'S SHOP

Log Book

Why not keep a day by day record of your walk in an easy to carry, pocket size booklet, with a page per section in which to record your daily journey round the Coast Path (all 630 miles / 1014 km!). Whether you do it all in one go or over a period of time, you will have a permanent record of your walks around some of the most beautiful country in the British Isles.

Price £3.50 including postage

2010 Association Calendar

Twelve gorgeous pictures in full colour.

Price £6.50 including postage

Polo Shirt

In an attractive jade green, with the Peninsula map embroidered on the shirt, with 'SOUTH WEST COAST PATH' embroidered around it.

A good quality garment, easy to wash (65% polyester / 35% cotton), in Small, Medium, Large, Extra Large and Extra Extra Large.

Price £18.25 including postage

Sweat Shirt

In bottle green or jade embroidered with the Peninsula map on the left side, and 'SOUTH WEST COAST PATH' around it (70% polyester / 30% cotton). It comes in five sizes, Small, Medium, Large, Extra Large and Extra Extra Large. Other colours are available on request.

Price £25.00 including postage

Sleeveless Fleece

In bottle green with the Peninsula map on the left side and two zip pockets. 100% pill resistant polyester and unlined. Sizes Small, Medium, Large, Extra Large, and Extra Extra Large.

Price £25.00 including postage

Polar Fleece Jacket

In bottle green with the Peninsula map on the left side and two zip pockets. 100% pill resistant, unlined, elasticated hem and cuffs. Sizes Small, Medium, Large, Extra Large, and Extra Extra Large. Other colours are available on request.

Price £27.50 including postage

Wombat Tops

In either navy or red, 100% washed cotton pique with Association logo embroidered in pale grey. Antique effect half zipper, contrasting corduroy inner collar. Dropped back hem. Sizes XS, S, M, L, XL

Price £35.00 including UK postage

Baseball Cap

Available in dark green or stone colour, 100% cotton with embroidered logo. One size adjustable to fit.

Price £7.95 including postage

If in Salcombe you may like to visit Salcombe Embroiderers who stock all the Association clothing with the Coast Path logo. You will find them at Hannaford's Landing, Island Street, Salcombe, TQ8 8FE telephone: 01548 842115

Cloth Badge

Good quality cloth badge, showing the Peninsula map, with 'SOUTH WEST COAST PATH' embroidered below, approximate size 4" x 3" (10 x 8 cm). Suitable for sewing onto shirt or rucksack, coloured map in green and yellow on a blue background.

Price £2.70 including postage

Metal Badge

30mm quality enamel badge suitable for clothing; rucksacks etc. Secured with "butterfly" pin.

Price £3.50 including postage

Coast Path Embroidery

We have designed this unique counted cross stitch embroidery to celebrate the South West Coast Path. The embroidery kit contains everything you need to complete the project. Guidance is also given on how to personalise your embroidery to include your own completion date of the Coast Path.

Price £25.00 including postage

Postcards

Large size, map postcards (35p each including postage) depicting map of whole Coast Path with information on the reverse.

Marker postcards (30p each including postage) depicting the magnificent markers at Minehead and South Haven Point.

Tea Towels

Full cotton tea towel 48 x 78 cm, depicting the end markers and scenes and flowers from locations on the trail. In the centre is a clear map of the whole South West Coast Path.

Price £3.50 including postage

Notelets

The Coast Path Embroidery has been used as the cover design for notelets, which come in packs of 10 and include envelopes.

Price £7.50 including postage

Tumblers

Cut glass tumblers with the Peninsula map sand-blasted on the glass. Suitably packaged.

Price £16.00 each including postage.

Glass Tankards

Glass tankards, plain glass with the Peninsula map sand-blasted onto the glass. Suitably packaged.

Price £12.99 including postage.

Certificates

These lovely colour certificates are available to people who have walked the whole path. They are free to members and cost £3.50 to non-members including postage. Contact the Administrator. Members can have them presented by the Chairman at our next AGM.

Map Poster

A large sized map poster showing the South West Coast Path with the path printed in white enabling walkers to mark off sections walked. Size 64cm x 45cm (25$\frac{1}{4}$" x 17$\frac{3}{4}$").

Price including postage £5.00 (member price), £6.50 (non-member price).

TO ORDER:- Please send details of the sizes of garments and / or quantity required, together with a cheque made payable to: **The South West Coast Path Association** to the Administrator.

We can also accept the credit/debit cards shown below, providing we have the following information:

Card Number - Start Date - Expiry Date
Full name as it appears on the card
Issue Number (if applicable)
Last 3 digits on the reverse of the card

We welcome...

Non UK orders: extra postage will be taken to a maximum of £4.00 depending on the number of items ordered.

BOOKS

These publications are available from bookshops. This list is not exhaustive; there are a number of other books available but we have tried hard to list all those which are really useful and even those not really useful that you might think would be.

South West Coast Path - Minehead to South Haven Point (ISBN 1-85284-379-9)

An excellent pocket sized book by Paddy Dillon. We can recommend it as most useful. It has stunning photographs and OS maps. Available from Cicerone Press, 2 Police Square, Milnthorpe, Cumbria, LA7 7PY at £12.95 and bookshops. Third print 2007 ISBN 978-1-85284-379-3.

National Trail Guides - published by Aurum Press in association with the Countryside Agency. They are available from bookshops, or in case of difficulty, from Aurum Press, 25 Bedford Avenue, London WC1B 3AT. These are good guide books with good maps. An excellent venture by those involved.

Minehead to Padstow by Roland Tarr (May 2004)

Padstow to Falmouth by John Macadam (May 2005)

Falmouth to Exmouth by Brian Le Messurier (June 2006)

Exmouth to Poole by Roland Tarr (May 2004)

LANDFALL WALKS BOOKS - Bob Acton of Devoran has written 16 splendid books that contain well over 100 circular walks in Cornwall. These feature sections of the Coast Path throughout the county. They will enable walkers to progress along the Coast Path by basing themselves at one location. Write to Landfall Publications, Landfall, Penpol, Devoran, Truro, TR3 6NR for full list, or Tel: 01872 862581. E-mail bob.acton@virgin.net

Most Tourist Information Centres (see our Accommodation section) have good supplies of leaflets and books relating to their local areas. We suggest you telephone or write to them and ask what is available.

Other Walking Routes

Two Moors Way - Devon's coast to coast trail links Lynmouth to Ivybridge in South Devon, and the Erme Plym trail links Ivybridge to the coast and Plymouth. There are various trail guides and accommodation guides available. The Two Moors Way Association provide lots of information including maps and certificates. www.twomoorsway.org.uk

Two Moors Way by John Macadam. This is a new recreational guide published by Aurum Press and Ordnance Survey. £12.99. ISBN 1854104586

We recommend the Long Distance Walkers' Handbook 7th edition. It is completely revised and updated, and contains details of 638 routes. Contact LDWA Merchandise, Tim Glenn, 2 Sandy Lane, Beeston, Nottingham, NG9 3GS (12.99 including postage). The Handbook can also be ordered at www.ldwa.org.uk To complement the Handbook there is The Long Distance Path Chart now in its 2nd edition, produced by Harvey's Maps. The chart costs £9.95 and can be ordered as above.

Information on Long Distance Routes can also be obtained from the Ramblers' Association, see page 19.

THE NATIONAL TRUST

THE NATIONAL TRUST 'COAST OF DEVON' LEAFLETS

A series of detailed leaflets with maps is available covering much of the coastline owned by the National Trust in Devon. Each leaflet contains good maps and information on the history, flora and fauna and general information of the areas.

They are available from the Arlington Court Shop, Arlington, Barnstaple, Devon, EX31 4LP tel: 01271 851116 at £1.00 each plus post and packing – see guidelines for 'Coast of Cornwall' leaflets overleaf.

The West Exmoor Coast	Wembury and Aymer Cove
Bideford Bay to Welcombe Mouth	Ilfracombe to Croyde

THE NATIONAL TRUST 'COAST OF CORNWALL' LEAFLETS

A series of detailed leaflets with maps, covering the coastline owned by the National Trust in Cornwall. Each leaflet contains information of the history, flora and fauna of the area as well as general information on points of interest. Available at £1 each from National Trust shops in Cornwall or from Lanhydrock House Shop, Lanhydrock, Bodmin, Cornwall PL30 5AD. Tel: 01208 265952.

Please make cheques payable to The National Trust and include postage & packing (see guidelines following).

No 1	Bude to Morwenstow	£1
No 2	Crackington Haven	£1
No 3	Boscastle	£1
No 4	Tintagel	£1
No 5	Polzeath to Port Quin	£1
No 6	Trevose to Watergate Bay, including Bedruthan Steps (not NT)	£1
No 7	Crantock to Holywell Bay	£1
No 8	St. Agnes and Chapel Porth	£1
No 9	Godrevy to Portreath	£1
No 10	West Penwith: St. Ives to Pendeen	£1
No 11	West Penwith: Levant to Penberth	£1
No 12	Loe Pool and Mount's Bay	£1
No 13	Lizard, West Coast	£1

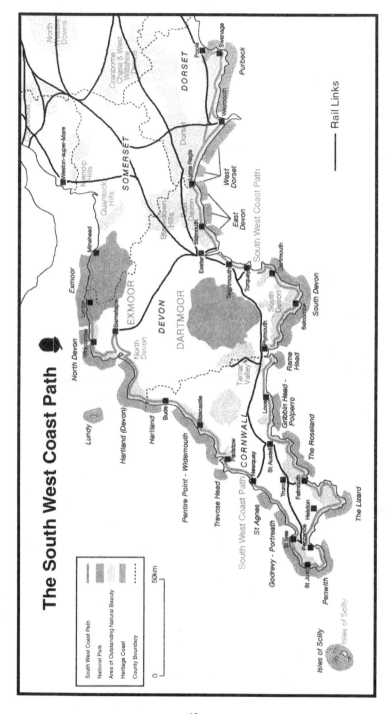

The South West Coast Path

Rail Links

South West Coast Path
National Park
Area of Outstanding Natural Beauty
Heritage Coast
County Boundary

0   50km

No 14	Lizard, Kynance, Lizard Point & Bass Point	£1
No 15	Lizard, East Coast, Landewednack to St. Keverne	£1
No 16	Helford River	£1
No 17	Trelissick	£1
No 18/19	The Roseland and St Anthony Head	£1
No 20	Nare Head and the Dodman	£1
No 21	Fowey	£1
No 22	East Cornwall	£1

Country Walks Leaflet : Cotehele Estate £1
Country Walks Leaflet : Lanhydrock £1

Godolphin £1

When ordering, please add the following rates for postage and packaging:

Quantity	1st Class
1-3	50p
4-8	75p
9-11	£1.00
12 & over	£2.00

THE NATIONAL TRUST WESSEX REGION

The following illustrated walks leaflets are available from the National Trust Holnicote Estate Office. To order, please send a cheque (including 50p postage) to the National Trust, Holnicote Estate Office, Selworthy, Minehead, Somerset, TA24 8TJ. Tel: 01643 862452.

Holnicote (Horner Wood)
- Valley Walk £0.60
- Hill Walk £0.60

Holnicote - Bossington and Coastline Walk £0.60

Holnicote - Allerford and Selworthy woods walk £0.60

Holnicote - Dunkery and Horner Wood £0.60

Holnicote - Luccombe and Woodland £0.60

Holnicote - Selworthy and Bury Castle £0.60

Holnicote - Upland Archaeology £0.60

(All the above leaflets are available as a walks pack priced £3.99)

Explore Holnicote £1.00

Holnicote - Selworthy £0.60

Holnicote - Working with Nature at Porlock Bay £1.00

Isle of Purbeck (5 walks) - telephone for current price

An illustrated walking pack entitled 'Circular walks along the Dorset and East Devon Coast' is available from the National Trust West Dorset office, priced at £3.95 per pack plus £1.00 post and packing. To order, please send a cheque to the National Trust, West Dorset Office, The Court, Charmouth, Bridport, Dorset, DT6 6PE. Telephone: 01297 561900.

NATIONAL TRUST REGIONAL MARKETING AND COMMUNICATIONS MANAGERS

Devon and Cornwall Regional Office, Killerton House, Broadclyst, Exeter, Devon EX5 3LE Tel: 01392 881691.

Wessex Regional Office, (for Dorset and Somerset) Eastleigh Court, Bishopstrow, Warminster, Wilts. BA12 9HW Tel: 01985 843600.

RAILWAYS

Throughout the year there is a regular service of direct First Great Western High Speed services linking London Paddington with Taunton, Exeter St. David's, Newton Abbot, Plymouth and Cornwall. There are also regular Arriva Cross Country Trains services linking Birmingham, the North West, North East and Scotland with Taunton, Exeter St. David's, Plymouth, Cornwall, Bournemouth and Poole. All these services offer a range of on-train facilities including catering and on most First Great Western High Speed services during the school holidays, coach E is dedicated for the use of families. During the high season (May to September), demand for seats is high so it is recommended that seats are reserved in advance to ensure a comfortable journey. On Saturdays, additional services run to and from the West Country to the Midlands, North of England and London with a direct service operated between London and Newquay during the summer only.

There is a regular South West Trains' service linking London Waterloo with Bournemouth, Poole, Wareham (for Swanage), and Weymouth for those who intend to walk the Dorset end of the Coast Path. East Devon is served by an approximate two hourly service from London Waterloo to Axminster (for Lyme Regis and Seaton) and Honiton (for Sidmouth). In addition to these services South West Trains also offer a service of trains linking London Waterloo, Basingstoke, Salisbury, Exeter Central, Paignton and Plymouth.

First Great Western West offers long distance and most local trains in the South West. The long distance trains link Cardiff and Bristol with Exeter, Penzance, Plymouth, Portsmouth, Salisbury, Southampton and Weymouth. The local services on the branch lines of Devon and Cornwall offer connections into and out of First Great Western High Speed, South West Trains and Arriva services. First Great Western West local routes run regular Sunday services on the routes listed below during the summer, with those asterisked* routes operating a Sunday service during the winter months also

* Westbury - Yeovil - Weymouth	Liskeard - Looe
* Exeter - Barnstaple	Par - Newquay
* Exeter - Exmouth	*Truro - Falmouth
* Newton Abbot -Torquay - Paignton	*St Erth - St Ives
* Plymouth - Gunnislake	

To obtain train information, book tickets and reserve seats call the National Rail Enquiries Service on 08457 484950 (24 hours a day) or via the website www.nationalrail.co.uk The web address for First Great Western High Speed and West services is www.firstgreatwestern.co.uk The web address for Arriva is www.crosscountrytrains.co.uk The web address for South West Trains is www.southwesttrains.co.uk

Private Branch Line Railways

Bishops Lydeard to Minehead - The West Somerset Railway PLC runs steam trains through 20 scenic miles (32 km) to Minehead. Bishops Lydeard is 4 miles (6 km) outside Taunton and easily accessible by bus. The service operates between March and October. For details contact the company at 'The Railway Station', Minehead TA24 5BG Tel: 01643 704996. The web address is www.west-somerset-railway.co.uk

Paignton to Kingswear (Dartmouth) - For the rambler who is also a railway enthusiast, the Paignton and Dartmouth Steam Railway is a `must'. This most attractive line runs from Paignton to Goodrington, Churston and Kingswear and operates preserved Great Western steam locomotives and rolling-stock. The line passes through some delightful coastal and river scenery, and a trip on the railway could easily be combined with a walk to make a very pleasant day out. Steam trains operate on selected dates in April, May and October; daily June - September; Santa specials in December. For details contact - Queens Park Station, Torbay Road, Paignton TQ4 6AF Tel: 01803 555872 www.paignton-steamrailway.co.uk.

The Bodmin & Wenford Railway runs between Bodmin Parkway to Bodmin Town is a service that could prove useful for those requiring bus transport to the coast. Tel: 0845 125 9678, www.bodminandwenfordrailway.co.uk.

The Swanage Railway which links a large park and ride facility to Swanage could also prove useful for those requiring car parking (not long stay) with access by rail to the Coast Path. If you require information contact the enquiry line on 01929 425800 or their web site at www.swanagerailway.co.uk

BUS SERVICES

A National Transport Enquiry Service has been established. For all timetable enquiries in South West England, call Traveline on 0871 200 2233 or www.travelinesw.com. The main bus operative contact details are: First Devon and Cornwall Tel: 0845 600 1420 www.firstgroup.com.

Tourist Information Centres can be very helpful with bus enquiries. For details of all coastal TICs see our Accommodation section at the back of this book.

ACCESS TO THE START OF THE PATH:
Access to the start of the path can be made locally and from outside the region, with First's bus service 28 linking Minehead to the mainline railway station at Taunton.

Service 28 Taunton-Minehead currently operates on an half-hourly frequency up to the early evenings from Monday to Saturdays. On Sundays service 28 operates less frequently. For service 28 timetable enquiries telephone First - Taunton. Tel: 01823 272033.

National Express operates some direct services to Minehead and others to Taunton where passengers can change to First Service 28 for Minehead. For more information about national coach services to the South West, telephone National Express Tel: 0870 580 8080 (this is charged at local call rates).

BUS INFORMATION:
Listed below, in path order, are details of services and information available from County Councils and local bus operators; it is intended for guidance use only. All information provided is correct at the time of going to print; responsibility for any inaccuracies or changes cannot be accepted by County Councils or bus operators. For up to date bus service information, telephone the relevant numbers given in the following paragraphs.

SOMERSET:
For service 28 from Taunton to Minehead and services 30/30A from Taunton to Lyme Regis and Weymouth via Axminster (change buses) contact First, The Bus Station, Tower Street, Taunton, TA1 4AF Tel: 01823 272033.

Somerset County Council produces 4 district area booklets detailing the timetables of all public bus services. It also produces a Sunday services leaflet, various tourist bus service leaflets and the Somerset Rail Guide, which details all train services operating through the county, along with information about the West Somerset Railway. All literature can be obtained from Transporting Somerset, County Hall, Taunton, TA1 4DY. Tel: 0845 345 9155
E-mail: transport@somerset.gov.uk Website: www.somerset.gov.uk/publictransport

NORTH DEVON:
The North Devon coast has a range of bus services which may be of use to coastal walkers. The greatest choice of coastal destinations is provided from Barnstaple. The principal services are: 309/310 Barnstaple to Lynton; Services 3, 30 Barnstaple to Ilfracombe and Combe Martin; 308 Barnstaple to Georgeham; 303 Barnstaple, 301 to Woolacombe; 1, Barnstaple to Bideford and Westward Ho!; 2 Barnstaple to Bideford and Appledore and 319 Barnstaple to Bideford, Clovelly and Hartland. Also 21 Barnstaple to Bideford and Westward Ho! and 21A Barnstaple to Bideford and Appledore. Note that the number prefix refers to the bus route number. During the Summer, Exmoor Coastlink 300 operates daily from Ilfracombe to Lynton, Lynmouth, Porlock and Minehead, with glorious coastal views along much of the route.

Those who are not walking the entire path in one go may find the First Devon and Cornwall X9 service from Exeter to Bude a useful link to or from the coast Western Greyhound 599.

The above services are operated by First Devon and Cornwall, Filers Travel, Quantock Motor Services, Stagecoach South West and TW Coaches. For timetable enquiries telephone Traveline - 0871 2002233, 0700-2100 daily, www.traveline.org.uk

Devon County Council produces timetable guides summer and winter entitled 'North Devon Public Transport Guide'. They are available from Tourist Information Centres, Libraries, bus operators or by telephoning the DevonBus enquiry line Barnstaple: 01271 382800 or Exeter 01392 382800, Monday - Friday 0900-1700. Email: devonbus@devon.gov.uk Website: www.devon.gov.uk/devonbus

CORNWALL:
Cornwall Council, in conjunction with local bus operators, produce a series of 4 public transport

guides covering the west, mid, north and south east parts of Cornwall. The guides are published twice yearly in May and September and cover the whole of Cornwall. They are available from Passenger Transport, Cornwall Council, Fal Building, County Hall, Truro, TR1 3AY, Tel: 0300 1234 222. The timetable can also be obtained locally from bus stations, Tourist Information Centres and libraries, as can a county public transport map showing all bus and rail routes with a summary of frequencies.

Public transport information can be obtained from Traveline 0871 200 22 33, www.traveline.org.uk. The main bus operative contact details are: First Devon and Cornwall Tel: 0845 600 1420 www.firstgroup.com; Western Greyhound Tel: 01637 871871 www.westerngreyhound.com

The principal routes serving coastal areas are:

First Services 1 Penzance to Land's End, 2 Penzance to Helston to Falmouth, 17 St Ives to Penzance to St Just, 25 St Austell to Fowey, 26 Mevagissey to St Austell, 33 The Lizard to Helston, 34 Helston to Truro, 81 Cremyll to Plymouth, 82 Truro to Helston, 85 Truro to St Agnes, 88 Truro to Falmouth, 300 Penzance to St Ives (summer only), X9 Exeter to Bude.

Western Greyhound services 500 Truro to Falmouth and Helford Passage, 501 Penzance to Land's End, 504 Penzance to Mousehole to Porthcurno to Land's End to St Just, 508 Penzance to Zennor to St Ives, 510 Newquay to Wadebridge to Camelford and Exeter, 515 Penzance to Hayle to Gwithian, 516 Penzance to Nancledra to St Ives, 524 (evenings and Sundays only) St Austell to Fowey, 525 St Austell to Par, 526 St Austell to Mevagissey to Gorran Haven, 550/551 Truro to Veryan and St Mawes, 555 Bodmin Parkway to Bodmin to Wadebridge to Padstow, 556 Newquay to Padstow, 572 Looe to Plymouth, 573 Polperro to Looe to Liskeard, 581 Liskeard to Torpoint, 584 Wadebridge to Port Isaac to Camelford, 587 Newquay to Perranporth to Truro, 594 Boscastle to Camelford to Wadebridge to St Columb Major, 595 Boscastle to Tintagel to Bude, 597 Truro to St Columb Major to Newquay, 599 Exeter to Bude.

Western Greyhound will also operate from Easter 2010 a service between Newquay and St Ives.

ERH Roadcar 281 Polruan to Looe; Summercourt Travel 403 Newquay to Perranporth to St Agnes.

SOUTH DEVON:
The coastline between Plymouth and Exeter is accessible by bus from many inland towns. The principal services are:

80/81 Plymouth to Torpoint; 34 and 34/B Plymouth City Centre and Admirals Hard for Cremyll Ferry (buses meet ferry and through ticket available); 7A Union Street (short walk from Cremyll Ferry) to Mount Batten (54 Bovisand in the summer); 49 Plymouth to Heybrook Bay; 48 Plymouth to Wembury; 94 Plymouth to Noss Mayo; 93 Plymouth to Kingsbridge & Dartmouth; X80 Plymouth to Paignton & Torquay; X38 Plymouth to Exeter; X64 Exeter to Kingsbridge, 164 Totnes to Kingsbridge; 111 Totnes to Dartmouth; 162 Kingsbridge to Hope Cove; 606 Kingsbridge to Salcombe; 120 Kingswear to Paignton; 22, 24 Kingswear to Brixham; 12 Brixham & Paignton to Torquay and Newton Abbot; 32T Torquay to Teignmouth; 2 (Newton Abbot) Teignmouth, Dawlish and Exeter. 85A Newton Abbot to Teignmouth, Dawlish and Exeter.

25 Goodrington to Paignton and Stoke Gabriel; 17 Brixham to Furzeham, Wall Park and The Quay; X46 Paignton to Torquay and Exeter; 88 Paignton to Totnes, Buckfastleigh, Ashburton and Newton Abbot; X80 Torquay to Paignton, Totnes, Ivybridge and Plymouth.

The above services are operated by First, Tally Ho, Plymouth Citybus, Stagecoach South West and Dart Pleasure Craft. For timetable enquiries telephone Traveline on 0871 200 2233.

Devon County Council produce timetables, guides summer and winter for the South Hams and Teignbridge areas. They are available from Devon bus on Traveline 0871 200 2233.

Plymouth Citybus map and services are available from from Plymouth Citybus on 01752 662271 or www.citycoach.co.uk.

EAST DEVON:
The East Devon coastline is accessible by bus from Exeter, Ottery St. Mary, Honiton and

Axminster. The principal services are:

X53 Exeter to Beer, Seaton, Lyme Regis, Bridport, West Bay and Weymouth; X53 Exeter to Wareham, Poole, Bournemouth; 20 Taunton to Seaton; 57 Exeter to Exmouth, change Exmouth for service 157 (through fares available) to Budleigh Salterton and Sidmouth; 52A Exeter to Sidmouth & Seaton; 52B Exeter to Sidmouth & Honiton; 382 Ottery St. Mary to Sidmouth; 885 Axminster to Seaton; 30 Taunton to Axminster change at Axminster for service 31 (through fares available) 31 Taunton to Axminster to Lyme Regis (and continues to Bridport, Dorchester and Weymouth); 899 Sidmouth to Branscombe, Beer and Seaton. On Summer Sundays service 379 operates between Sidmouth, Honiton, Ottery St Mary & Exeter.

The above services are operated by Stagecoach South West, Axe Valley Mini-Travel and First Hampshire and Dorset. For timetable enquiries telephone Traveline public transport info. (Tel: 0871 200 2233) daily 0700-2100.

Devon County Council produces timetable guides summer and winter, entitled 'East Devon Public Transport Guide'- they are available from Tourist Information Centres, libraries, bus operators or by telephoning the DevonBus enquiry line on Exeter (Tel: 01392 382800) Monday-Friday 0900-1700.

Bus Map - Other useful information provided by Devon County Council includes the public transport map. This depicts all bus routes and railway lines throughout the county and gives a summary of service frequency. It is available from Tourist Information Centres, libraries and bus stations or by telephoning the DevonBus enquiry line on Barnstaple (Tel: 01271 382800) or Exeter (Tel: 01392 382800) Monday-Friday 0900-1700.

DORSET:
The Dorset Coast is accessible by bus from various inland points with train connections for the distant traveller. The principal routes are listed below.

Service 31 provides hourly journeys from Mondays to Saturdays between Weymouth-Dorchester-Bridport-Lyme Regis and Axminster, calling at Axminster and Dorchester South rail stations for onward travel. The service operates until late in the evening. There is a two hourly service along the same route on Sundays. Passengers benefit from low floor buses that provide easy access and greater comfort. Contact First Hampshire and Dorset. Tel: 01305 783645.

Service 103 operates from Mondays to Saturdays between Dorchester-Lulworth-Durdle Door-Wool and Bovington. This service is a mixture of fixed and bookable journeys. Tel: 'door to dorset' on 0845 6024547 for information.

Service X53 is fully accessible and operates several journeys each day between Poole-Wareham-Weymouth-Lyme Regis and Exeter. During the winter, the Sunday service is reduced and operates between Waymouth and Exeter. Details from First Hampshire and Dorset, see above.

Service 40 runs daily between Poole, Swanage and Wareham. Service 44 operates between Swanage, Harmans Cross and Worth Matravers from Monday to Saturday. Details from Wilts & Dorset Bus Company, Tel: 01202 673555.

Service 50 operates daily between Bournemouth and Swanage via the Sandbanks Ferry. Service 52 runs from the ferry into Poole daily during the summer and from Mondays to Saturdays during the winter (NB no Sunday service). Details from Wilts & Dorset Bus Company, see above.

Frequent services run to Portland from Weymouth and Dorchester. They are mainly operated by First Hampshire and Dorset, details above.

Dorset County Council produces comprehensive timetable information including a countywide Bus and Rail Map along with two Jurassic Coast Maps – one for Purbeck and one for West Dorset. The Jurassic Maps include enhanced map details and timetables. All information is available from Tourist Information Centres or Dorset Passenger Transport, County Hall, Dorchester, DT1 1XJ. Tel: 01305 225165 or E-mail dorsetpassegertransport@dorsetcc.gov.uk. Timetables can be downloaded at www.dorsetforyou.com/bustimes

KIT TRANSFER AND ARRANGED COAST PATH WALKS

KIT TRANSFER
Coast Path walking can be arduous in places but some of the hard work can be eliminated. We

have been informed that the use of local taxis can ease the muscles. Transport is not for the walker, naturally, but for rucksack transfer from B&B to B&B. Local taxi firms will be pleased to give a price for the service. Consult yellow pages or ask the locals for details of taxi operators.

By referring to our accommodation section it will be seen that many of our B&Bs will, for a fee, move your kit along.

LUGGAGE TRANSFERS SOUTH WEST

2009 saw the start of a new service by South West Coast Path Association member Ben Charity and his partner Mike Kearon. They have formed a luggage transfer business called Luggage Transfers.

Walkers can now access this service along the South West Coast Path from just £13 per transfer of two bags, a price that is attracting literally thousands of transfers in just the opening months of the business. The volume movement of bags means that deliveries can be 'daisy chained' along the various routes.

They also insure luggage at £250 per bag during the transfer process to provide peace of mind. Luggage Transfers can be contacted on 0800 043 7927 or visit www.luggagetransfers.co.uk. You can book your entire route on-line, just make sure you have your accommodation details to hand and you will have a quote back within hours.

As well as offering a great service to walkers the company will also be helping raise money to help the South West Coast Path Association's improvement fund.

WALKING HOLIDAY COMPANIES

For those who require a Coast Path walk without carrying rucksacks and have their accommodation fixed in advance there are several businesses that will arrange everything. All you have to do is let them know your requirements and pay them. Also there are some excellent organisations that run walking holidays with guides. The South West Coast Path Association realised that there are too many to be listed in this guide so we have created a small booklet with these companies listed. We will supply it at a cost of £1.50. Contact the Administrator at Bowker House, see page 2.

SEA TRANSPORT AND COASTAL CRUISES

The famous pleasure steamers Waverley and Balmoral provide both cruises and transport, to and from the Exmoor Coast.

From May until late September these sea-going ships provide transport to South Wales, Bristol, North Somerset, Lundy Island and the Exmoor Coast.

Sailings are to and from Ilfracombe, Bideford & Minehead. The timetable is subject to the Bristol Channel tides which have the second highest rise and fall in the world. Free copies of the full programme are available from Waverley Excursions Ltd., The Waverley Terminal, 36 Lancefield Quay, Glasgow G3 8HA www.waverleyexcursions.co.uk - telephone 0845 1304647, or from Tourist Information Centres in West Somerset and North Devon.

AIRPORTS

There are airports in or near towns close to the Coast Path. In path order, they are:

Newquay Airport (for flights to and from Plymouth and flights to and from the Isles of Scilly): St Mawgan, NEWQUAY, TR8 4RQ.
Tel: 01637 860600 Website: www.newquaycornwallairport.com

Land's End (for flights to the Isles of Scilly): Information from Isles of Scilly Travel, Steamship House, Quay Street, PENZANCE, TR18 4BZ.
Tel: 01736 334220 Website: www.islesofscilly-travel.co.uk

Penzance (for flights to the Isles of Scilly): British International, Eastern Green, Jelbert Way, PENZANCE, TR18 3AP.
Tel: 01736 363871 Website: www.islesofscillyhelicopter.com

Plymouth: Plymouth City Airport, North Quay House, Sutton Harbour, PLYMOUTH. PL4 0RA.
Tel: 01752 204090 Website: www.plymouthairport.com

Exeter: Exeter International Airport, EXETER, EX5 2BD.
Tel: 01392 446446 Website: www.exeter-airport.co.uk

Bournemouth: Bournemouth Airport Ltd., CHRISTCHURCH, BH23 6SE.
Tel: 01202 364000 Website: www.bournemouthairport.com

USEFUL ADDRESSES

COAST PATH MANAGERS

South West Coast Path Team, Matford Lane Offices, County Hall, Exeter, EX2 4QW. Tel: 01392 383560
Natural England, Level 8, Renslade House, Bonhay Road, Exeter, EX4 3AW. Tel: 01392 889770
Exmoor National Park Authority, Exmoor House, Dulverton, Somerset, TA22 9HL.
Tel: 01398 323665; Fax: 01398 323150; E-mail: info@exmoor-nationalpark.gov.uk
Website: www.exmoor-nationalpark.gov.uk
Devon County Council, County Hall, Exeter, Devon, EX2 4QD.Tel: 0845 155 1015
Cornwall Council, County Hall, Truro, Cornwall, TR1 3AY. Tel: 0300 1234 100
Dorset County Council, County Hall, Dorchester, Dorset, DT1 1XJ. Tel: 01305 221000

RAMBLERS' ASSOCIATION CONTACTS

Ramblers' Association, Second Floor, Camelford House, 87-90 Albert Embankment, London,
SE1 7TW. Tel: 0207 339 8500; Fax: 0207 339 8501; E-mail: ramblers@ramblers.org.uk;
Website: www.ramblers.org.uk
Somerset – www.somersetramblers.co.uk
Devon – www.devonramblers.co.uk
Cornwall – www.racornwall.org.uk
Dorset – www.dorset-ramblers.co.uk

MAPS

We are sometimes asked if you require a map sheet as well as a guide book and our advice is
certainly yes. One does not get as badly lost on the Coast Path as you can on inland paths, but a
map is an asset nonetheless. Furthermore many walkers derive much interest from looking at
their route in relation to the rest of the countryside on ordinary walks, and the same applies just
as much, if not more so, on our Coast Path. The National Trail Guides offer a partial solution with
their maps, but even these are not as useful as a map sheet.

Harvey Maps

Walk for a week with just one map - those who have walked in the Scottish Highlands or the
Lake District will know of Harvey Maps.

Produced at a scale of 1:40 000 the walkers' maps for the South West Coast Path are ideal for
this National Trail which, because it is following a geological feature, i.e. the coast, route finding
does not usually present any real difficulties.

Six maps cover the entire route of the Coast Path compared with fourteen OS Landranger maps
or seventeen OS Explorer/Outdoor Leisure maps. The maps have a similar amount of detail as
Landranger maps for the walker yet without the administrative symbols that sometimes
obscure the detail. The maps are of a more manageable size (folding to approx 240 x 120mm
or 9.52" x 4.68") and are waterproof. Weight wise (without the wallet) they are a mere 58 g
compared with Landrangers at 82 g and Explorers at 110 g (without their card covers). Another
useful feature is the provision on areas of the map not needed for walking (in this case the sea)
of much important information about the Trail and services along the way.

Map 1   Minehead to Bude
Map 2   Bude to Portreath
Map 3   Portreath to Lizard
Map 4   Lizard to Plymouth
Map 5   Plymouth to Sidmouth
Map 6   Sidmouth to Poole

They are priced at £9.95 each and are becoming more widely available at branches of Waterstone's and Cotswold Outdoors (or direct from Harvey Maps). For further details visit www.harveymaps.co.uk or telephone 01786 841202, fax 01786 841098, sales@harveymaps.co.uk,   They offer the complete set for £49.75.

1:50 000 Ordnance Survey Maps

The Metric 1:50 000 Landranger Series needed to cover the coast from Minehead in Somerset to Studland in Dorset are as follows, working round the coast from Minehead.

181	Minehead & Brendon Hills	200	Newquay & Bodmin
180	Barnstaple & Ilfracombe	201	Plymouth & Launceston
190	Bude & Clovelly	202	Torbay & South Dartmoor
200	Newquay & Bodmin	192	Exeter & Sidmouth
204	Truro & Falmouth	193	Taunton & Lyme Regis
203	Land's End & The Lizard	194	Dorchester & Weymouth
204	Truro & Falmouth	195	Bournemouth & Purbeck

1:25 000 Ordnance Survey Maps

In path order, from Minehead the Coast Path is on $2\frac{1}{2}$" maps.

Outdoor Leisure 9	- Exmoor
Explorer 139	- Bideford, Ilfracombe and Barnstaple
Explorer 126	- Clovelly and Hartland
Explorer 111	- Bude, Boscastle and Tintagel
Explorer 109	- Bodmin Moor (depicts Coast Path from Boscastle to Portgaverne)
Explorer 106	- Newquay and Padstow
Explorer 104	- Redruth, St Agnes, Camborne and Perranporth
Explorer 102	- Land's End
Explorer 103	- The Lizard
Explorer 105	- Falmouth and Mevagissey
Explorer 107	- St Austell and Liskeard
Explorer 108	- Lower Tamar Valley and Plymouth
Explorer OL20	- South Devon
Explorer 110	- Torquay and Dawlish
Explorer 115	- Exmouth and Sidmouth
Explorer 116	- Lyme Regis and Bridport
Outdoor Leisure 15	- Purbeck and South Dorset

All Harvey and OS maps can be obtained from most bookshops. They, including Harvey Maps, may also be obtained from KenRoy Thompson Limited, 25 Cobourg Street, Plymouth, PL1 1SR (Tel: 01752 227693 E-mail: maps@kenroythompson.co.uk Website: kenroythompson.co.uk) POST FREE TO UK MEMBERS OF THE SOUTH WEST COAST PATH ASSOCIATION (Credit cards accepted).

BANKS

We suggest you contact your own bank for a list of where their branches along the trail are located. There are small Post Offices in most villages. Overseas visitors, we suggest, will find their cashpoint cards very useful.

TELEPHONES

Mobile phones sometimes will not work in remote places and it's reassuring to see a public telephone box just when you need it. However, many of these remote telephones have recently been converted to only take debit cards. You can use the following cards in these boxes - Switch; Maestro; Delta; Solo; Visa Debit but not Electron. There are still some telephone boxes which will accept BT Phonecards and all boxes will accept BT Chargecards (these are only available to BT landline customers).   (Continued on page 23)

TIDE TABLES 2009 (BASED ON DEVONPORT)

MARCH 2010
LOW WATER
From 28th, add 1 hour for BST

Days		Morning Time	Afternoon Time
1	Mo	0002	1229
2	Tu	0047	1312
3	We	0128	1351
4	Th	0206	1428
5	Fr	0241	1501
6	Sa	0315	1534
7	Su	0351	1611
8	Mo	0435	1700
9	Tu	0538	1812
10	We	0710	2015
11	Th	0913	2133
12	Fr	1003	2219
13	Sa	1044	2259
14	Su	1121	2335
15	Mo	1155	----
16	Tu	0007	1225
17	We	0037	1253
18	Th	0103	1319
19	Fr	0129	1345
20	Sa	0155	1412
21	Su	0224	1442
22	Mo	0300	1521
23	Tu	0347	1616
24	We	0501	1749
25	Th	0655	1937
26	Fr	0827	2058
27	Sa	0935	2200
28	Su	1031	2252
29	Mo	1120	2339
30	Tu	----	1205
31	We	0023	1247

APRIL 2010
LOW WATER
add 1 hour for BST

Days		Morning Time	Afternoon Time
1	Th	0103	1325
2	Fr	0141	1401
3	Sa	0216	1434
4	Su	0250	1506
5	Mo	0326	1542
6	Tu	0409	1630
7	We	0509	1739
8	Th	0627	1905
9	Fr	0811	2039
10	Sa	0917	2135
11	Su	1001	2218
12	Mo	1039	2256
13	Tu	1115	2331
14	We	1149	----
15	Th	0005	1222
16	Fr	0037	1254
17	Sa	0109	1325
18	Su	0140	1357
19	Mo	0215	1434
20	Tu	0256	1518
21	We	0349	1618
22	Th	0504	1742
23	Fr	0639	1915
24	Sa	0802	2031
25	Su	0908	2133
26	Mo	1004	2226
27	Tu	1053	2314
28	We	1139	2358
29	Th	----	1221
30	Fr	0039	1300

MAY 2010
LOW WATER
add 1 hour for BST

Days		Morning Time	Afternoon Time
1	Sa	0118	1337
2	Su	0154	1411
3	Mo	0230	1445
4	Tu	0306	1521
5	We	0348	1606
6	Th	0441	1704
7	Fr	0545	1813
8	Sa	0654	1924
9	Su	0801	2029
10	Mo	0858	2123
11	Tu	0947	2210
12	We	1031	2253
13	Th	1113	2334
14	Fr	1153	----
15	Sa	0014	1233
16	Su	0054	1312
17	Mo	0134	1353
18	Tu	0216	1436
19	We	0303	1524
20	Th	0356	1620
21	Fr	0500	1727
22	Sa	0613	1843
23	Su	0727	1956
24	Mo	0835	2101
25	Tu	0934	2158
26	We	1026	2249
27	Th	1114	2336
28	Fr	1158	----
29	Sa	0020	1240
30	Su	0101	1318
31	Mo	0138	1354

JUNE 2010
LOW WATER
add 1 hour for BST

Days		Morning Time	Afternoon Time	Days		Morning Time	Afternoon Time
1	Tu	0214	1428	17	Th	0304	1523
2	We	0250	1503	18	Fr	0352	1611
3	Th	0326	1539	19	Sa	0443	1704
4	Fr	0407	1623	20	Su	0539	1805
5	Sa	0457	1719	21	Mo	0645	1915
6	Su	0555	1823	22	Tu	0757	2028
7	Mo	0658	1928	23	We	0905	2134
8	Tu	0759	2029	24	Th	1004	2231
9	We	0857	2126	25	Fr	1056	2321
10	Th	0951	2219	26	Sa	1143	----
11	Fr	1041	2309	27	Su	0006	1226
12	Sa	1130	2357	28	Mo	0048	1305
13	Su	----	1218	29	Tu	0125	1340
14	Mo	0044	1305	30	We	0159	1411
15	Tu	0131	1351				
16	We	0218	1436				

JULY 2010
LOW WATER
add 1 hour for BST

Days		Morning Time	Afternoon Time	Days		Morning Time	Afternoon Time
1	Th	0230	1440	16	Fr	0253	1509
2	Fr	0259	1508	17	Sa	0335	1551
3	Sa	0328	1537	18	Su	0417	1635
4	Su	0402	1615	19	Mo	0503	1726
5	Mo	0447	1710	20	Tu	0600	1832
6	Tu	0552	1827	21	We	0715	1957
7	We	0707	1943	22	Th	0841	2119
8	Th	0816	2051	23	Fr	0950	2220
9	Fr	0919	2152	24	Sa	1044	2310
10	Sa	1018	2250	25	Su	1130	2354
11	Su	1114	2344	26	Mo	----	1211
12	Mo	----	1206	27	Tu	0033	1248
13	Tu	0035	1256	28	We	0108	1321
14	We	0124	1343	29	Th	0138	1349
15	Th	0210	1427	30	Fr	0204	1412
				31	Sa	0227	1434

AUGUST 2010
LOW WATER
add 1 hour for BST

Days	Morning Time	Afternoon Time
1 Su	0250	1458
2 Mo	0316	1529
3 Tu	0352	1612
4 We	0443	1719
5 Th	0611	1905
6 Fr	0744	2026
7 Sa	0858	2135
8 Su	1002	2236
9 Mo	1100	2331
10 Tu	1153	----
11 We	0021	1242
12 Th	0108	1327
13 Fr	0151	1408
14 Sa	0232	1447
15 Su	0310	1525
16 Mo	0347	1605
17 Tu	0428	1652
18 We	0519	1754
19 Th	0634	1933
20 Fr	0828	2111
21 Sa	0938	2208
22 Su	1028	2253
23 Mo	1111	2333
24 Tu	1149	----
25 We	0010	1225
26 Th	0042	1255
27 Fr	0110	1320
28 Sa	0133	1342
29 Su	0154	1403
30 Mo	0216	1426
31 Tu	0242	1457

SEPTEMBER 2010
LOW WATER
add 1 hour for BST

Days	Morning Time	Afternoon Time
1 We	0316	1537
2 Th	0403	1639
3 Fr	0524	1837
4 Sa	0722	2009
5 Su	0842	2120
6 Mo	0948	2220
7 Tu	1044	2312
8 We	1134	----
9 Th	0000	1221
10 Fr	0046	1304
11 Sa	0127	1344
12 Su	0206	1422
13 Mo	0242	1459
14 Tu	0317	1537
15 We	0355	1622
16 Th	0445	1724
17 Fr	0558	1905
18 Sa	0805	2051
19 Su	0914	2143
20 Mo	1001	2225
21 Tu	1042	2303
22 We	1119	2338
23 Th	1152	----
24 Fr	0008	1223
25 Sa	0036	1249
26 Su	0101	1313
27 Mo	0125	1337
28 Tu	0150	1404
29 We	0218	1436
30 Th	0254	1519

OCTOBER 2010
LOW WATER
add 1 hour for BST until 31st

Days	Morning Time	Afternoon Time
1 Fr	0342	1623
2 Sa	0504	1817
3 Su	0701	1951
4 Mo	0824	2101
5 Tu	0928	2158
6 We	1022	2249
7 Th	1111	2336
8 Fr	1157	----
9 Sa	0020	1240
10 Su	0101	1320
11 Mo	0140	1358
12 Tu	0216	1435
13 We	0251	1513
14 Th	0329	1558
15 Fr	0417	1656
16 Sa	0524	1815
17 Su	0658	2001
18 Mo	0829	2101
19 Tu	0921	2145
20 We	1003	2223
21 Th	1041	2258
22 Fr	1116	2331
23 Sa	1149	----
24 Su	0002	1220
25 Mo	0033	1250
26 Tu	0103	1320
27 We	0133	1353
28 Th	0207	1430
29 Fr	0247	1517
30 Sa	0340	1623
31 Su	0456	1755

NOVEMBER 2010
LOW WATER

Days	Morning Time	Afternoon Time	Days	Morning Time	Afternoon Time
1 Mo	0633	1923	17 We	0816	2045
2 Tu	0756	2033	18 Th	0910	2132
3 We	0901	2132	19 Fr	0956	2215
4 Th	0957	2224	20 Sa	1038	2254
5 Fr	1047	2311	21 Su	1117	2333
6 Sa	1134	2356	22 Mo	1156	----
7 Su	----	1217	23 Tu	0011	1234
8 Mo	0038	1259	24 We	0049	1313
9 Tu	0118	1339	25 Th	0127	1352
10 We	0155	1417	26 Fr	0207	1435
11 Th	0231	1455	27 Sa	0251	1523
12 Fr	0308	1537	28 Su	0341	1619
13 Sa	0351	1626	29 Mo	0442	1727
14 Su	0445	1726	30 Tu	0556	1844
15 Mo	0553	1836			
16 Tu	0708	1946			

DECEMBER 2010
LOW WATER

Days	Morning Time	Afternoon Time	Days	Morning Time	Afternoon Time
1 We	0717	1958	17 Fr	0811	2038
2 Th	0829	2103	18 Sa	0910	2133
3 Fr	0931	2159	19 Su	1002	2223
4 Sa	1025	2250	20 Mo	1051	2310
5 Su	1115	2337	21 Tu	1138	2356
6 Mo	----	1201	22 We	----	1223
7 Tu	0021	1245	23 Th	0040	1308
8 We	0102	1326	24 Fr	0124	1352
9 Th	0140	1403	25 Sa	0207	1436
10 Fr	0216	1439	26 Su	0250	1519
11 Sa	0250	1515	27 Mo	0334	1605
12 Su	0324	1552	28 Tu	0422	1656
13 Mo	0403	1635	29 We	0518	1758
14 Tu	0452	1729	30 Th	0629	1915
15 We	0555	1833	31 Fr	0753	2034
16 Th	0705	1938			

Mobile phones are always useful to have whilst on the Coast Path. However, do not rely on them as coverage is not always good in the South West. You may also have difficulty in obtaining top-up in some areas.

RIVER CROSSINGS

The walker tends to view feet as the only certain method of progress - and why not? Unfortunately, the absolute purist would need to be an olympic-class swimmer not to have to use ferries on the South West Coast Path. However, a certain amount of scepticism is helpful, absolute reliance on ferries is not advised.

There are other ferries available on the path which walkers may wish to use for diversions or shortcuts. We have attempted to list those directly necessary.

Tide Tables (see pages 21 and 22)

The tide tables included in this edition refer to the times of low water at Devonport. These tables will act as a guide for those wishing to paddle across the Gannel (Newquay), Gillan Creek, and the Erme and Avon (Bigbury-on-Sea). Please be sure to read the warnings given under each section. We have been criticised for being too cautious over the times we suggest for paddling across the rivers, and know that some walkers cross at other times. We believe our attitude is correct as there certainly are dangers, but you may wish to try at low tide on other occasions to see if conditions will permit a safe crossing. Variations in barometric pressure can affect tide levels. Remember there are different levels daily of low water; if in doubt seek local knowledge.

Newquay (The Gannel)	Deduct 30 minutes	Gillan Harbour	Deduct 15 minutes
R. Erme	As at Devonport	Bigbury/Bantham (R.Avon)	As at Devonport

DOGS

1. Beaches

For many years most district councils and unitary authorities have implemented dog bans on beaches generally from 1st May to 31st October. Our Association and most of the general public regard this as a sensible measure.

There are several sections of the South West Coast Path that cross beaches and are officially marked as such. These beaches are Croyde Bay in Devon, Harlyn Bay, Constantine, Treyarnon, Perranporth and Penberth slipway in Cornwall, and Studland in Dorset.
The routing of the Coast Path (with its designation as a National Trail) across these beaches means that they are public rights of way. Our enquiries reveal that a public right of way DOES carry precedence over seasonal regulations banning dogs, and ultimately any walker in the process of walking along, but not stopping on, these sections of the path may be accompanied by a dog under TOTAL control.

However we strongly recommend the following:-
a) If an alternative route is provided and signposted, that you use it.
b) That residents near to dog ban beaches use other walks and do not use the beach path during the ban period.
c) Total control means that the dog should be on a short (not extendable) lead.
d) That your progress should be as unobtrusive as possible to other beach users. To aid this, close attention should be paid to the actual route marked on the map.
e) Lastly, but most importantly, should the worst happen, any dog mess MUST be removed from the beach.

2. Along the Coast Path

Many walk the Coast Path with their dogs and all have an enjoyable time. We receive many reports of not only humans but dogs completing the whole path.

However we do urge caution because the Coast Path is very high along many sections and it takes only an excited dog to go chasing after a rabbit, thus causing much grief if it goes over the edge.

If your dog is well-trained and you can trust it, then please enjoy your Coast Path walk with your four-legged friend. If it is not and you cannot, then do take care.

Many sections along the South West Coast Path will have farm livestock grazing. Again, walkers should maintain proper control of their dogs.

NATIONAL COASTWATCH INSTITUTION (NCI)

This information could be very useful to Coast Path walkers in an emergency situation. Lookouts are served by watchkeepers in daylight hours when a flag is flying and they keep an eye on walkers, vessels at sea, aircraft, divers and grazing animals. They work with the nearest Coastguard Station, Police and Lifeboat service.

When a lookout is on duty a flag is flown and, where there are Visitor Centres at the stations, walkers can enter to see pictures and receive information. If an incident is not in progress visitors can be invited into the station itself. See www.nci.org.uk

For the South West Coast Path there are stations at:

Station	Telephone Number	OS Grid reference
North Cornwall		
Boscastle	01840 250965	SX 091 913
Stepper Point	07810 898041	SW 913 784
St Agnes Head	01872 552073	SW 610 514
West Cornwall		
St Ives	01736 799398	SW 522 412
Cape Cornwall	01736 787890	SW 349 318
Gwennap Head	01736 871351	SW 365 217
Penzance	01736 367063	SW 478 309
Bass Point, Lizard	01326 290212	SW 716 119
Nare Point	01326 231113	SW 800 251
East Cornwall		
Portscatho	01872 580180	SW 882 360
Charlestown	01726 817068	SX 046 516
Polruan	01726 870291	SX 125 510
Rame Head	01752 823706	SX 421 487
South Devon		
Prawle Point	01548 511259	SX 773 351
Froward Point	07976 505649	SX 903 496
Teignmouth	01626 772377	SX 945 732
Exmouth	01395 222492	SY 003 802
Dorset		
Portland Bill	01305 860178	SY 676 692
St Alban's Head	01929 439220	SY 961 755
Peveril Point	01929 422596	SZ 040 786

SUGGESTED ITINERARY

For some the fun of planning their own itinerary is a major part of the enjoyment of their holiday. If you are one of these, DO NOT READ THIS SECTION.

On the other hand there are some who have been put off tackling our path because they just could not see how to pack 630 miles (1014 km) walking into a normal holiday. The answer is, of course, you cannot. Our path, we reckon, needs about eight weeks to accomplish. That being so, we have tried to divide it up sensibly into eight roughly equal sections. Obviously, if we are going to suggest weekly stages, the beginning and end of each one must have reasonable accommodation and public transport. That presents a problem in itself, so after some thought we have broken it down into four 7-day and four 6-day weeks. Obviously not everybody will take a day off per week on their walk. That being the case, some will find they progress further along the Coast Path than our suggested itinerary. As usual, we would be very glad to hear from anyone who has tried one of our weeks and to hear their comments on it.

If you are a seasoned walker then there is a lot to be said for walking the whole path, albeit at different times, in our usual anticlockwise order. However, if you are not experienced, then obviously we should point out that the North Cornwall week, the third one in our schedule, is much the easiest if you want to start with something less demanding.

To keep the weeks set out below in a simple format the information is only an outline. IT IS ESSENTIAL TO CONSULT THE DETAIL IN THE REST OF THE GUIDE TO EFFECTIVELY PLAN YOUR HOLIDAY. Distances can vary depending on where you actually stay. Furthermore, our distances are only approximate because they are all 'rounded'.

After some of the place names we have added 'River Crossing'. You are advised to consult the appropriate section in this book for ferry and low tide suggestions.

Kilometres	Miles	Week 1 (Seven days)	
		MINEHEAD Rail Services to Taunton & bus to Minehead	
		Direct Nat. Express coach services.	
15	10	PORLOCK WEIR	
20	12	LYNMOUTH/LYNTON	
21	13	COMBE MARTIN	
20	13	WOOLACOMBE	
27	16	BRAUNTON	
20	12	INSTOW	
18	11	WESTWARD HO! (via Bideford)	Bus to Barnstaple
			& Rail services to Exeter.
141	87		Direct Nat. Express coach services.

		Week 2 (Seven days)	
		WESTWARD HO! Rail services to Barnstaple & Bus to	
		Westward Ho! Direct Nat. Express coach services	
18	11	CLOVELLY	
16	10	HARTLAND QUAY	
25	15	BUDE	
16	10	CRACKINGTON HAVEN	
18	11	TINTAGEL	
15	9	PORT ISAAC	
19	12	PADSTOW (River Crossing)	Bus to Bodmin Parkway Railway
			Station (Great Western Main Line)
127	78		

		Week 3 (Six days)	
		PADSTOW Rail services to Bodmin Parkway (Great Western	
		Main Line). Bus to Padstow	
22	14	PORTHCOTHAN	
18	11	NEWQUAY (River Crossing)	
18	11	PERRANPORTH	
20	12	PORTREATH	
20	12	HAYLE	
9	6	ST IVES	Numerous bus services or rail service to St Erth
			(Great Western Main Line)
107	66		

Kilometres	Miles	Week 4 (Six days)	
		ST IVES	Numerous bus services or rail service from St Erth (Great Western Main Line)
22	14	PENDEEN	
15	9	SENNEN COVE	
19	12	LAMORNA	
15	9	MARAZION	
17	11	PORTHLEVEN	
22	13	LIZARD TOWN	Bus service to Truro Railway Station (Great Western Main Line)
110	68		

Week 5 (Six days)

Kilometres	Miles		
		LIZARD TOWN	Rail service to Truro (Great Western Main Line) & bus services
17	11	COVERACK	
21	13	HELFORD (River Crossing)	
16	10	FALMOUTH (River Crossing)	
22	14	PORTLOE	
20	12	MEVAGISSEY	
19	12	PAR	Rail services (Great Western Main Line)
115	72		

Week 6 (Seven days)

Kilometres	Miles		
		PAR	Rail services (Great Western Main Line)
21	13	POLPERRO	
20	12	PORTWRINKLE	
21	13	PLYMOUTH (River Crossing)	
24	15	WEMBURY POINT (River Crossing)	
22	14	BIGBURY-ON-SEA (River Crossing)	
22	14	SALCOMBE	
21	13	TORCROSS	Bus service Dartmouth - Kingsbridge - Plymouth
151	94		

Week 7 (Six days)

Kilometres	Miles		
		TORCROSS	Bus service Plymouth - Kingsbridge - Dartmouth
16	10	DARTMOUTH (River Crossing)	
17	11	BRIXHAM	
17	11	BABBACOMBE	
27	16	EXMOUTH (via Starcross/Exmouth Ferry)	
21	13	SIDMOUTH	
17	11	SEATON	Bus services to Sidmouth, Lyme Regis, Honiton and Exeter
115	72		

Week 8 (Seven days)

Kilometres	Miles		
		SEATON	Bus services from Exeter, Honiton, Lyme Regis and Sidmouth
23	14	SEATOWN (Dorset)	
19	12	ABBOTSBURY	
17	11	FERRY BRIDGE (Wyke Regis)	
21	13	ISLE OF PORTLAND	
23	14	LULWORTH	
23	14	WORTH MATRAVERS *	
22	14	SOUTH HAVEN POINT	Ferry-Sandbanks, bus to Poole or Bournemouth & Rail services Nat. Express coach services from Bournemouth to London
148	92		

* See page 99 for opening times of Army Ranges and alternative routes.

THE SOUTH WEST COAST PATH NATIONAL TRAIL

General

This is a series of notes on the state of the path, which we hope will help you in your walking. Obviously it is very difficult to keep something as extensive as this both up-to-date and concise. Suggestions for improvement or amendments will always be welcome. We can only keep you right up-to-date with the state of the path if YOU will keep us posted about conditions as you find them on any stretch of the path. Your fellow members will be grateful, and so will we.

If you have any complaints about ordinary maintenance or signposting on the path, please write either to the Exmoor National Park Authority or the relevant County Council, Devon, Cornwall or Dorset. They should see this is done, and what is generally not realised is that any work carried out is 75% grant aided from Natural England for official National Trails such as the South West Coast Path. If you have any major problems or difficulties we would always be glad to be advised as well.

Each section has a reference to the Ordnance Survey map relevant to it - Outdoor Leisure (OS OL) and Explorer (OS E).

Towns and villages are now marked T or V respectively, but the places at the end of each section appear as the first entry in the next one. We obviously stick our necks out to try and classify towns and villages. To us a town should have a reasonable range of shops, maybe even something as exotic as a laundrette. Villages should at least have a pub and a village store open all the year round, and a bus service. There are, of course, numerous other places you can get refreshment in season, but precious few out of it. Please note that all sections end at reasonable access points, usually having parking facilities.

Places which can be reached by rail are marked.

Distances

The South West Coast Path Team's 1999/2000 survey using a Global Positioning System revealed that the total length of the South West Coast Path, including the Isle of Portland, is 630 miles (1014 km).

The section distances are shown in four columns.

    The first - distance of the section in kilometres
    The second - cumulative distance in kilometres
    The third - distance of the section in miles
    The fourth - cumulative distance in miles

The distances are measured along the officially designated route of the Coast Path, not along any diversions we suggest offering more scenic experiences than the route installed by the authorities.

Grading

Each section is graded as Easy, Moderate, Strenuous or Severe. Please note we no longer take into consideration lack of escape routes, distances from public transport, etc; it is purely a question of physical difficulty. We will try to highlight in the sections other considerations when they apply.

We would like to underline one point; the whole of our path is certainly not easy. Some parts of it are but other parts are not. We have had a number of letters from people who have walked The Pennine Way and who have been literally amazed at the severity of some of our tougher sections. Perhaps as a further comment we may add that recently we walked two 6 mile (10 km) adjacent sections. The time taken for one was 50% more than the time taken for the other. This may give additional emphasis to the importance of studying terrain if you wish to compute time.

Ascent

During a 3 year walk of the entire Coast Path, an Association member used a sophisticated altimeter to calculate that the walker who has completed the whole Coast Path will have climbed 115000 feet (35030 m), which is just a little short of walking the height of Mount Everest from sea level four times! We have therefore been able to calculate the total ascent per section, and this is now shown. The sections height gain are shown in four columns:

The first - height gain in metres
The second - cumulative height gain in metres
The third - height gain in feet
The fourth - cumulative height gain in feet

Section Timing

We have introduced estimated timings for those wanting to know approximately how long each section may take to walk.

We consider these times to be a fair average. There are those who will complete sections quicker or slower than our estimations. We have NOT allowed for refreshment stops or for looking at views. However, it is important to remember that many factors can influence the speed at which you walk, e.g. weather, the amount of gear carried, an unexpected diversion etc., and you should always allow adequate time for your walk, especially if you are relying on public transport at the end of your walk.

These timings relate to the official route of the South West Coast Path only, and not to any of our suggested alternatives.

WEB SITE NEWS

Any news concerning the state of the Coast Path received after this book is printed will be published in newsletters and on our web site www.southwestcoastpath.org.uk

THE TRAIL DESCRIPTION - Minehead to Poole

FOLLOW THE NATIONAL TRAIL WAYMARK (THE ACORN SYMBOL)
CAUTION

Our literature generally describes the walked and maintained route of the National Trail known as the South West Coast Path. Along its whole length the managing authorities mentioned below have a duty to maintain the path. Walkers should be warned – using out-of-date Association books could prove risky. Things change over the years, including the actual route of the South West Coast Path.

Where you find we have little to say about the route we consider that it is highly unlikely that the walker will run the risk of going astray.

Those who set forth upon this beautiful trail must remember it is mainly a cliff top path - in places it can be a very high cliff top. Those who manage the Coast Path want to keep it safe, but we remind walkers that it is unwise to leave the path at any point on the seaward side. We are not responsible for the maintenance of the cliff tops themselves, which can be unstable and extremely unsafe.

Now and again we suggest an alternative path away from the officially designated route. This will be for a more scenic and enjoyable experience.

These alternative, recommended paths, follow rights of way and in a few instances 'permissive routes' which are maintained by the landowner.

THIS ASSOCIATION STRESSES THAT ALL PERSONS USING THE PATH SHOULD NOT WANDER OFF IT, ESPECIALLY ON THE SEAWARD SIDE, AS TO DO SO WOULD BE PUTTING YOURSELF AND POSSIBLY OTHERS IN GRAVE DANGER OF SEVERE PERSONAL INJURY OR EVEN DEATH.

MANAGEMENT OF THE SOUTH WEST COAST PATH

The management of the 630 miles of the Coast Path is the responsibility of;-
The County Councils of Devon, Cornwall and Dorset
The City Council of Plymouth
Torbay Coast and Countryside Trust
Exmoor National Park and
The National Trust Regions of Devon/Cornwall and Wessex

Natural England has overall responsibility and provides most of the funding.

The South West Coast Path Association has, over the past 36 years, been the premier information source for those wanting to walk the Coast Path. Over those years it has been the 'user' organisation and, we like to think, has been responsible, by persistent lobbying, for the enjoyable experience it is to walk it today.

IMPORTANT - PLEASE NOTE

Information included or available through the South West Coast Path Association (SWCPA) is given in good faith and is believed to be accurate and correct at the time of going to print - however it cannot be guaranteed not to include inaccuracies or typographical errors.

Advice received via the SWCPA should not be relied upon for personal decisions and you should take into account the weather and your own capabilities before following the walks set out in this Guide. It is for the individual concerned to weigh up the risks of each of the walks described in this book.

The SWCPA makes no representations about the suitability of walks to any one person and will accept no liability for any loss or damage suffered as a result of relying on this book: it should be used for guidance only.

In no event shall the SWCPA be liable for any personal injury or any loss suffered as a result of using this publication.

COAST PATH SAFETY ADVICE

Your safety is your responsibility – please look after yourself and other members of your group.

Keep to the path and stay away from cliff edges – please follow advisory signs and waymarks.

Supervise children and dogs – please look out for your children and pets at all times.

Be prepared and well equipped – wear suitable clothing and footwear and be ready for possible changes in the weather.

Stay within your capabilities – some sections of the Coast Path can be strenuous and/or remote.

In an emergency dial 999 and ask for the coastguard.

WEATHER

The South West Coast Path is more exposed to wind than any other long distance trail, so please pay attention to gale forecasts as well as rain. Along some sections, strong winds can be dangerous, especially when rounding exposed headlands and crossing bridges; a high backpack can act like a sail. Detailed local forecasts are available from the UK Meteorological Office on 0870 900 0100 (24 hours) or www.metoffice.gov.uk/weather/uk

---

Grading: Official Route - Moderate
Alternative - Strenuous

Distance - 15.3 15.3 9.5 9.5

Ascent: 698 698 2290 2290

Timing: 4.5 hours

See also our Minehead to Porlock Weir Path Description.

The South West Coast Path starts from the celebratory marker on the sea front, approximately 100 yards (91 m) beyond the Quay Inn. The celebratory marker sculpture of a pair of hands holding a map was done by Owen Cunningham to the design of local art student Sarah Ward, and was opened on 14th February 2001. The construction of this striking piece of art was managed by the South West Coast Path Team and part-funded by donations from our South West Coast Path Association Members.

A new route, lobbied for and part-funded by the Association, has been waymarked along the sea front, past the quay towards Culver Cliff and then just before Greenaleigh Farm you turn left onto the ascending zigzag through trees to the old route to North Hill.

When you have gained the summit of North Hill, there is an acorn sign pointing to Selworthy and Bossington. Follow the line of this until you come to the next Coast Path sign, where there is a right fork marked 'Rugged Cliff Top Path'. Ordinary walkers should proceed forward on the official route but the more adventurous can fork right and proceed, walking seaward by what is a well-defined path.

Alternative - Rugged Coast Path

Please do not be put off by the description of the path as 'Rugged' – it is a splendid alternative and not difficult, and will give you much better views than the official Coast Path. It is well marked, but there are signs prohibiting dogs.

At the stile with a National Trust information board, you must take the left fork towards a bench, then continue downhill to take the lower path by a 'Rugged Path' signpost, which takes you down into Grexy Combe at 937 481. From here take the well-defined diagonal path leading up the hill to the wall which is the National Trust boundary. This wall can be followed towards the sea at first and then along parallel to the sea all the way to Western Brockholes. After Western Brockholes the path bears inland, but is well signposted and rejoins the official path behind Hurlstone Point. (If you take this route you should add an extra hour plus to your walk.)

Coast Path Continues

Those who have taken the official route, when reaching Bossington Hill should take the definitive right of way which goes down Hurlstone Combe. There is a much more spectacular route around Hurlstone Point which can be used apart from gale force conditions. If you stay on the official path, take care to descend the path to the left of Hurlstone Point and do not be tempted to take the more obvious path to the left (no signpost) contouring round Bossington Hill.

The path goes inland from Hurlstone Point to Bossington village and then just past the car park out towards the sea again. The original coast path followed the path behind the beach to Porlock Weir, but this is not now possible for safety reasons, as high storms have caused a breach in the pebble ridge and a deep and dangerous impassable gully has been formed. A new route has now been installed across the marsh to Porlock Weir - this is another section that the South West Coast Path Association has part-funded. The new route across the marsh is easy to follow, however, because of high spring tides the route can become impassable: for tide information please refer to local tide tables at Minehead - the TIC is a good source (see page 162). DO NOT use the Devonport tide table published in this book.

If this route is impassable then ample signs will direct you to Porlock village. If you have to take this diversion then you need to leave the village on the Toll Road past the Village Hall - do not take the road signposted Porlock Weir. Just up the Toll Road you bear right on a footpath that takes you behind West Porlock to Porlock Weir.

Grading: Moderate, Strenuous in parts   Distance -   **19.8**   **35.1**   **12.3**   **21.8**

Ascent: 934   1632   3064   5354

Timing: 5.5 hours

See also our Porlock Weir to Lynmouth Path Description

The official path is signposted to the left of the Anchor Hotel but you can go in front of the hotel, past the craft shops and then turn left signposted to Culbone.

At Culbone turn right if you want to visit the small church and we recommend this. There was once a do-it-yourself refreshment hut here which had to close down due to some local regulations – it may have re-opened.

From the church retrace your steps and turn right uphill onto the Coast Path. After about 300 yards (275 m), bear right through Culbone and Embelle Woods to Yenworthy Woods. This official route has been subject to land slippages but is now open again. An alternative route continues uphill to Silcombe Farm, an excellent B&B, as listed in our accommodation section.

PINETUM DIVERSION: When you get to Yenworthy Combe there is a sign to the Pinetum, where there is a pleasant diversion. There are some unusually mature examples of trees planted between 1840 and 1860 and several are over 100 feet tall. There is also a trout pond off the stream and an icehouse which was cut into the cool, shaded bank of the stream. A tunnel leads to a deep cemented pit which was sealed by two tightly fitting doors to hold ice throughout the year for use in the kitchens before electricity.

BEN'S PATH DIVERSION: At the end of the Pinetum is a new permissive path through woods south of Home Farm, called 'Ben's Path', that rejoins the Coast Path. Before you get on to Ben's Path you may like to go to Glenthorne Beach. You will see the remains of a jetty, which was built to land heavy building materials for the estate when overland routes were impractical. There is also the remains of a boathouse, coal store and lime kiln. The limestone and coal were brought over from South Wales.

Proceed to Sister's Fountain, where there is a legend that Jesus drank here with Joseph of Arimathea on his way to Glastonbury. Continue uphill through a pair of wild boar head gateposts, which was the entrance to the Victorian Woodland Lodge, which usually has barking Jack Russell dogs in its garden - take care not to miss the narrow signposted path 300 yards (275m) past the cottage as the drive bears left.

At Coddow Combe, the official route is again signposted inland `Countisbury 1.5 miles'. The surefooted might prefer the right of way signposted 'Lighthouse' which proceeds out to the Foreland Point Lighthouse. Just before the entrance to the lighthouse, where the wall commences on the right, the path takes off up the bank to the left. The beginning is clearly marked because the authorities tell you they no longer maintain the path. This path is more exposed than the official route and careful walking is advised. It has magnificent views if you are surefooted and the weather is calm.

The National Trust has a good path which can be taken down the seaward side of the main A39 coastal road, so avoiding the upper reaches of Countisbury Hill. Lower down the hill the path joins the road but a new path on the seaward side ensures that you will not get run down.

You come out on the foreshore. Walk along into Lynmouth, crossing the footbridge, and there turn right down to the sea front, turning left up the steps before the cliff railway (that is assuming you are a purist and are not actually going to use the railway, which you can well do if you wish!) If you use the railway you do suffer slightly at the top in that you will have to walk nearly into Lynton and then out again to regain the North Walk. After all, it serves you right for not having walked the whole way! An alternative and much more traditional route than the tarmac path and cliff railway has recently been opened. Continue along the sea front to the Esplanade car park and after about 250 yards (229 m) bear left up a pleasant path, signposted Lynton - on a steep wooded hillside, to emerge on the tarmac path beyond North Walk.

It is interesting to know that at Lynmouth you can now walk Devon's coast to coast route by using the Two Moors Way to Ivybridge then the Erme Valley Trail which links into the Erme - Plym Trail to Plymouth. Guide books to the above are available from Lynton TIC (see page 162).

Grading: Strenuous				Distance -	21.4	56.5	13.3	35.1

Ascent: 1350   2982   4429   9783

Timing: 7 hours

See also our Lynmouth to Ilfracombe Path Description.

Please note there is a long, lonely section onward from Heddon's Mouth to Combe Martin without any chance of refreshment.

The path itself out from Lynton is a Victorian idea for a coastal footpath called the North Walk and although to our modern ideas, tarmac might not be the ideal footpath medium, it is a very fine high level walk indeed. This takes you very happily out to Castle Rock.

There are diversions which will save you some road walking. The first takes off to the right after the turning circle (roundabout) at the end of the Valley of Rocks and then goes in a loop back, to come out by the Lodge at the beginning of Lee Abbey. The second alternative is a left turn immediately opposite Lee Abbey which is labelled 'Woodland Walk' (each end) and rejoins the road about 0.75 mile (1200 m) further along.

If you do not follow the 'Woodland Walk' but follow the road past the toll house and refreshment stop (seasonal), you will climb up a hill and come across a path on your right, that goes along the field edge to Crock Point and through the woods at Crock Pits. This will take you off a busy road with some stunning coastal views.

From now on this is one of the finest pieces of Coast Path in North Devon and should not be missed by anyone who is reasonably surefooted, or unless weather conditions are very bad. The path takes off just before the Woody Bay Hotel opposite the Red House and the beginning of the path is marked by a signpost on the right which says 'Coast Path 2.5 Heddon's Mouth'. This path comes out on another road, where you turn up left. There will be another sign 'Coast Path Hunter's Inn'. You will cross a stile with a sign 'Heddon Valley Hunter's Inn'. This is a superb path which is now the new official route. It is much nearer the coast giving splendid views. When the path reaches the Heddon Valley path, the official route is as follows. Continue ahead/left towards Hunter's Inn. On reaching the stone bridge over the Heddon River on your right, cross over it, immediately bear right and carry on through the gate and on reaching the next path across, turn hard left. Continue for 100 yards (91 m) or so to the signpost on the right to Combe Martin.

Alternative Route
For a very pleasant alternative down to the beach and restored lime kiln follow these directions. Turn hard right and walk down by the river to Heddon's Mouth, crossing the bridge by the picnic area. Carry on to the beach and the lime kiln. Return to the picnic area by the bridge and continue through the picnic area, keeping the river on your left. In a while ignore the path going down on your left. Pass through the gate and continue for 100 yards (91 m) or so to the signpost on the right to Combe Martin.

Coast Path continues
Whichever route you have taken, continue as follows. Follow this path up to the right, through the gate and on up; there are seats on the way up! Continue up the path and various steps and on reaching the few steps near the top, carry on round to your right, where the path now levels off. More lovely views of the Heddon Valley open up. Carry on round the headland at Peter Rock (beware if windy) and along the Coast Path for a good 0.5 mile (800 m) until you start heading inland and reach the path going across you by the stone wall, with the Coast Path sign up to your left. Whilst in the valley of Heddon's Mouth, those requiring refreshment have easy access to the Hunter's Inn and the National Trust shop selling very good ice cream.

Just west of East Cleave you will regain the old official route passing along High Cliff and North Cleave. At map reference 628 482 take the short walk across open heathland to avoid the walk up to the old Trentishoe Down Road.

As there are many sheep tracks by Sherrycombe, we suggest you follow the grass track along the top of the combe to the inland end of it to pick up the path down.

When ascending Great Hangman from Sherrycombe you reach a seat. Keep alongside the wall on your left. There are a number of well-walked paths going out to the right but they are all wrong! From Great Hangman the path is clear to Little Hangman, where more stunning views are available.

When you come to the shelter above Combe Martin, turn right on the unmarked path; this has the better views.

---

4 | Combe Martin to Ilfracombe (Harbour)   OS OL9 (T) Combe Martin

---

Grading: Moderate, Strenuous in parts	Distance-	8.6	65.1	5.3	40.4

Ascent: 550   3532   1804   11587

Timing: 2.5 hours

See also our Lynmouth to Ilfracombe Path Description.

Before setting forth on this section some words of caution. Check the times of high tide at Watermouth by contacting Ilfracombe or Combe Martin TICs (see page 162). DO NOT use the Devonport tide table published in this book. There is a low tide route; however, if you cannot avoid having to walk the section when the tide is too high, then the only walking route is along the dangerous road where you will have to exercise extreme caution. Devon County Council has removed the direction signs that used to be there in case a walker adhering to that signed route was involved in an accident and was looking for someone to sue.

The Association has been telling Devon County Council for years that the road is dangerous and it was only towards the end of 2007 that they realised the potential hazard for walkers. A raised walkway, avoiding the road and not reliant on the tides, was being planned and this Association had offered to part fund it to the tune of £60 000 of the cost; unfortunately, the plans and overall costings have since been the subject of major amendment by Devon County Council, with the possibility that the project will not now start until 2010.

The path leaves the lime kiln car park, passing Combe Martin TIC; fork right and join the A399 road. Turn right (Seaside Hill Road) above the beach. Turn right onto a narrow tarmac lane, which climbs steeply to rejoin the A399 road.

Walk on the slightly raised path along the road side through two gates. Having gone along a path beside a field to the flight of steps, you should turn left up the newish slip road back to the main road and to the brow, passing the bus shelter. You then turn right to follow the road down to the old main road, with a bus shelter over to the right, which is now used as an information point for the Heritage Coast. Here you turn left beside the entrance to the Sandy Cove Hotel to follow a track towards Watermouth Cove.

Watermouth Castle, built 1825, comes into view. At Watermouth it is possible to cross the foreshore to a flight of steps some 110 yards (100 m) away at most times other than at high tide; however, take care as the rocks can be slippery. If you do need to take the road, please take extra care. We recommend that you cross over the road at the Watermouth Cove caravan park entrance. From here you get a better view of the traffic, away from the blind bend. Once you have crossed over the road, walk along the grass verge past the castle. When the verge peters out you will find that you have a good view to cross back again. Then walk facing the traffic to the cut-through back to the signed Coast Path.

(If you are approaching Watermouth from the Ilfracombe direction and you need to walk the road, please take extra care. You will be coming through the woods with the cove down to your left. If the tide is too far in for you to walk from the bottom of the steps, then return to the cut-through to the main road. Please take extra care especially in this direction. We suggest that you cross over quickly from the cut-through so that vehicles get a better view of you. As soon as you can, walk along the elevated verge to pass the castle. From this side of the road, you can safely cross back to the Coast Path as the view along the road is better from here.)

The next section of the path is very pleasant on the western side of Watermouth and continues out and around Widmouth Head. This section provides some very spectacular walking; we particularly commend the view back from Widmouth Head over Watermouth, whatever the state of the tide or sea. This will be your last good viewpoint of the dramatic setting of the Great Hangman and the Little Hangman eastwards above Combe Martin. After Widmouth Head the path continues in front of the coastguard cottages going to Rillage Point.

This fine section ends with a road walk down into Hele. Turn right and look out for some steps on the far left of the beach. The path then zigzags passing Beacon Point with a fine view of Ilfracombe, until it reaches the top of Hillsborough. Follow the waymarks down the hill till you reach the harbour road.

Grading: Easy to moderate   Distance-   5.3   70.4   3.3   43.7

Ascent: 350   3882   1148   12735

Timing: 1.5 hours

See also our Ilfracombe to Croyde Bay Path Description.

Walk along the edge of the harbour, bear left at the slip and then right into Broad Street. At a T-junction, turn left into Capstone Road next to the Sandpiper Inn. The Capstone Point Path has been reopened, so after about 170 yards (150 m) turn right and walk around Capstone Point. Then take the flight of steps that goes up the back of the Landmark Theatre. Follow this path up to the top of the gardens and the gate by a shelter. Pass through this gate and bear right to walk along Granville road, before bearing right onto an unmetalled road which takes you to the Torrs Walk: it is well waymarked.

At the top of the Torrs Walk bear right and follow the path down the field to the stile in the corner. Continue ahead around the hill and beware of the steep drop on your right, to the stile. Now cross the field to the old coach road ahead, bearing right onto it and follow it all the way to Flat Point. Along Flat Point the Coast Path follows the route of the old coach road. (Flat Point is National Trust land with its open access policy, and it can be roamed at your own risk and offers good sites for picnic stops.) Passing through a field gate your route is along a narrow, pleasant road down into Lee.

Refreshments are available all year round at the Grampus Inn in Lee village, which is only a minor diversion from the coast.

| 6 | Lee Bay to Woolacombe | OS E139 (V) Lee Bay |

Grading: Strenuous, becoming easy   Distance -   6.4   76.8   4.0   47.7

Ascent: 397   4279   1302   14037

Timing: 2 hours

See also our Ilfracombe to Croyde Bay Path Description.

This section will take you longer to walk than you think as it includes some up and down work but is a lovely piece of path to walk.

Proceed up the road from Lee, and at the top of the hill turn right through a brick- pillared gate that might easily be mistaken for a garden gate. To the left of the path are the remains of a pre war golf course. Before Bull Point the path crosses two steep valleys, Hilly Mouth and Bennets Water. Rockham has a fine stretch of sand that is very popular in the summer. Morte Point is a spectacular jagged slate ridge rather like a dinosaur's back emerging from the sea. Offshore is the often submerged Morte Stone and this 'Rock of Death' was aptly named in the 19th century. At certain states of the tide an awesome tidal race can be seen; many ships have been wrecked off here.

| 7 | Woolacombe to Croyde Bay (Beach) | OS E139 (T) Woolacombe |

Grading: Moderate   Distance -   10.2   87.0   6.3   54.0

Ascent: 168   4447   551   14588

Timing: 3 hours

See also our Ilfracombe to Croyde Bay Path Description.

This section starts at the Watersmeet Hotel and runs parallel to the Esplanade road, then turns up Challacombe road. This is now waymarked but a vital waymark has been removed to indicate where the route turns off the road into the Warren. The path is about where the National Trust sign has been placed. The official route stays in the Warren; the alignment shown on 139 OS Explorer map is incorrect.

The path tries hard to lose itself in the enormous dunes, but the waymarking however has been improved and you should not go astray. A possible alternative is to walk the Marine Drive which gives fine views. If the tide is out it is easier to walk Woolacombe Beach but it should not be attempted on a flood tide as you may not be able to get off the beach at Vention.

If you have used the official path, it leaves the Warren by a set of steep steps. At the top turn right and after 500 yards (460 m) a path leaves the official route; this takes you down to a car park (refreshments and toilets). Pass to the left of the caravan site, over a stile and up the cliff slope to rejoin the official route to Baggy Point.

The high level path out to Baggy Point is pleasant. If the visibility is good you will get a good chance as you turn the corner to look at the path for a number of miles ahead across Bideford Bay. At Baggy Point itself, when you have turned the corner, do bear right on to the lower path; it is no further and provides much better sea views.

Passing the National Trust car park, there is a road walk of about 545 yards (500 m) before the turn off to the beach. Do not be tempted to use the first slipway as it would be very difficult walking over the rocks.

8 Croyde Bay to Barnstaple (Long Bridge)   OS E139 (V) Croyde

Grading: Easy				Distance -	23.1	110.1	14.4	68.4
Ascent:	128	4575	420	15008				

Timing: 5.25 hours

See also our Croyde Bay to Barnstaple Path Description.

Distances are measured walking via Crow Point, and around Horsey Island, through Velator to join the disused railway track all the way to Barnstaple.

The path crosses the top of Croyde beach (walkers are advised NOT to take their dogs onto this beach between May and September), and on to the low cliffs at Down End, turns left after reaching the old coastguard lookout, and then crosses the B3231 road. This is a very busy road so take great care as you cross over the road, which has to be done at this point. Turn left and walk downhill a short way to reach some stone steps. After a short climb, the path contours round Saunton Down, parallel to and above the road.

From this path there are some spectacular views down the length of Saunton Sands, and if clear, across the estuary to Appledore. On the hillside to the left some ancient cultivation terraces can be seen. The path ends on the road opposite the hotel. This large flat-roofed building is the five-star Saunton Sands Hotel owned by the Brend family. Wonderful food; they welcome all, including walkers.

At this point you are confronted with three routes from which to choose:-

1. *The official route* crosses the B3231 road and passes around the Saunton Sands Hotel and descends to the large Saunton Sands car park. Refreshments and other facilities are available here from Easter to the end of September.

    Leave the car park by the main entrance/exit at the foot of the hill and after 55 yards (50 m) rejoin the waymarked path on the right along a sandy lane. At the end of this lane you return to the B3231 road (some Coast Path!)

    Take care as there is 400 yards (365 m) of that road to walk along. You pass the driveway into Saunton Golf Club and then turn right at the red brick/partially rendered house; the path is signed, but not particularly clear. From here you cross a field and then enter the edge of the golf course and Braunton Burrows. The route has recently been slightly diverted, but this has been well signed.

2. At the bottom of the slope, before the road, opposite the Saunton Sands Hotel, turn left onto a public footpath. You climb steeply with the path bearing right at the top of the hill. After descending it passes near to Saunton Court and continues on to the B3231 road opposite the red brick house. After crossing you then follow the official route as described in Option

1 above.

This diversion eliminates 400 yards (365 m) of very dangerous road walking. The North Devon Coast and Countryside Service suggests this route and we have asked for signs to be installed.

3. This third choice is probably the one preferred by most walkers. Cross over the B3231. Pass around the Saunton Sands Hotel and descend to the large car park. Walk south along the beach via Airy Point to Crow Point. After 3.5 miles (5.5 km) along the beach, just after the groyne, watch out for a slatted wooden catwalk on your left. This is your beach exit so walk along this to Broad Sands. As you do so you will have regained the official route.

The official route after options 1 and 2 now enters the Braunton Burrows nature reserve.

These burrows are renowned for the great wealth and diversity of plant life, and over 400 species of flowering plants have been recorded here.

Skirt around the Burrows (options 1 & 2) and join the so-called American road, which is then followed south for approximately 1.5 miles (2.5 km) to Broad Sands.

Arriving at Broad Sands, either by the Burrows walk or the beach walk (Option 3), the path becomes a little vague, but keep the estuary on your right hand side and you cannot go wrong. Head for the white cottage on the estuary side.

The route now follows the estuary side on top of the Great Sea Bank. The path keeps to the top of this sea wall all the way to Velator. If you wish to visit Braunton turn left at Velator and walk along the old railway track into the village.

From Velator the route now follows the old Barnstaple to Ilfracombe railway track into Barnstaple: the railway was closed in 1970.

In the summer months, the walker will have a problem on this section of the path, as not only is it the South West Coast Path, but it is also a cycle track used by many hundreds of cyclists. Few bikes seem to have any audible means of warning you of their approach, so walking can become very hazardous. After leaving Velator you will pass the old railway station at Wrafton and after about 1 mile (1500 m) the path suddenly emerges onto the estuary side. When the tide is high it presents a very fine picture and in the winter months there are many ducks and waders to observe.

After the Tarka Inn (previously Heanton Court), a possible stop for refreshments, continue following the old railway track along the banks of the estuary. The new Barnstaple bridge is now open and this is signposted as an alternative route across the estuary, thus avoiding the town (and reducing the walk by just over 1 mile or 2 km). The official path continues into Barnstaple and if this is walked, cross the river Yeo bridge and continue along beside the wharf towards the old Long Bridge over the river Taw in Barnstaple.

Having passed the old Barnstaple railway station, you soon pass a new recreation area with seating, a good spot for a break. Continue along beside the river to the Long Bridge and take the steps up to the left which bring you onto the bridge.

9 | Barnstaple to Westward Ho! (Amusement Arcade)
OS E139 & OS E126 (T) Barnstaple (Trains); (T) Bideford

Grading: Easy				Distance -	30.7	140.8	19.1	87.5
Ascent:	162	4737	531	15539				

Timing: 7 hours

See also our Barnstaple to Westward Ho! Path Description.

Cross the Long Bridge – there is no need to cross the road. Keep to the right of the large roundabout, pass the Leaderflush and Shapland factory, then cross a mini roundabout to follow a new path which curves around to a subway under the approach road to the new bridge. The path, which is also part of the Tarka Trail, then links up with the old railway line. There is an alternative path here, not signed, which runs closer to the estuary, first along the left hand side of the Leaderflush and Shapland factory and then under the new bridge, curving around to link up with the old railway line.

There is an excellent café, open all year, at the delightfully restored Fremington Quay, together with an informative museum attached to the former railway station building: for further information please see www.fremingtonquaycafe.co.uk Again be aware of cyclists as you follow the old railway line, which itself goes to Instow. The official Coast Path turns right, just past the RSPB site to reach the side of the estuary and continues round until reaching Instow.

Continue on to Bideford under the new Bideford bridge. The old Bideford railway station is the base of the North Devon Coast and Countryside Service. Refreshments are available in season in the reconditioned railway carriage.

Cross the Bideford Long Bridge, turn right and walk along the quay. Continue walking by the riverside path now named Landivisau Walk (Bideford's twin town in France) keeping the car park on your left. At the end of the car park there is a waymarked lane passing the Bideford RFC stadium. Continue walking on a road to pass under the new high level road bridge, then up a rough track, turn right by the waymark, and walk down a narrow track. This rejoins the riverside by a small beach at Lower Cleave. There is some more road walking passing the Yeoldon House Hotel. Be sure to keep to the waymarked lane; do not stray up any of the many private drives. After the Second World War tank traps, fork right and the route enters the National Trust property of Burrough Farm. This is a very pleasant section through some riverside woods with fine views back up the river to Bideford.

There is now a steep descent to another small beach with a boardwalk over a marshy area. After the second National Trust sign turn right. There are now two options here. The low tide route can now be used again (following the removal of a temporary closure notice) after a breach in the sea wall has been filled in, or the high tide route, which is well waymarked. Follow the waymarked route around Appledore shipyard to reach the road, turn right and into Appledore via Myrtle Street.

At Appledore plenty of accommodation and refreshment places are available. The route now continues into old Appledore, passing the homes of the old sailing captains to near the lifeboat house. Pass the Royal George Inn and walk along Irsha Street, then, keeping in front of the lifeboat station, pick up the path which goes along the edge of low cliffs and across a field before descending some steps to a slipway to join the road by the old Hinks' boatyard (now a garage) and follow this for approximately 0.3 mile (0.5 km) to reach a crossroads. (At low tide it is possible to walk along the beach from the lifeboat station to Appledore bridge and the entrance to Northam Burrows.)

Here for some distance you are walking on the seaward side of the dunes, turning to the golf links side to pass Sandy Mere, then it is a straight walk into Westward Ho!. At most states of the tide it is possible to walk the beach, but be warned, the sand can be rather soft in places. Westward Ho! has plenty of accommodation but refreshment places are limited out of season.

10 | Westward Ho! to Clovelly (Mount Pleasant)   OS E126 (T) Westward Ho!

Grading: Strenuous   Distance -   18   158.8   11.2   98.7

Ascent: 789   5526   2589   18128

Timing: 6 hours

See also our Westward Ho! to Clovelly Path Description.

After passing the last of the holiday chalets, the path follows the track of the old Bideford to Westward Ho! railway. This is a fine stretch of the Coast Path over Cornborough and Abbotsham cliffs. At Greencliff a very poor coal was once mined. The path now climbs steeply over Cockington cliffs, only to drop again to sea level to cross a pebble beach, before climbing again via a wooden staircase to cross Babbacombe cliffs. At Peppercombe turn inland to cross the stream and then the path meanders through Sloo Woods to join the new section through Worthygate Wood.

NOTE: The route shown on OS Explorer map 126 at Gauter Pool is wrong. The path does not turn to the south but goes on through the woods dropping to Buck's Mills.

At Buck's Mills a walk down to the old Quay is worthwhile. On leaving Barton Wood, keep to the bottom edge of the field until you cross a bridge into Hobby Drive. The walk along the Hobby Drive is nearly 3 miles (5 km) long, and takes longer than you think. There is a path which takes you off the Hobby Drive, linking up with Clovelly's main street and on down to the harbour, but this is little used, rather overgrown and eroded in places.

Grading: Moderate to strenuous Distance - 16.6 175.4 10.3 109.0

Ascent: 708 6234 2323 20451

Timing: 5 hours

See also our Clovelly to Hartland Quay Path Description.

If walking from Clovelly the landowner asks you to use the main (estate) car park. There is a charge for this, but never mind, take comfort that the fee assists in maintaining the Clovelly section of the Coast Path, including tree planting, seats and view points such as Angels Wings (referred to below). Following negotiations with the owner the charge has been reduced to bona fide Coast Path walkers for groups of up to four people to £7.50 per vehicle. Walkers are requested to introduce themselves at the Visitor Centre, sign a book saying they are Coast Path walkers and obtain a ticket.

Having parked in the main car park walk out of the entrance and turn right down the road for some 200 yards to a white gate on your left, which bring you onto the Coast Path.

This is a very fine section indeed, what coastal walking is all about! Allow yourself plenty of time to really enjoy it. You leave the top of Clovelly westwards on the road and follow the Coast Path sign through the large gate in the wall/fence on the left at the top of the hill - do not go down the hill. Follow the track first to the left and round to the right, to the Coast Path signpost, where you follow the path down to the right (yellow waymark). After a while you pass through the kissing-gate and follow the fence on your right until reaching the small kissing-gate in the shrubbery. Follow this path and soon a covered seat appears on the right. Carry on through the shrubbery and through the next two kissing-gates. After a while turn right at the T-junction, following the Coast Path sign, and right again at the next fork.

Soon you come to an original seat called the 'Angel's Wings', with nice woodcarvings. On reaching the track, take the Coast Path hard to the right - do not go along the track. Follow this path to a wonderful viewpoint before it descends steeply into a valley to a track. Go right and before going immediately left and immediately right again there is an easy detour that is very worthwhile (signposted - permissive path to viewpoint 0.5 mile). Having turned right off the steep descent, go ahead instead of sharp left up the track beside the cliff edge. The Coast Path is signed inland, but there is a permissive path signed "To Viewpoint" going right - take this. Watch for little flights of stone steps on the right, the first is about 75 yards and the third which you want is about 200 yards from the junction, unsigned at the time of writing. The steps lead to an arch and a surprise view of the sea, that is a gem.

Return back through the rock cutting to the Coast Path sign, bearing right down to the main track, where you turn hard right to follow this track down the valley to the shore at Mouth Mill. Go down the narrow path, crossing the stream by the stepping stones. Pause at the shore and notice the rock formations and the waterfall along the coast to your left (at low tide). Also note the old lime kiln. Now follow the grass track inland past the lime kiln and old building. Shortly take the Coast Path up to your right. Half way up, follow the steps to the right ignoring the path going on ahead. On reaching the top, cross the stile by the National Trust sign for Brownsham.

The path proceeds through one field and over another stile, which is multi-stepped on the eastern side, then across another field to the stile in the right hand fence. Then proceed down the zigzags, across the bridge at the bottom, turning left, and then take the first turning on the right. This is the more seaward route and is now the official path. We asked for this path and are grateful to the National Trust for having provided it. At Windbury Castle (earthworks) there is a small memorial plaque in memory of the crew of a Wellington bomber that crashed into these cliffs in April 1942.

The route now continues practically on the coast all the way to Eldern Point and then on to Shipload Bay. (There is a seasonal refreshment hut at Hartland Point car park, serving excellent light meals and freshly made snacks. The hut is open from Palm Sunday until the end of September.)

As you approach the gate to the lighthouse note the water catchment area on your left. The path turns sharp left towards the coastguard lookout and a short diversion here brings you to a good view of the wreck below and a memorial to the hospital ship Glenart Castle, which was torpedoed and sunk in 1918.

The path down into the Smoothlands Valley and out to Damehole Point is a wonderful part of the Coast Path. To cross Abbey River the path goes inland behind the cottage to a stone bridge.

On reaching the old Rocket House by the road inland to Stoke, bear right to follow the path downhill to Hartland Quay, soon picking up the small road down to the seasonal refreshments, museum, toilets and hotel.

12 | Hartland Quay to Bude (Canal Bridge)   OS E126 & E111

Grading: Severe			Distance -	24.8	200.2	15.4	124.4
Ascent:	1302	7536	4272	24723			

Timing: 8.5 hours

See also our Hartland Quay to Bude Path Description.

This is probably the most difficult section of the whole Coast Path – before you reach Bude you will have crossed ten river valleys. It has been suggested it should be split into two sections – Hartland Quay to Morwenstow (12.0 km, 7.5 miles) and Morwenstow to Bude (12.8 km, 7.9 miles) and some walkers may want to take this option. There is accommodation available in the Morwenstow area.

A word of caution - there are no refreshment facilities other than the seasonal opportunities at Morwenstow and Sandy Mouth, so you should consider adding to your load at Hartland Quay.

The path from Hartland Quay is largely track and becomes a grassy footpath behind St Catherine's Tor. There is then a climb up and down to the waterfall at Speke's Mill Mouth. In our opinion this is the most dramatic waterfall on the whole of the path and we do not forget Pentargon ahead.

The path keeps to the eastern side of the stream for about 150 yards (135 m) then crosses it by a new wooden footbridge. Follow the signs up the valley to the east of Swansford Hill. The path over Swansford Hill is still walkable but should not be attempted in strong wind conditions.

Take care at Sandhole Cliff, after joining the metalled road, to watch for the signpost after about a 0.33 mile (500 m) directing you to turn right to rejoin the Coast Path. Our Association has been urging the Northern Devon Coast and Countryside Service to install a true Coast Path along Sandhole Cliff; those who have been this way before will notice that they have installed half of what we requested. It is hoped that the stretch of road walking will be eliminated in the not too distant future. On the descent into Marsland Mouth, look out for a little stone building, once the seaside lookout of the author Ronald Duncan. It will provide a shelter from the elements.

As you come across the Cornish border you will start to find a series of extremely helpful and well-thought-out posts. You might smile at the first which says 'Cornwall' but thereafter not only do they point the way in each direction, but they also tell you where you are down the shank of the post. Our thanks and appreciation to whoever had this idea - surely the best yet!

The diversion to visit Morwenstow Church is worth consideration. In season refreshments are available at the old rectory. The eccentric Parson Hawker was vicar here in 1830; look out for his hut which he constructed out of driftwood on Vicarage Cliff, when you regain the Coast Path.

At Steeple Point there is a tendency to keep too far inland. The official path keeps well to seaward. To cross the stream in Coombe Valley (where there are refreshments and toilets), there is a footbridge.

At Duckpool, because of an erosion problem, a new path has been created which takes you slightly away from the original path, where you will soon cross a new footbridge and rejoin the original path.

At Sandy Mouth there is a National Trust café, which is usually open from April to November.

The walking now becomes easier. Soon after Northcott Mouth, Crooklets Beach is reached. Keep to the cliffs passing the cricket pitch. This is the official route and the best way into Bude.

13   Bude to Crackington Haven (Beach)   OS E111 (T) Bude

Grading: Strenuous   Distance -   16.4   216.6   10.2   134.6

Ascent: 812   8348   2664   27387

Timing: 4.75 hours

See also our Bude to Crackington Haven Path Description.

A colourful free guide to the coast is available at the Bude Tourist Information Centre.

Bude has good shops and accommodation, being a fair-sized town. Before you leave do try a short beach walk to the north on the falling tide and look at those cliffs - alternating bands of sandstone and shale in beautiful curving waves and with eroding continuations of the strata extending out across the beach. This pattern has been with you since Hartland, but as you go south there will soon be a series of changes - from tightly compressed folds to violent crumplings and igneous intrusions of a much more complex nature.

The southbound path starts from the sea lock on the historic Bude Canal, climbs to the cliff top at Compass Point and on to Efford Beacon. Looking back if the tide is out, the magnificent beach stretches before you for several miles going absolutely due north, with the dish aerials of the satellite tracking station visible beyond. To the south-east, if the weather is clear, the high tors of Dartmoor can be seen, and to the south-west the prominent outline of Cambeak on the south side of the Crackington Haven inlet.

The path over Efford Down and on to Upton is easy enough to follow, and then it is sandwiched between the cliff edge and the road to Widemouth. The beach at Widemouth is popular for swimming and surfing. Toilets, cafés and accommodation are available, but apart from the fine beach with its prominent Black Rock, an unusual stack of slump breccia, Widemouth is not attractive; but be prepared, there will be no more facilities until you reach Crackington Haven.

South of Widemouth the path follows the low cliff for a short distance and then diverts inland slightly at Wanson Mouth to join the coast road by the stream valley. Turn west and climb up to Penhalt Cliff. Major subsidence is occurring and the old coast path has long gone. At the southern end of the cliff top car park the Coast Path proper recommences through a field and then descends steeply into Millook Haven.

Those with a geological interest should go on to the stony beach to view the remarkable chevron folded rock strata in the cliff on the north side - a classic textbook photograph and in sharp contrast to the curving folds to the north beyond Widemouth.

Follow the steep road beyond the stream crossing in Millook for a short distance, then branch right on to the cliff top path at Raven's Beak. From here the path climbs steadily but is fairly easy going all the way to Chipman Point. Note the ancient stunted oak wood in the area of Dizzard Point. The stream valley at Chipman Point is steep and deep, one of a series ahead, with spectacular waterfalls cascading over into the rocky beach below. There is a tough ascent, then a further drop into the valley at Cleave Strand, followed by a ridge walk at Castle Point giving tremendous views. The descent to the Coxford Water stream is severe and the climb onwards to Pencannow Point will certainly exercise the heart/lung system. Pause to recover and enjoy the views before the descent into Crackington Haven.

14   Crackington Haven to Boscastle (Footbridge) OS E111 (V) Crackington Haven

Grading: Strenuous   Distance -   10.9   227.5   6.8   141.4

Ascent: 744   9092   2441   29828

Timing: 3.75 hours

See also our Crackington Haven to Tintagel Path Description.

At Crackington Haven it is usually safe for a swim, but never go out of your depth on Cornwall's north coast. There are toilets and a seasonal shop, pub and café, which survived the floods of 2004, and a long, tough, remote stretch ahead. The folds in the rock strata are remarkable, with interesting patterns down on the beach at Tremoutha Haven. Take particular care to the west of the Cambeak headland - keep away from the cliff edges and just admire the views - Hartland and Lundy Island to the north; Tintagel and Rumps Point to the south.

The path is now relatively level and generally stays above the massive landslip zone at Strangles Beach. There is a good path down through the landslip to the beach, which is interesting and pleasant at low tide, but it is an arduous climb back. At the northern end of the beach is the conspicuous Northern Door rock arch. There is access to the road and car parking at the National Trust Trevigue Farm (Coast Information Centre).

Ahead looms High Cliff, the highest point on the Coast Path in Cornwall and best avoided when a gale is blowing. The southbound descent from High Cliff is precipitously steep so take it slowly, then the path up through the massive landfall at Rusey Cliff twists and turns through the brambles and gorse. This is a major geological fault zone. The path is easier to follow than it used to be, but the ground here is soily and the vegetation grows rampantly in summer, presenting a continuing problem to the County Council, which has difficulty keeping it cleared back.

Once at the top of Rusey Cliff there follows an easier stretch through grassy sheep fields, with the approach to Buckator now being more coastal than shown in earlier guides.

The sheer black cliff of Buckator hangs over the sea inlet, with impressive white bands of quartz running through, quite different from the brown and grey cliffs of predominantly sandstone to the north. The path dips slightly to cross a bridge, then onto some stepping stones, which provide firm footing, then continues on at high level to Fire Beacon Point. Here the descent is steep but there are attractive slate steps on the most precipitous part. The path then keeps close to the cliff edge and into the Pentargon inlet where an impressive waterfall cascades down to the sea. The best view of this is now from the southern side, cliff falls having caused the path on the north side to be diverted and the old viewpoint has been lost. You are advised NOT to leave the official Coast Path to attempt a better view of this waterfall. It is a long way down.

Further cliff falls seem imminent on the south side of Pentargon, but from here on it is easy going into Boscastle. Aim for the white mast atop Penally Hill, then follow the path to the beautiful harbour inlet and past the Youth Hostel into the village of Boscastle. Penally Point is well worth the detour, an exciting viewpoint, but the slate rock is dangerously slippery when wet. Note the extraordinary small scale distortions in the strata alongside the path.

15   Boscastle to Tintagel (Haven)   OS E109 (V) Boscastle

Grading: Moderate				Distance -	7.4	234.9	4.6	146.0
Ascent:	489	9581	1604	31432				

Timing: 2.25 hours

See also our Crackington Haven to Tintagel Path Description.

There are some shops, pubs, toilets, accommodation and a new Heritage Centre which have all been rebuilt in Boscastle after the floods of 2004.

The next section on to Tintagel is shorter and easier then the two previous sections. The path leaves from the south side of the harbour and climbs steeply past the gully to Eastern Blackapit, to the Willapark headland, with its prominent white watch tower, which was restored as a National Coastwatch Institution lookout station in 2003. Go up to the watch tower, or take the short cut across the back of the headland past the ancient Forrabury strip field system, now preserved by the National Trust. The path soon descends into the stream valley of Grower Gut - there is a bridge to help you if the water is in flood. Further on the path turns sharp right to keep to the seaward side of the Manor House and onto a prominent headland which overlooks Short Island. If you are a birdwatcher, here is a good place to stop, picnic and observe through binoculars. Both Short Island and its neighbour Long Island are densely populated with breeding seabirds during the early summer, including guillemots, razorbills and a few puffins. Always look down on the water; they tend to float around in groups when off duty.

As you go on past Firebeacon Hill look for the Ladies Window rock arch in the gully to the right - walking west it is easy to miss this attractive photo opportunity. From here to Rocky Valley the going is level, but do look back to the dramatic pinnacles below Trevalga Cliff. On your left you are soon confronted by a conspicuous cliff top caravan/camp site - the path runs seaward of it. Trewethet Gut is a dangerous and eroding inlet that has necessitated a slight diversion of the path, and then you descend into the exquisite Rocky Valley. Look for seals in the surging sea as you cross the footbridge, and for the dippers that feed in the water of the stream. There is a path through Rocky Valley to the coast road, where cars may be parked.

From the footbridge there is a steep climb to high level again, and you find yourself overlooking Bossiney Haven. There is a crossroad of paths giving access to the beach from Bossinney village, and indeed this is an excellent place for a swim just after low tide. But the Coast Path goes on straight ahead and bears right to another prominent headland called Willapark, the second in just 2 miles. Again birdwatchers should go to the end and scan The Sisters and the ocean through binoculars. There are often terns, gannets and even shearwaters further out, but beware the precipitous cliff edge as you return to the path. Then on to Barras Nose headland, dominated by that awful hotel eyesore, and down to Tintagel Haven below the Castle ruins. Here there are toilets, a café and a gift shop, which also shows an introductory film 'Searching for King Arthur'.

16 | Tintagel to Port Isaac (Beach)   OS E9 & E106 (T) Tintagel

Grading: Severe				Distance -	14.7	249.6	9.1	155.1
Ascent:	835	10416	2740	34172				

Timing: 4.75 hours

See also our Tintagel to Port Isaac Path Description.

Tintagel has many shops, cafés and guest houses. The Old Post Office, owned and restored by the National Trust, dates back to the fourteenth century when it was no doubt a house of some importance.

Around The Island and down in Tintagel Haven there is some interesting and complex geology, with older rocks (Devonian) overthrust on top of more recent rocks (carboniferous), and bands of lava and tuff. The severe erosion, which is no doubt compounded by these faults and thrusts, is making access to The Island increasingly difficult to maintain. In the shelter of Tintagel Haven sailing ships used to be loaded with the high quality slate that is still extracted from several quarries inland away from this highly disturbed coastal zone.

The path to Trebarwith Strand climbs up from Tintagel Haven below and to the left of the Castle entrance and gives an excellent view of the rocks on the south face of The Island. From here on it is easy going. The Youth Hostel at Dunderhole Point was once a quarry office building. The National Trust path around the headlands of Penhallic offers glorious views. There are further old quarries ahead as you approach Hole Beach and Trebarwith Strand, and surprisingly sailing ships were loaded under the cliffs at Penhallic Point, where the remains of the wharf can still be seen. The path drops down by the toilets in Trebarwith Strand, and opposite is a welcome pub serving hot food and which has accommodation. The beach is worth exploring at low tide, but watch that you don't get cut off, and do be warned that swimming can be dangerous here.

From here to Port Isaac the path is long and very tough in parts. The descents to the valley streams and up again on the other side are about the steepest on the whole of the Coast Path. Do not leave Trebarwith Strand unless you have food, energy and plenty of time in hand. The climb up out of Trebarwith Strand, which is stepped almost all the way, will give you a foretaste of what lies ahead. And having reached the top, you must go all the way down again into Backways Cove, then up again to a more restful level stretch for about 1 mile (1.5 km) to the stream valley behind Tregardock Beach, where you are confronted by a detached and eroding piece of the cliff known as The Mountain. As you descend on the inland side of The Mountain you will meet a crossroad of paths from Tregardock village to the beach. The beach is worth a visit at low tide but your route lies straight ahead and you have quite a long way to go.

From here the stretch marked on the maps as Tregardock Cliff is easy enough, but at Jacket's Point the deepest and steepest valley of all lies before you - the commencement of the National Trust Dannonchapel property. An excellent job has been done on the path, the stream crossing and the staircase of steps on the ascent on the south side. However having reached the top, you drop down again into yet another deep valley. There are more steps up on the south side of the valley, then you go over to the Barrett's Zawn stream valley where another mineworking adit faces you. This gave donkeys burdened with slate access to Barrett's Zawn beach - don't even think about it as this tunnel is collapsing.

On the climb up round the Barrett's Zawn cliffs you will certainly see that there have been massive rock falls and that another will occur any time. You then descend very steeply on the south side into the next stream valley at Ranie Point, and as you slide down the stony slope you may well feel that the path here could be improved. Some walkers evidently complain about the staircases of steps on these valley sides, but they are so exceptionally steep we believe that steps are the best option and we have been urging the hard-pressed County Council to put some here.

Now at last the path levels out through the sheep meadows, with just a small valley to cross at St Illickswell Gug, where a boardwalk takes you across the marsh. When you reach the road at Cartway Cove the official path is directly opposite and drops down by the side of the hotel at Portgaverne. But, for the best views, take the path to the right and go round the headland and, if the tide is out, walk along the old harbour quay, where sailing ships were once loaded with slate. Either way there is then a short road walk up to the cliff car park at Port Isaac. Go through this, past the public toilets and follow the well-signed path round to overlook the attractive inlet and thence the village street.

17 | Port Isaac to Polzeath (Beach) — OS E106 (V) Port Isaac

Grading: Strenuous   Distance -   14.2   263.8   8.8   163.9

Ascent: 729   11145   2392   36564

Timing: 4.25 hours

See also our Port Isaac to Padstow Path Description.

Port Isaac is a gem, with narrow streets and tiny cottages which are no doubt easier to look at than to live in. There are two excellent pubs and one of the cafés is in an extremely old and crooked little building. Do take time to explore the back streets and the small fish market, and see if you can find Squeeze-ee-belly Alley!

Another tough walk lies ahead and there are no facilities until you reach Polzeath, but the scenery is superb. Take the road to the right behind the fish market and past more toilets. The path bears right along the cliff in front of two prominent guest houses and takes you on past Lobber Point then down into Pine Haven. From here on the path is magnificent, and keeps close to the cliff edge all the way to Port Quin. At Varley Sand the path cuts straight across a field. However it is worth taking the cliff walk around Varley Head and rejoining the Coast Path at the next stile. The fence stays on your left for over a mile of steep ups and downs, but it does protect you from the enormous herd of beef cattle that generally roams the meadows during the summer. Watch out for the peregrines that hunt along this stretch, the occasional adder basking in the sun, and seals on the rocks below.

At Kellan Head The Rumps promontory faces you at the far end of Portquin Bay. Then as you turn the corner the path overlooks the beautiful Port Quin inlet and descends to the village, once a busy little pilchard port, but there are no facilities here now, although there is a tap marked drinking water on the wall in front of you as you descend the steps into the harbour. Follow the road westbound until half way up the steep hill, where a new slate stile gives access to the south side of the inlet. You are on National Trust land and free to explore Doyden Point, formed from rocks of greenstone. The path follows the stream valley some distance in front of the old Prison Governor's House, and soon passes two fenced mineshafts, where you might still find interesting mineral samples amongst the loose spoil material nearby - but keep away from the dangerous cliff edge.

At Trevan Point there is a sharp descent to Epphaven Cove which, with its neighbour Lundy Bay, has a beautiful beach at low tide. You then enter a surprisingly wooded valley, where in late spring you will hear the delightful call of the willow warbler. As you climb up out of the bay look out for the startling Lundy Hole behind a protective wall on your right. On the cliff top again as you approach The Rumps you will see the earth ramparts of an Iron Age Fort in the lower ground in front of the headland. When you get there the detour through the entrance and on round the rocks overlooking The Mouls island is well worthwhile and can give good seabird watching; puffins nest on The Mouls most years.

It is then quite easy going on to Pentire Point, another headland formed from pillow lava. A perfect cross-section can be seen in the small vertical rock face on your left as you leave The Rumps headland, the rounded hollow shapes having been formed of molten lava under the sea. The walling stone alongside the path reveals the structure of small holes in the rock caused by gases and steam, but do not remove pieces as samples; the National Trust spends much time and money maintaining these walls and they provide wind shelter for the sheep. Just before you get to Pentire Point look out for the Memorial Plaque to Laurence Binyon which contains an exerpt from his epic war poem "The Fallen".

There are many good viewpoints on the Coast Path, but that from Pentire Point is one of the best. In clear conditions south to Trevose Head and beyond, and north to Bude, the satellite tracking station and even Hartland Quay and Lundy Island are visible, but you will need binoculars! Then follows an easy descent into Polzeath with the Camel Estuary before you and Stepper Point with its Daymark Tower on the opposite side. In contrast to the last 20 miles of perfection, the cliff top housing and car parking in New and Old Polzeath are unfortunate, but the sea, the sand and the surf are magnificent. There are toilets on the left as you reach the road beyond Pentireglaze Haven. The path continues along the cliff edge to the village centre and gives access to the beach on the way.

18 Polzeath to Padstow (Harbour)   OS E106 (V) Polzeath; (V) Rock

Grading: Easy		Distance -	4.7	268.5	2.9	166.8
Ascent:	125	11270	410	36974		

Timing: 1.25 hours

See also our Port Isaac to Padstow Path Description.

Polzeath is a surfers' paradise with several shops, cafés, accommodation and campsites. On the left by the park is a small Tourist Information Centre and there are toilets opposite.

Follow the road past the beach car park and take the path right by the cottages, where the road bends sharp left on the steep hill. The path follows the edge of Tristram Cliff, where you can watch the expertise of the surfers. From here to Daymer Bay the path along The Greenaway is intensively walked throughout the year, and measures have had to be taken to discourage people from wandering off the route and scarring the fragile turf with alternative tracks. In fact this path is so good it is now classed as suitable for wheelchair users, which is almost unique on the Coast Path. There are houses on your left, but the coastal scene is beautiful with a rocky sea-washed platform below - the haunt of curlews, redshanks, grey plover and oystercatchers, with the headlands of Stepper Point and Pentire Point in the background. Many fishing and pleasure boats can be observed entering and leaving from Padstow, some 2 miles (3 km) up the Camel Estuary.

Just off Trebetherick Point is the Doom Bar, noticeable only at low tide when the waves are breaking over the sand; there were many wrecks here during the days of sail, when ships were largely at the mercy of wind and tide. There are toilets and a café in Daymer Bay car park and the beach is one of the safest for a swim - but keep out of the estuary channel at low tide.

The Coast Path goes down the steps on to the beach and then through the dunes and over a footbridge just below Brea Hill. To visit little St Enodoc Church, which was once buried beneath the blown sand, turn left midway along the dunes and follow the white markers across the golf course. You must then retrace your route back to the dunes, or you can go on through the golf course to rejoin the Coast Path in the dunes on the far side of Brea Hill, but this is a busy golf course and you may wish you had a protective helmet and visor. Your route through the golf course is marked by large white painted rocks. From the footbridge you can go either way round Brea Hill, or straight over the top! Alternatively, if the tide is out you can walk along the beach to Rock and the Padstow ferry. All routes are pleasant and the sheltered estuary surroundings make quite a change from the exposed cliffs that you have been used to. The official path goes through a hollow just behind the dunes on the south side of Brea Hill, a Site of Special Scientific Interest for the rare plant life that thrives on the calcium-rich sand. At the southern end the path branches left to a higher level and on to Rock car park, but you can continue on along the beach, except at very high tide. There are toilets in the car park and the ferry landing is on the shore below. Be warned however that at exceptionally low tides the ferry may sail from quite some distance downstream in front of the dunes, so keep a lookout as you walk.

Rock/Padstow (River Camel)
Black Tor Ferry
Padstow Harbour Commissioners,
Harbour Office, West Quay,
Padstow, Cornwall PL28 8AQ.
Tel: Padstow 01841 532239
Mobile: 07773 081574
Fax: 01841 533346
Website: www.padstow-harbour.co.uk
E-mail: info@padstow-harbour.co.uk

Ferry operates all year at 20 min intervals
0800 - 1950 (summer)
0800 - 1650 (winter)
June-mid July 0800 - 1850
mid July - end August 0800 - 1950

A water taxi also operates between Rock and Padstow between 1900 and midnight from Easter to 31st October, weather and tides permitting. Contact: GB Smith & Son, Tel: 01208 862815 (office hours), Fax: 01208 863090, Website: www.rock-watertaxis.co.uk E-mail: info@rock-watertaxi.co.uk or contact the boat direct on 07778 105297 (operating hours only).

We urge you to contact the ferry operators direct if you are relying on this service, particularly if you are anticipating a fairly late finish and need to confirm the time of its last run.

The Saints' Way, Cornwall's coast to Coast Path from Padstow to Fowey starts here. A guide book is available from Padstow TIC (see page 162).

19 | Padstow to Trevone (Car Park)   OS E106 (T) Padstow

Grading: Easy				Distance -	9.1	277.6	5.7	172.5
Ascent:	403	11673	1322	38296				

Timing: 2.5 hours

See also our Padstow to Porthcothan Path Description.

Normally the Padstow ferry will take you into the harbour, but at low tide it will deposit you a short distance downstream at St Saviour's Point, just below the path to Stepper Point. Do not take this as an opportunity to cut out Padstow; you should go into the town and explore. The harbour area, the narrow lanes in the old town and up to St Petroc's Church are attractive and fairly traffic free. A glass of beer and a genuine Cornish steak pasty make an excellent traditional lunch. A visit to the Tourist Information Centre on the harbour is recommended, and on your way it is interesting to look at the places of origin of the many fishing boats - all ports from the Hebrides to the Channel Islands!

The Coast Path starts on your left at the north end of the harbour and is wide and well trodden. In the early summer blackcaps and warblers sing in the wooded stream valley at St George's Cove. From Gun Point you can, if the tide is out, take a short cut across the beach to Hawker's Cove by the prominent old Lifeboat House. If the tide is in you can enjoy a quiet swim; this is a very pleasant and usually wind sheltered beach. Go round the back of the old pilots' houses from Hawker's Cove and then climb up to Stepper Point, with its stone-built Daymark Tower. From this high ground there is a remarkable panorama behind you and on a clear day you will see the granite tors of Bodmin Moor in the distance.

So now you are back on the exposed Atlantic Coast. Approaching the precipitous inlet of Butter Hole Cove, look out for the small Pepper Hole a few yards to the right of the path. There follows a long easy stretch to Gunver Head, followed by a steep descent to the small stream valley. The rocky pinnacles of the Merope Islands just behind you are spectacular. After a short climb up again you will see the Marble Cliff and Porthmissen Bridge ahead. The cliff comprises many bands of hard limestone and softer shale on which razorbills, guillemots and kittiwakes nest in the summer. At Roundhole Point the path skirts the impressive Round Hole collapsed cave, which should be approached with caution, and then descends to the car park at Trevone.

20   Trevone to Porthcothan (Footbridge)   OS E106

Grading: Easy   Distance -   12.7   290.3   7.9   180.4

Ascent: 367   12040   1204   39500

Timing: 3.5 hours

See also our Padstow to Porthcothan Path Description.

There are toilets, a café, pub and a good beach in Trevone, plus some bed and breakfast accommodation. The path passes behind the little headland on the south side of the bay and follows the cliff edge round rocky Newtrain Bay. There are refreshments, toilets and a beautiful beach at Harlyn.

The stream generally has to be crossed via the road bridge, and then the path follows the beach for about 330 yards (300 m) before climbing slightly into the dunes and so on past the end of the bay to Cataclews Point. The hard erosion-resistant dolerite rock here was used to make the polished font in Padstow Church. Access to the headland by the new Padstow Lifeboat Station is barred by an ugly concrete and mesh fence, reminiscent of prison camps, which is in sharp contrast to the old tamarisk hedges nearby. How sadly all this compares with the painstaking remedial and conservation work that has been carried out by the National Trust on long stretches of the coast to the north of the Camel Estuary.

At Trevose Head you can generally visit the immaculately kept lighthouse, but keep away when the fog horn is blowing. On a clear day you will see the granite hills of West Penwith behind St Ives to the south and the satellite tracking dish aerials beyond Bude to the north. Turning south, the path passes yet another large Round Hole as it descends to Booby's Bay. There is something of a rocky scramble to get through to Constantine Bay, but it is beautiful here with a particularly attractive beach at low tide - not really safe for swimming unfortunately. Beyond the dunes the path leaves the beach to go round Treyarnon Point, revealing another attractive beach at Treyarnon Bay. The Youth Hostel is on the left, and there are toilets and possibly refreshments. If you are intent on swimming, observe the safety notices which will certainly tell you not to do so at low tide.

An unusually indented coastline follows beyond Trethias Island, but the path cuts across the narrower headlands. Between Pepper Cove and Warren Cove are the ramparts of an Iron Age Fort, and in Fox Cove you may see the remains of a ship which ran aground in 1969. Minnows Islands and the cove beyond are quite spectacular. The path turns into Porthcothan Bay, descending through the protected National Trust strip which contrasts with the housing development on the opposite side. To reach Porthcothan's pub, the Tredrea Inn, take the road before the bridge and go uphill for approximately 500 yards (458 m).

21   Porthcothan to Newquay (Harbour)   OS E106

Grading: Moderate   Distance -   17.9   308.2   11.1   191.5

Ascent: 535   12575   1755   41255

Timing: 5 hours

See also our Porthcothan to Newquay Path Description.

Porthcothan has toilets, a shop, limited accommodation and a pub. The path leaves past the shop and keeps in front of the houses and on round the headland overlooking Trescore Islands. There is a short steep descent into Porth Mear valley, a popular spot for birdwatchers, and an equally short steep climb up again, then it is an easy walk to Park Head, another spectacular viewpoint. As you approach Park Head you will come across a National Trust landmark stone - keep to the path to the left of the landmark as there are numerous landslips here and signs warn to keep well inland of the white posts because of cliff falls. Ahead lies the famous Carnewas property of the National Trust, with a beautiful beach at low tide. As you leave Park Head you will see that the cliff is slowly sliding down, although it has been like this for many years. Bedruthan beach itself has a recurring accessibility problem due to the dangerous condition of the cliffs, but a great deal of money is being spent on the long flight of steps down. If the tide is on its way out, it is worth going down to explore the pools, caves and the rock stacks, Bedruthan Steps, but don't get cut off and don't even think about swimming. The National Trust café and

Information Centre in the car park are open throughout the summer.

Bedruthan Steps can be busy, but you will soon find yourself on a quieter stretch of path to Trenance Point. The path descends from Trenance Point to Mawgan Porth through an inconspicuous ditch which was once a canal that was intended to link, in a semi-circular route, Mawgan Porth, via St Columb Major and Minor, with St Columb Porth further down the coast. It's aim was to carry mainly sea-sand inland. The canal was never finished, although the section from Trenance to St Columb was completed by 1779. Mawgan Porth has one of the few beaches in North Cornwall where dogs are permitted in the summer. At Mawgan Porth there are toilets, shops, cafés, and a pub. The road must be used here for a very short distance in order to cross the stream. The westbound path leaves to the right on the sharp road bend on the hill out of Mawgan Porth. Then follows a long high level stretch to Watergate Bay, with minor descents at Beacon Cove and Stem Cove, between which across Griffin's Point headland are the ramparts of another Iron Age Fort. Just inland is Newquay Airport and you may experience exciting views of low-flying aircraft coming into land. Ahead lies the magnificent Watergate Beach, but the path remains at high level until it crosses to the road behind the Watergate Bay Hotel into Watergate itself, where there are toilets, cafés and a pub.

After crossing the stream bridge by the car park, where there are toilets, the path leaves to the right from the road to Newquay and again climbs to the high cliff top, where it remains all the way to Whipsiderry. Here some ugly cliff top development has been permitted, but the coastal scene is great, with Newquay and Towan Head in the background. The cliffs at Whipsiderry are high and precipitous, but there are steps down to the beach and some caves to explore. There are Coast Path signs here, which take you along the pavement down the hill to Porth Beach. However you might prefer to take the original route that starts with a narrow path between a hotel and the cliff edge, and then leads you on to Trevelgue Head. You might then choose to cross the footbridge onto the island, where a rough sea can be most spectacular.

You must now return to Porth Beach, where there are toilets, cafés, beach shops and pubs. The official route then goes along the road and descends steps by the road bridge on the left, by the bus shelter. Alternatively you may walk across the beach, which is signposted down steps at the Mermaid Inn, and re-join the path opposite the Beach House apartment block at the Porth Beach car park. From here the path crosses the headland between Porth and Lusty Glaze. This short cut avoids the road and takes you round the cliff edge at Lusty Glaze and into the Barrowfields Park. With reference to the canal earlier mentioned, looking back from the Western side of Lusty Glaze a faint vertical scar can be seen running down the cliffs. This was the route of the incline plane or hoist to and from vessels on the beach and this, no doubt, is how the problem was to be solved at Trenance as well. There is a new seasonal café and shop at Tolcarne Beach. You are then on the road into Newquay town centre, but if the tide is out, you can walk along the magnificent beach from Lusty Glaze or from Barrowfields all the way to the harbour.

22 | Newquay to Holywell (Beach)   OS E104 (T) Newquay (Trains); (V) Crantock

Grading: Moderate   Distance -   10.2   318.4   6.3   197.8

Ascent: 334   12909   1096   42351

Timing: 3.5 hours (Official Route)

See also our Newquay to Perranporth Path Description.

Newquay is the biggest town on the north coast and the pedestrianised shopping centre is quite attractive. There is no shortage of restaurants, pubs and accommodation here, and there is even a railway station! But do explore the beaches and the harbour before you leave, and if the tide is out you can gain access to the Coast Path by the steps at the back of the harbour.

The Coast Path leaves just above the harbour and climbs past the old Huer's Hut to Towan Head. In the cliffs below the Hut is a noisy kittiwake colony and this is a very good spot to observe the differences between kittiwakes, fulmars, black-headed gulls and the rest. Towan Head is particularly good for seabird watching; with binoculars you may spot gannets, petrels and shearwaters further out.

From Towan Head the path follows along the back of Fistral Beach. This is probably the most popular surfing beach in the British Isles and international competitions are held here. The path climbs to the cliffs at the southern end, passing in front of the housing development at Pentire, then across the headland at the Warren over to the Gannel river estuary.

A much better and enjoyable walk is from the southern end of Fistral Beach out and onto Pentire Point East, then return along the Warren to the ferry or footbridge. The Point has fantastic views and makes a perfect picnic site.

There are four ways that you can cross the River Gannel, three of which are available, tide permitting, throughout the year. The distances via the Penpol crossing assume that you have walked via Fern Pit; the same applies to the other two crossings of Trenance Footbridge and the A3075 main road route. However, it is possible to reach the Trenance and Trevemper crossings from the town itself.

1. Newquay to Crantock via Penpol

Up river there is a tidal footbridge off Trevean Lane which crosses over to Penpol Creek. This is the official crossing of the River Gannel and during 2006 it was superbly refurbished by Cornwall County Council, and our thanks go to them. It is useful to know that this footbridge can be crossed 3-4 hours either side of low water, depending on the state of the tide and wind direction.

If you at Fern Pit and need to go upstream, go east (inland) along Riverside Crescent, Riverside Avenue, Fistral Crescent, turn right into Pentire Crescent, continue along Penmere Drive and turn right into Trevean Way, then turn right at the Coast Path sign. Be warned; there is an earlier footpath sign to Crantock - DO NOT take it because you may find it is under water. Having crossed the Gannel, turn right to follow an estuary side path. Presently it becomes a track and you pass a house on the right, then some bungalows and can soon turn right down into the National Trust's Crantock Beach car park. Take the exit practically opposite where you came in. There is a seasonal café close to the car park. (Note that the National Trail Guide refers to this crossing as being at the bottom of Trethellan Hill.)

2. Newquay to Crantock via Fern Pit Ferry Crossing (summer only); (deduct approx. 2 miles / 3 km)

Newquay/Crantock (River Gannel)	Spring Bank Holiday
Fern Pit Café and Ferry	End of May to mid-September
Proprietors - G A Northey & G King	continuous 7 days a week
Fern Pit, Riverside Crescent, Newquay. TR7 1PJ.	1000-1800 hrs
Tel: 01637 873181	

E-mail: mail@fernpit.co.uk Website: www.fernpit.co.uk

We urge you to contact the ferry operator direct if you are relying on this service, particularly if you are anticipating a fairly late finish and need to confirm the time of its last run.

You have to pass Fern Pit to reach the official crossing of the Gannel. If the ferry is running, it is a comfortable and scenic way to cross; there is even a café on the Newquay side so that you can while away your waiting time with refreshment. However, neither the ferry nor the footbridge, which is used at low tide instead of the ferry, is available when the café is closed.

3. Newquay to Crantock via Trenance Footbridge (add approx. 3 miles / 4.8 km)

Further up stream again, just before the estuary becomes a river, there is another footbridge which we call 'Trenance'. It is beside the A3075 Gannel Road just before the boating lake on the left and its junction with Trevemper Road. If you are in Newquay and know the tides are against you, the quickest way to get here is to walk down the Gannel Road (A3075). On the other side of the footbridge, walk forward for about 165 yards (150 m) keeping the hawthorn hedge on your left, until you come to a clearing on your left, offering various routes for you to choose. You can either turn right through the pedestrian gate that is a permissive path (this path is dependent on the tide, and should be navigable for two hours either side of low tide) or, if you have any doubts about the tide, you are advised to take the old bridleway through the big gate going towards Trevemper. Proceed forwards uphill and having gone over the brow, turn right before you get to the tarmac. You walk via Treringey coming to Penpol Creek and so on, to the National Trust's Crantock Beach car park as described above.

4. Newquay to Crantock via the A3075 (add approx. 4.5 miles / 7.2 km)

However if all these crossings fail there is the A3075 main road itself, which is the only all-states-of-the-tide and all-seasons route. Those taking the A3075 should proceed along it until just after the roundabout where the A392 branches off. In about 100 yards (90 m) take the little unsigned lane on the right. You immediately pass a partly ruined barn on your right and soon you pass a house on the outskirts of Trevemper. Then as the road bears left, go forward and right. Pass through a gate and turn left to go via Treringey to Penpol Creek and so on to the National Trust's Crantock Beach car park. Needless to say the A3075, although the one route that is always certain is quite the longest and certainly the most uninteresting.

Crantock Beach is attractive at low tide and can give good views of terns fishing in the Gannel below the cliffs of Pentire Point East. The path goes westwards through the dunes to the cliffs of Pentire Point West. On the west side of Crantock Beach, in the deep cleft of Piper's Hole at low tide, the first cave on the right can be entered and a flat slab will be seen on which the outline of a female figure is carved and a few lines have been cut. These carvings were the work of a local man, Joseph Prater and are thought to have been completed in the early 1900s.

Porth Joke is a sheltered sandy inlet, then follows a climb to Kelsey Head, another Iron Age site. From here in the distance can be seen St Agnes Head with Bawden Rocks offshore. Holywell Beach lies before you and the path descends to the dunes and then into Holywell. Those continuing onwards can take advantage of the splendid new National Trust footbridge across the river seaward of the village.

23 | Holywell to Perranporth (Beach car park)   OS E104

Grading: Moderate. Sand dune route - Strenuous.   Distances -   7.3   325.7   4.5   202.3

Ascent: 148   13057   486   42837

Timing: 2 hours

See also our Newquay to Perranporth Path Description.

The path cuts across Penhale Point headland and then skirts the seaward edge of the rather ugly Penhale Camp, where there is a short fenced section. The army presence here has however served to preserve the beautiful wild dunes area inland from being overrun by campsites and chalets, and it now deserves to be protected as a nature reserve. The path goes out to Ligger Point and you get the first good view of the long Perran Beach.

The easiest path, if the tide permits, is now along the great stretch of firm beach to Perranporth, rather than over the dunes. Even if, as is sometimes the case, you can only walk part-way along the beach it is worth going down to do this, there being a number of 'escape routes' up from the beach going west. The important point to watch if you want an easy descent to the beach is to fork left along the sandy path after the old wooden stile; the right fork is quicker but much steeper. It is essential that you stay on the marked route through the dunes as there has been news of collapsing mine shafts.

The official path takes you towards the dunes, where you will see the rusty coloured Perran Iron Lode in the cliff quarry. The path descends behind this and follows the back of the beach for almost a mile, then climbs up through the dunes behind the rock cliff at Cotty's Point. The incoming tide will reach the foot of the cliff here but there are escape steps to the dunes at each side, and if the tide is out you can continue on along the beach rather than going over the top. The path descends to the back of the beach just south of Cotty's Point, crosses the stream by a footbridge and so takes you into the town or the car park, where there are toilets.

24 | Perranporth to St Agnes (Trevaunance Cove)   OS E104 (T) Perranporth

Grading: Moderate   Distance -   6.0   331.7   3.7   206.0

Ascent: 314   13371   1030   43867

Timing: 2 hours

See also our Perranporth to Portreath Path Description.

Perranporth is a busy holiday centre during the summer and has good shops and accommodation. The eroding rock stacks at the western end of the beach are interesting, and may be explored using the beach access at the far end of the car park in front of the hotel terrace. Round the corner you will find a staircase from the beach up to the cliff car park at Droskyn Point. The official route leaves west from the town car park and follows the hill up Cliff Road, but just to the left of the Atlantic House Hotel there are some steps up and a footpath which takes you past the Droskyn Point car park. Whichever way you have chosen, keep inland of the prominent castellated building and on along Tregundy Lane to the end of the houses. The westbound Coast Path is signposted half left at the entrance drive to the Youth Hostel and the South West Water sewage pumping station. It then descends slightly to the right, before climbing to the cliffs overlooking Shag Rock.

From here on you will see increasing evidence of mining activity. The path is fairly level going, passing the small outcrop of granite at Cligga Head, which has been quarried and displays conspicuous stripes of greisen (for the chemistry of which you must consult the textbooks!). The mineralisation along the coast here and to the west is attributable to the intrusion of the granite which extends over a considerable area below the surface. Walking westbound through the quarry and mineworkings, you are unlikely to lose the path. Hanover Cove is named after a shipwreck. The Hanover was lost in a storm in December 1763 on route from Lisbon to Falmouth: all hands were lost plus a cargo of gold. It is rumoured that there is £50m of gold still onboard. The rock formations around the cove are dramatic and green copper stains the cliffs. There are many mineshafts in this area capped with conical steel mesh which allows access for bats.

The long stretch to Trevellas Porth is level easy going alongside the airfield perimeter; you will progress much faster here than you did further east. There is a sharp descent into Trevellas Coombe, where there are many mine workings with their decaying buildings. Go upstream to the bridge which crosses the stream in front of the Blue Hills engine house and then right over the top to Trevaunance Cove. The western path is the recommended route here, as the current official path passes close to the cliff edge. Cross over the road and turn right behind the four storey grey rendered housing block to pick up the official path. If you go down into the cove, where there is a seasonal café and toilets, a footpath behind the Jubilee Terrace and steps take you back up to the Coast Path.

25 | St Agnes to Porthtowan (The Unicorn pub)   OS E104 (V) St Agnes

Grading: Moderate   Distance -   7.4   339.1   4.6   210.6

Ascent: 262   13633   860   44727

Timing: 2 hours

See also our Perranporth to Portreath Path Description.

From the top the Coast Path stays at high level out to St Agnes Head, passing many mineshafts and waste tips on the way. Here you are circumnavigating St Agnes Beacon, a small outcrop of granite 0.5 mile (800 m) back from the coast. As the path turns west, you will see Godrevy Lighthouse across the bay, with St Ives and the massive granite of Penwith beyond. The going is relatively easy and soon you will pass the much-photographed Towanroath Engine House, part of the Wheal Coates tin and copper mine and now preserved by the National Trust. The path then descends into Chapel Porth, where there is a car park, toilets and a seasonal café which sells the legendary hedgehog ice cream! At low tide, if you walk some distance east along the beach, you will see a streak of copper ore in the cliff beneath the Towanroath shaft.

The westbound path leaves the National Trust car park, travelling inland for 200 yards (185 m) on the right of the small stream, before joining the wide rough track to Mulgram Hill, then there is a good cliff top walk to Porthtowan. The path descends to the back of the beach and on past the car park, where there are toilets. The transition from mining to tourism here has produced some unattractive features, but the beach is beautiful and extensive at low tide, from Tobban Horse to Chapel Porth.

26 | Porthtowan to Portreath (Harbour)   OS E104 (V) Porthtowan

Grading: Strenuous   Distance -   6.3   345.4   3.9   214.5

Ascent: 172   13805   564   45291

Timing: 1.75 hours

See also our Perranporth to Portreath Path Description.

Porthtowan is popular for surfing and has accommodation, a pub, a few shops and seasonal cafés. To find the westbound path, turn right along West Beach Road, then left up the narrow road to the cliff top. On the headland the path turns west, passing many mineworkings, and keeps some distance back from the crumbling and dangerous cliff edge. At the steep valley, drop to Sally's

Bottom, where steps have been installed on either side, then on reaching high level again you find yourself walking alongside the unattractive Nancekuke fence which encloses the large military establishment just inland. It stays with you for over a mile and almost to Portreath, where the Daymark above the harbour entrance can be seen ahead. The path turns west just before you reach the Daymark, avoiding another dangerous cliff edge, and joins the road down to the harbour. The long narrow inlet is unusual, but the protective pier that extends over the rocks on the west side is now out of bounds; too many people have been swept off by waves breaking over.

27 | Portreath to Hayle (White Hart Hotel)   OS E104 & E102 (V) Portreath

Grading: Moderate   Distance -   19.9   365.3   12.4   226.9

Ascent: 418   14223   1371   46662

Timing: 5.5 hours

See also our Portreath to Hayle Path Description.

There are shops, cafés and bed and breakfast accommodation in Portreath, but the beach is small in comparison to most on this coast. To gain the southbound path go round the harbour to the beach car park, then to the right up Battery Hill. Where this road drops to the beach again at the western end, the Coast Path branches left up the valley. In approximately 10 yards (10 m) there is a low National Trust sign marking Western Hill. The official Coast Path begins with a right turn up well made steps and carries on up Western Hill; you have views from here after your initial effort to gain the cliff top.

At Basset's Cove you go through a big car park and start several miles of easy cliff top walking. There are practically no signs but you are unlikely to go astray. After 1.5 miles (2.5 km) you get closer to the road between two car parks and then start to get away from it again.

You pass Hell's Mouth, which has a seasonal café just across the road. The path strikes up to the north-west and becomes narrow. From the highest point you may just see the top of St Michael's Mount to the south-west. Be careful to avoid a path to the right which eventually drops steeply to the beach. Pass through stone posts onto a farm track, which soon bears left towards a house and other buildings; here you take the stone stile into the field on your right. Keep to the seaward field boundary and cross another stone stile. Almost immediately cross a wooden stile placed to keep in the Shetland ponies used to maintain the habitat of the Knavocks.

There is then a very pleasant walk round Navax and Godrevy Points; there are good views out to sea and ahead to St Ives. You then have to negotiate a big car park but by keeping well to seaward you can miss most of it and the road that leads to it.

You will find Godrevy Café, which may be open all year round. To find the Red River footbridge leave the car park's south-western corner along a board walk. You will see the bridge to your left. After crossing it the path goes left for some 30 yards before turning right following the new large slate waymarkings through the former Hanson quarry which is now left to return to nature. Carry on through the Towans following the signposts through the dunes.

You can walk along the beach after crossing the Red River but beware the tide which can come in behind you and then cut you off near Black Cliff, some 3 miles (4.5 km) away. The walking is easier on top of the shingle bank. From here you will see a lifeguard hut, slightly to your right. You then begin a stretch through the dunes following way-posts which are well sited and lead you accurately.

If you have come along the beach, leave it at the lifeguard hut near the foot of Black Cliff to rejoin the dunes path. If you come through the dunes, avoid turning left (up a very narrow passage between houses) at the confusing waymark just above the lifeguard hut, but carry on (in front of the convenient pub garden) to turn left up some steep steps just before two holiday chalets. Turn right and walk towards a house called Silver Spray. Leave this house to your right and walk along a line of chalets on your left. Keep straight on. Part of the path is slightly overgrown here but it soon opens out to become a track and heads towards a car park.

There is no ferry and the river cannot be forded, so you have to follow the estuary inland. Walk along the old quay until you cross the swing bridge. Then turn right on the main road and follow it to the railway viaduct by the White Hart Hotel.

28 | Hayle to St Ives (Western Pier) OS E102 (T) Hayle (Trains); (V) Lelant (Trains)

| Grading: Moderate | | | | Distance - | 9.0 | 374.3 | 5.6 | 232.5 |
| Ascent: | 202 | 14425 | 663 | 47325 | | | | |

Timing: 2.5 hours

See also our Hayle to Pendeen Watch Path Description.

Distance is measured from the railway viaduct/the White Hart Hotel at Hayle, around the estuary to Lelant then along the coast road to St Ives.

At Hayle, double back under the railway viaduct and continue along Carnsew Road. You can either walk all the way to Griggs Quay along the road or take a detour around a lagoon in the estuary which offers more opportunities for bird-watching. To detour take the footpath to the right, signposted 'The Weir 0.5 mile'. Walk round the embankment and, when you come out again on the main road, turn right.

At Griggs Quay bear right off the Causeway on the A3074, passing the Old Quay House. After passing under the railway bridge, turn right - it is signed St Ives Park and Ride. When you come to a toilet block cut through to the road on your left in front of the board showing car park charges. Follow the road, passing Lelant railway station, all the way to Lelant Church.

At the church continue ahead on the same line to go across a golf course and under the railway again. Here turn left along the seaward side of the railway. The path narrows and becomes winding but stay with it.

Just before Carrack Gladden, where you are close to the sea, there are several paths going down to the beach. If the tide is well out you can go down and save yourself several ups and downs by walking along the beach to Carbis Bay. If you stay on the path you come up alongside a pedestrian railway crossing and then bear right. On the descent avoid the two beach paths on your right.

At Carbis Bay circle round the inland side of the café complex and leave on a tarmac path above the beach but to seaward of the hotel. Climb up, crossing a railway footbridge, then keep ahead avoiding the path on the left, which is where St Michael's Way leaves the Coast Path. Continue along ignoring the 'Private road - pedestrians only' sign on the right. The path becomes a minor road and, where there is another private road on your right, go straight ahead. Cross the railway again on a more substantial old fashioned bridge, to bear right and downhill. This brings you to Porthminster Café and then out below the railway station in St Ives.

For those interested, there is a cross-peninsula path, St Michael's Way between St Ives and Marazion. The waymark is a cockleshell and the path can be picked up at St Uny Church in Lelant. There is a guide leaflet to the St Michael's Way available from St Ives TIC (see page 162).

29 | St Ives to Pendeen Watch (Lighthouse)   OS E102 (T) St Ives (Trains)

| Grading: Severe | | | | Distance - | 22.3 | 396.6 | 13.9 | 246.4 |
| Ascent: | 971 | 15396 | 3186 | 50511 | | | | |

Timing: 7 hours

See also our Hayle to Pendeen Watch Path Description.

You are now starting the longest and most deserted stretch of coast on the whole South West Coast Path, so think about refreshments and accommodation. You will have to walk for some 22 miles (35 km) before finding refreshment (at Sennen Cove) actually on the path. You can divert inland as listed below but all suggestions are subject to some seasonal closing and opening hours. There is not even a telephone box on the path. It is magnificent walking, but do not start out unprepared.

In summer you might consider using one accommodation base as there are good bus services around the Land's End peninsula.

Refreshment possibilities are Zennor (0.5 mile/0.8 km off the path, inland), Gurnard's Head (0.6 mile/1 km inland) Pendeen (1 mile/1.6 km inland), Botallack (0.4 mile/0.6 km inland) and St Just (1.5 miles/2.4 km inland). In summer there is a mobile snack wagon in Cape Cornwall car park (on the path).

One other warning, the path is often rough and rocky, the terrain is severe and in places after rain surprisingly boggy; few will average 2 miles (3 km) an hour; in other words it may take you longer than you expect.

Many use St Ives as a staging post; if however you should just want to walk through continue along the path below the railway station by which you enter. This becomes a tarmac lane which proves to be called The Warren at its end. Keep as close as you can to the harbour, until you reach its north-west corner. Here you have a choice; the purists will stay with the harbour and walk out round what is called The Island or St Ives Head; it is a pleasant walk. The less pure or perhaps those with lots of miles to cover can cut the corner by following signs to the Tate St Ives - this will bring you out behind Porthmeor Beach. Those going out to The Island can walk right round the harbour to turn left, signposted The Museum.

You can walk round The Island but the interesting little St Nicholas Chapel is on the high point in the middle. When you have completed your circuit you turn right to pass along in front of the Tate St Ives.

Go along behind Porthmeor Beach, ignoring the ramp going down to it. The road starts to rise - there is a car park on your right and the path you want starts to bear off right by some public conveniences. You pass a putting green and continue along the tarmac path, which becomes the true Coast Path.

Shortly after the National Trust Hellesveor Cliff sign turn right on the track rather than going inland. At Pen Enys Point the Coast Path cuts behind the National Trust property. If you have time it is a pleasant extension out to the headland.

If the weather is clear Carn Naun Point (where there is a trig point) is the place to look back and gloat at what you have done. On a clear day you can see St Agnes Beacon and sometimes Trevose Head. Be careful though a little later, just before the stream, where there is a path down to the beach which you should avoid and shortly after the stream, a path running inland which you should also ignore. Look out for seals on the Carracks; you may even hear them 'singing'.

Just before you reach Zennor Head a Coast Path sign takes you down to the right, then shortly the path divides. At this point take the lower, seaward path to go out round Zennor Head, or take the upward path to avoid eroded cliffs and miss out on the headland. As you come inland again the Coast Path soon turns right to descend steeply down steps. Zennor itself is ahead along the track, so the miles you have planned ahead will no doubt help you decide whether to make a diversion in search of refreshment.

Back on the path you pass some of the most beautiful coastal scenery of this section, with plenty of ups and downs before Treen Cove and Gurnard's Head. If you have time it is a splendid diversion out onto the latter, once an Iron Age settlement.

Bosigran is difficult to negotiate but there is now better signing. As you drop off Carn Veslan look ahead to the ridge of Bosigran cliff and aim for the high point on the cliff. Follow the path to its highest point and just after passing through a gap in a low wall, turn right up to top of the ridge. From here descend to the stream by the obvious path, with good views of the Coast Path continuing ahead. Cross a small bridge just inland of a ruined building and follow the path uphill, just to the seaward side of the furthest field boundary. If you turn and look back you may see (and hear) the rock climbers on the cliff.

As you descend from Chypraze Cliff you see the lighthouse of Pendeen Watch ahead. You can take the inland path to your left to Rose Valley for accommodation at Morvah, Bojewyan and Pendeen, or continue on round Portheras Cove to the lighthouse and a road walk back into Pendeen.

Grading: Moderate   Distance -   6.5   403.1   4.0   250.4

Ascent: 271   15667   889   51400

Timing: 1.75 hours

See also our Pendeen Watch to Porthcurno Path Description.

Remember what was said about refreshment in Section 29.

In summer you might consider using one accommodation base as there are good bus services around the Land's End peninsula.

The official path from Pendeen Watch starts at the car park and goes along the road to the far end of the row of white ex-coastguard cottages on your left. Here you turn right, off the road. A granite marker tells you it is 3.5 miles (5.25 km) to Cape Cornwall.

The route is well-defined and brings you to the old Levant Mine dressing floors. A minor inland diversion is recommended to Geevor Tin Mine (closed Saturdays), where you will find a museum, underground tour, refreshments and toilets. If you can find time for a visit you should - the glittering displays of minerals are breathtaking.

Refreshments may also be obtained a pleasant 0.75 mile (1.2 km) walk away by turning left at the Levant Beam Engine up a track that becomes Levant Road, into Trewellard, where there is a pub and a seasonal tea-room.

From the Beam Engine House the path is a broad gravel-type that goes straight on to Roscommon and stays well inland of many interesting diversions. With care you can take paths closer to the cliff edge, and see the remains of old mine workings and the spectacular Stamps and Jowl Zawn, but be prepared to retrace your steps and turn inland again to the main path. As you approach Botallack look for the famous Crowns mine engine houses down below.

About 300 yards (275 m) past Wheal Edward keep a sharp lookout for a sign directing you to the right off the granite-set driveway. Your route now leads you towards the sea and the ancient settlement at Kenidjack Castle.

Proceeding on round the headland you descend into the Kenidjack valley. The path drops to a broad gravel track where it turns left, upstream. Continue until you reach a cottage and then turn right over a footbridge. The path then bears right to a junction by a ditch. The official path bears left and zigzags uphill, then goes right at the top. An alternative route continues right at the junction (and is not recommended in summer or early autumn when it can be very overgrown). If you take this, proceed along the path and, as you near the sea, scramble up a few yards to turn right on a similar path above, which leads to the road.

Turn right at this road and right again down the path which leads to Old Forge Cottage, at which you should head left again in a westerly direction, following the right of way downhill between stone walls. The path then passes into National Trust owned fields and over a stile, turning first left by the wall and then right to join the easy path to the viewpoint, from where there are wonderful views – there could be dolphins, sharks and seals to see. You now descend on the stepped path past Cape House, to turn right just past Cape Cottage, down a wide path with granite steps. In the nearby car park there are public toilets and seasonal refreshments are available.

31 | **Cape Cornwall to Sennen Cove (Beach Car Park)**   **OS E102**

Grading: Moderate   Distance -   8.1   411.2   5.0   255.4

Ascent: 315   15982   1033   52433

Timing: 2.5 hours

See also our Pendeen Watch to Porthcurno Path Description.

In summer you might consider using one accommodation base as there are good bus services around the Land's End peninsula.

From the car park descend into a small field. At the bottom you turn left and descend granite steps, then turn sharp left up a concrete-covered drive, then take a right turn onto a granite gravel covered track. The steep climb ends at Carn Gloose, where the road bears off left to Ballowall Barrow and St Just, but the path bears right down to Cot Valley. Half way down a new waymarked path will take you straight down to the Porth Nanven beach.

Following the Coast Path in Cot Valley, turn right down the road and head towards the beach at Porth Nanven, then cross the stream and climb up on the path. There are several zigzag paths to make the climbs easier as you proceed around Gribba Point towards Nanquidno.

From here to Gwynver Beach the path is fairly level and the walking is moderate (with one difficult step) but the Coast Path is everything a coast path should be - we predict that everyone will enjoy this section! Look out for rare flowers in early summer in fields near to Nanquidno.

Below Escalls cliff, between Gwynver Beach and the sands of Sennen Cove, the path runs along the edge of fast-eroding low cliffs. It is suggested you might consider walking the firm sands of Sennen Cove, at any time but very high tide, rather than the official soft sand route in the dunes at the back of the beach.

32   Sennen Cove to Porthcurno (Beach)   OS E102 (V) Sennen Cove

Grading: Moderate				Distance -	10.6	421.8	6.6	262.0
Ascent:	565	16547	1854	54287				

Timing: 3.25 hours

See also our Pendeen Watch to Porthcurno Path Description.

In summer you might consider using one accommodation base as there are good bus services around the Land's End peninsula.

We recommend that during your planning of this section, you should allow a good hour for a visit to and exploration of the scenic Minack Theatre. Entry can be gained when there is no performance. Please remember that any visit you make to the theatre is not included in our estimated timing for this section. However, we need to warn you about your accommodation requirements to Penzance. From mid May to mid September there are performances at the theatre, and theatregoers take up many B&Bs, so bear this in mind and perhaps book ahead.

Leaving Sennen Cove you pass the Round House; go on into the car park area and turn left at the public toilets. Proceed ahead shortly to turn right and then head for the battlemented lookout post. From the lookout there are many well-worn paths to Land's End - needless to say, the best is the most seaward - just keep heading on towards the hotel block at Land's End. The Coast Path provides free access to the Land's End complex, indeed the route passes through it. By keeping to the seaward paths you may avoid some of the crowds, although you may want to use the cafés and other facilities.

Proceeding on, be careful to watch for path rerouting. The proprietors of Land's End are trying to encourage the growth of grasses on areas badly affected by foot erosion. The path leads to Greeb Cottage which now houses an animal collection.

From Land's End to Porthcurno is one of the finest sections of the path, and effects of the sun on the water make you conscious of having turned to walk in a southerly direction. As you approach Nanjizal Beach look across to see where the Coast Path turns right and uphill after the small stream. Once across the stream by a small wooden bridge proceed ahead for 40 yards (36 m) and then turn right to go steeply uphill on a stepped path.

Care should be taken to keep to the seaward path out to Gwennap Head. It is the official route but it can be tempting to keep to the easier, wider, inland path and you will miss many grand sights. Tol-Pedn-Penwith means the 'holed headland of Penwith' and that hole is easy to miss. From the Coastwatch hut walk on a bearing of 140 degrees for 153 yards (140 m) then walk along a path which bears 190 degrees. It is up to you but if you do go to walk across the natural arch then take GREAT care and, having crossed over, bear left along a path to rejoin the higher Coast Path.

The path drops into Porthgwarra where, if tide permits, a walk down the granite slipway towards the beach is rewarding. From the beach you can walk up through a fisherman's passage, out the other end then return to the refreshment hut (open early April - October).

The path leaves Porthgwarra along a track in front of cottages, then turns slightly inland to go behind another. The path is now easy to follow and is well-marked along Carn Barges. As you descend towards Porth Chapel beach take a short excursion out to a granite point for glorious views of the beach. The path descends to the back of the beach, passing by St Levan's Holy Well. You can descend to the beach for a swim or bear off left within 10 yards (9 m) of the bridge. The path traverses cliffs behind the beach then climbs towards the headland of Pedn-mên-an-mere. Another rewarding diversion is to go out and round the headland.

You come out into the car park behind the Minack Theatre through a kissing gate. Go through the car park to leave at the other end on a path parallel to and behind the Theatre entrance. The path drops very steeply, with steps, to Porthcurno Beach. A notice warns 'A difficult descent not recommended for young children or elderly persons', and we could add that if one suffers badly from vertigo then go, have a look and make up your own mind. An alternative path around by the road can be used.

At the bottom turn left and unless you want a swim do not go onto the beach but keep along the path contouring above the beach. Drop down to the path from the car park to the beach. You may detour left for transport or refreshments, or to visit the museum at Porthcurno that celebrates the history of submarine telegraphy.

33 | Porthcurno to Lamorna Cove (Harbour) OS E102

Grading: Strenuous		Distance -	8.8	430.6	5.5	267.5
Ascent:	371	16918	1217	55504		

Timing: 3.25 hours

See also our Porthcurno to Penzance Path Description.

In summer you might consider using one accommodation base as there are good bus services around the Land's End peninsula.

There is again fine walking in this section and some of it easy going; however parts of it are not easy and it may well take you longer than you expect.

The path starts at the back of Porthcurno beach. You join a steep track, overlooking the beach to Percella Point.

Just beyond the Telegraph Cable sign the National Trust has put in a short path which loops round the next headland and keeps you nearer to the sea. Along this path there is a very steep path to Pednvounder beach which many use for swimming.

The path then crosses behind the earthworks of Treryn Dinas (fortress settlement) with an Iron Age cliff castle. A diversion can be made to see the Logan Rock on the headland but you have to return to the path where you left it.

At Penberth Cove there is currently a tedious 400 yard (366 m) inland diversion for dog walkers to try to ensure that dogs do not foul the fishing slipway there. For dogless walkers, cross the slipway, pass the old capstan and go up the other side outside the house to climb a cove-side path.

As you progress east along Trevedran Cliff the path veers away from the cliff edge and you cross a heathlike stretch of cliff top and then come upon a well-marked turn right, with a white painted sign on a granite boulder, directing you to turn sharply right. Turn down here and follow the waymarks.

Nearing St Loy the path gradually moves inland. You will pass a house seaward and below you - after passing it watch out for a sign and stile. You will descend steeply through woodlands. You will find a B&B here in this tranquil spot at Cove Cottage but, sadly, the owners have retired to spend more time gardening and their cafe is now closed. The path continues on to the bouldered beach. There are only 55 yards (50 m) of boulders to cross before you leave them to regain the Coast Path. Watch carefully for the beach exit: in the past several have missed it and continued walking on the boulders to have to return.

After you pass the path down to the lighthouse at Tater-du, you cross a tumbled granite landscape to Lamorna. You will pass the entrance to the Oliver Land Reserve, 'a place of solitude', purchased by Derek and Jeannie Tangye to create a wildlife sanctuary and now protected by the Minack Chronicles Nature Trust.

Be careful on Carn Barges not to be diverted on to the inland path to Lamorna - the better and official route is round the coast.

34 Lamorna Cove to Penzance (Railway Station)   OS E102 (V) Mousehole; (V) Newlyn

Grading: Strenuous and then easy				Distance -	9.7	440.3	6.0	273.5
Ascent:	169	17087	554	56058				

Timing: 2.5 hours

See also our Porthcurno to Penzance Path Description.

In summer you might consider using one accommodation base as there are good bus services around the Land's End peninsula.

After the café at Lamorna you bear right, behind the harbour, and cross the bridge. You go up past a complicated waymark which, unless you look at it carefully, almost sends you the wrong way. However, keep right with only one house still on your right.

Few find the correct route into Mousehole. When you have passed the Bird Hospital on your left there is a post box on your right with a Coast Path sign pointing the way you have come, but not the way you are going! Turn right opposite 'Lowena', and at the sign for Merlin Place head towards the rocks (St Clement's Isle) which you can see out to sea.

Just before the foreshore bear left along a terrace and fork right into a car park. Go to the bottom right end of the car park to continue briefly along the harbour side. You then have to turn in again left and first right. However, those with an interest in history should go past the house with the pillars, the Keigwin, the oldest and most attractive house in the village. It has a large porch with granite columns. The turn brings you out on to a busier street; bear right along it to come behind the harbour again.

The official Coast Path leaving Mousehole goes up a narrow road. We suggest you pass through the car park at the other end of the harbour, near some toilets, and along a concrete path. Go round the corner and up steps into a small car park with a café. At the top turn right along a pavement.

A new cycle/walkway has been opened seaward of the road to Newlyn. Follow the signs and when you reach Newlyn go round the back of the harbour, passing the War Memorial. Then bear right over the little bridge; the Seaman's Mission is on the right. Over the bridge bear right to come out once more behind the beach. Walk along the promenade into Penzance.

Pass the open air Jubilee swimming pool and continue to pass Penzance Harbour then keep to the right on the seaward side of the car park, where, at the far side you will join the waterfront walkway/cycleway which leads onto the seaward side of the railway.

35 Penzance to Marazion (Market Place)   OS E102 (T) Penzance (Trains)

Grading: Easy				Distance -	5.4	445.7	3.4	276.9
Ascent:	14	17101	46	56104				

Timing: 1 hour

See also our Penzance to Porthleven Path Description

Leave Penzance by the walkway/cycleway from the seaward north east corner of the harbour car park. The Railway and Bus Stations and the Tourist Information Centre are all within 150 yards (135 m) of this waterfront walkway. The walkway is a scenic and safe way out of Penzance with good views over Mounts Bay. It follows the top of the sea wall to Marazion.

If the tide is right it is possible to walk all the way from Penzance to Marazion along the beach, though you will have to ford some small streams on the way.

Further along, where the railway veers away from the beach, you will come upon Marazion Bridge, which has a large car park.

You will have to cross the Red River either by the road bridge or a footbridge to bring you to a grass car park known locally as Folly Field. Follow the edge of the field past the sailing dinghy compound, across a car park and into historic Marazion, behind the new sea defence wall.

Between Marazion and Lelant there is a cross-peninsula path, St Michael's Way. This could be used to make a circular trip round Penwith by walking round the Coast Path and coming back inland from Marazion to Carbis Bay, Lelant or St Ives. There is a guide leaflet to the St Michael's Way available from St Ives TIC (see page 162).

36 | Marazion to Prussia Cove (Bessy's Cove)   OS E102 (V) Marazion

Grading: Moderate   Distance -   6.8   452.5   4.2   281.1

Ascent: 195   17296   640   56744

Timing: 1.75 hours

See also our Penzance to Porthleven Path Description.

Walkers are treated badly at the beginning of this section, as there is no path at all for a while and then the first coastal length is on a beach.

You go up the road in Marazion for some way and pass the 40 speed restriction sign. Shortly after this you see the sign which thanks drivers for driving carefully and turn right into a driveway. As the driveway bears right, into a private house, you go left down a little concrete staircase and then follow the path down to the shoreline. Walk along the beach (but not when the tide is very high) and ascend some hideous metal steps. There is a marked diversion at Trenow Cove. Follow the diverted track for 274 yards (250 m) and look out for a yellow arrow pointing you back to the coast.

After that you will have no trouble getting to Perranuthnoe where there are refreshments in season. The path comes out onto a tarmac road by a car park. Walk on into the tarmac lane immediately opposite and to seaward of the car park. Go right at the fork by Blue Burrow Cottage and bear right. Just before you get to the beach the path turns left into a field.

At Cudden Point the path cuts slightly inland but then the true Coast Path goes seaward again towards Little Cudden. The view from Cudden Point takes in the whole of Mount's Bay from Lizard Point to Tater-du. Notice particularly the unusual view of Mousehole.

At Bessy's Cove the path goes up to join a track by a letter box. Continue ahead bearing right beside a pair of granite gate posts.

37 | Prussia Cove to Porthleven (Harbour)   OS E102 & E103

Grading: Strenuous   Distance -   10.3   462.8   6.4   287.5

Ascent: 338   17634   1109   57853

Timing: 3 hours

See also our Penzance to Porthleven Path Description.

The path at Prussia Cove is quite a surprise, a sunken lane between two large stone buildings. You continue along a lane, with the row of old coastguard cottages up on your left, to pass through a gate, after which the track becomes a path and you should fork right at the first junction.

The path later becomes a green track down to Praa Sands, where there are plenty of refreshments in season, and one café opens on Friday, Saturday, Sunday and Monday through the winter months, although it is closed from January to mid February.

The official route is along the road but it is preferable to continue on near the sea, so turn right down onto the beach onto a slipway between the Welloe Rock public house and the car park. Walk along the front of the pub and the beach shop, then take the steps off the beach beside the shop/café. Turn right across the top of the sand dunes, going left when signed, into a small estate of houses. As you come out of the estate bear right and pick up the path in the dunes once more.

The path now takes you across Rinsey Head, with a diversion sign taking you inland to cut off the point. Go through the National Trust car park. As you drop down to the restored engine house you will see two paths ahead, one going uphill, which you do not want, the other going down, which you do. When you reach the engine house pick up the path below it on the other side.

At Trewavas Head the path bears inland of the old mine ruins and is well marked. Between Trewavas Head and Bullion Cliff the coastal route changes often due to constant erosion. It is well to be cautious and always take the newest track even if the old one does appear to be intact. You will see evidence of recent landslides. The advice is keep well away from the edge.

As you approach Porthleven you pass a cross erected in memory of drowned sailors buried in unconsecrated ground.

On entering Porthleven you join a lane and then take the first road down to the right, which will lead you down into the town and harbour.

38 Porthleven to Mullion Cove (Harbour)   OS E103 (V) Porthleven

Grading: Moderate				Distance -	11.4	474.2	7.1	294.6
Ascent:	335	17969	1099	58952				

Timing: 3.25 hours

See also our Porthleven to The Lizard Path Description.

At Porthleven walk around the back of the harbour over the Green and head for the Bickford Smith Institute, the building with a clocktower at the beginning of the pier. Follow the road around the building to the start of the beach and keep to the coastal road. This is Loe Bar Road. The Old Chapel 1790-1820 was the first of three Methodist churches in Porthleven. Turn right into Mount's Road, although it says it is a cul-de-sac.

Carry on along Highburrow Road, following the coast road past the Coach House and Dolphin Cottage, the last building before the car park. The sign at the steps in the car park says 'Church Cove 3.75 miles'. Go up the steps and proceed along the coast and down to the beach of Loe Bar.

Keep to the seaward side and head for the red life saving equipment box on the far side of the beach. Keep to the less conspicuous right hand path going uphill past the cross. The path levels out and you pass a wooden seat. 87 yards (80 m) after this, fork right downhill hugging the old coast route. Before Gunwalloe Cove pass the old pilchard fishery building and old rusting winches alongside the path.

You come out onto a gravelly road. First right takes you down to the beach but the path goes straight ahead, before bearing right. It looks like you are heading up a private drive but this is an illusion. Heading onto the National Trust land of Baulk Head pass to the left of the house and then go over or through a series of stiles and gates. Left is the crenellated house of Halzephron Farm.

Follow the path past the tamarisk hedges above Halzephron Cove, where you join a path following the road towards a small car park. Bear right at the National Trust sign for Halzephron Cliff across the top of the cliffs, where there is crop farming to the left not even a yard from your feet. Turning right, a gate takes you to Dollar Cove. Follow the signs down to Church Cove, which diverts one around the continually eroding cliffs - a reminder of what is happening along the whole of the Coast Path.

At Church Cove you can view the spectacularly placed church that has seemingly been hewn out of the very rock that it nestles in. From the church, skirt the back of the beach and head for the visible path going up the cliff. The alternative to heading for the church is to follow the official route veering left to the buildings along the hidden road: these are public conveniences. Follow the road to a turning space, ignoring the bridge that leads onto a golf course. There is a path leading from the turning space to another bridge over a freshwater stream.

Cross the bridge and go across or around the back of the beach, up the path to the top, where there is a car park. Be aware that the Coast Path turns right straight after the car park, off the road, seaward to Poldhu Cove. If you pass two white pillars of a cottage on your left, you have missed the Coast Path on the right, opposite one of the golf course tees. The path rejoins the road to go around the back of Poldhu Cove. There is a seasonal café here, situated at the back of the beach road. Walk over the bridge (noting the unusual black post box on the brow of the thinnest part of the bridge) and take the road signposted to the Marconi Centre. 110 yards (100 m) up the hill, turn right off the driveway to go onto the path round the large residential home which was once a luxury hotel. One passes the Marconi monument and carry on downhill, past a house perched on the cliff at Polurrian Cove. Take the steps up to the Polurrian Hotel and take a track to the right continuing uphill.

Join a road, keeping right, and when the road veers to the left, the path continues ahead along the coast past the coastguard lookout. Continue to the Mullion Cove Hotel, looking for the path to the right, next to a cannon in the car park - follow this down to the quay. Turn left. Refreshments are here with toilets 110 yards (100 m) up the hill.

39 | Mullion Cove to The Lizard (Lighthouse)   OS E103

Grading: Moderate		Distance -	10.9	485.1	6.8	301.4
Ascent:	405	18374	1329	60281		

Timing: 3.25 hours

See also our Porthleven to The Lizard Path Description.

Some of the most popular coastal walking in Cornwall features in this section. The scenery is spectacular and well worth the uphill effort at the start of this section. From the quay the sign for the path is after the first house, on the right, up the hill past the café, which is on the left. Take your time and enjoy the views to your right over Mount's Bay where on clear days St Michael's Mount stands proud. As you trek up the hill notice that the vegetation changes. Underfoot the geology is changing from schists to serpentine. In July and August Natural England takes short two hour circular walks around Mullion, Kynance and the Lizard (telephone 01326 240808 for details).

After the first climb there is a wooden walkway at the brow of the hill. Keep to the right path, hugging the coastline. You can be rewarded with nesting seabirds and many varieties of unique flora that you cannot see elsewhere in the South West. You are now in Chough country, so keep a look out and listen for their unique cry.

Having rounded Parc Bean Cove at Lower Predannack Cliff, look back towards Ogo-dour Cave as you progress around Vellan Head. Go down and then uphill at Gew Graze (Soapy Cove at Kynance Farm) then just after, if you have a head for heights, look into the cave at Pigeon Ogo.

It is not well signposted from Soapy Cove to Kynance, so when in doubt keep coastward. The café at Kynance is well stocked for food and the new eco toilets are worthy of your patronage, in the knowledge that all is being recycled and treated without any harm to the environment. Electricity is sustainable too. There is a choice of paths up to the car park. Either go uphill along the wider track from the café, or, if the tide is favourable, go across the back of the beach and up the other side, following the path and looking for a sign on your right indicating the Lizard. Take it or continue to the car park. Whichever path you choose from the café, the Coast Path continues from the car park just before the public toilets.

From Soapy Cove and across Vellan Head all the way to the Lizard keep an eye out for seals and choughs. From Kynance all the way around to Church Cove on the other side of Lizard Point there are paths that lead inland to Lizard Town (actually a village), so a variety of circular walks can be taken – it is handy for accommodation too.

The path at all times of the year is well trodden and signposted all the way to Lizard Point and the Most Southerly Café at the tip of the Lizard.

40 The Lizard to Coverack (Dolor Point) OS E103 1 mile to (V) Lizard Town

Grading: Moderate but strenuous in parts		Distance -	17.1	502.2	10.6	312.0
Ascent:	654	19028	2146	62427		

Timing: 5.75 hours

See also our The Lizard to Coverack Path Description.

From the Café go uphill and turn right along in front of the lighthouse, shortly after which is the Lion's Den, that a series of paths lead to and from. Worth the slight detour.

The Housel Bay Hotel offers all year round facilities. Its gardens reach down to the sea and you follow the path that edges their property. A little further on you pass the Lizard Wireless Station hut - originally set up by Marconi to contact shipping and also to carry out research. It is open for limited hours in season (ring 01326 561407 for details). Passing the Lloyds Signal Station go along the drive past a house and then the path veers right.

At Kilcobben Cove you pass inland of the Lifeboat Station. Turn right down the steps directly next to the Station but veer left. Do not continue down the steps. On your left is a single bench dedicated to HSM Unsworth (Popeye) who 'misbehaved all his life'. Therein lies a story.

You come downhill into Church Cove to a signpost indicating the direction to follow. The road goes up towards Lizard village but take the gate 22 yards (20 m) up on the right, which follows the line of the coast. Keep to the path up the hill, ignoring any paths that intersect and seem to lead closer to the coast. At the top of the hill there is a stile to be negotiated.

The Coast Path inclines downhill and round into Polgwidden Cove, where you encounter another rocky stile. Do not take the path to the left, which is in sight of the isolated house. Turn right and pass in front of it where there are evergreen shrubs, South African Proteas, jockeying for space along the tight path.

Climbing slightly uphill the signs for the National Trust's Devil's Frying Pan greet you. The cove is steep sided and the path narrows as you negotiate around it heading towards Cadgwith Cove. The path into the village is well signposted, but keep right and do not take the road into the village, take the path descending between houses, before the road which you join finally to enter the village. A beach, refreshments, art gallery and pub with accommodation await.

Continue on the road up the hill and turn right on the path on reaching Veneth Cottage. This takes you around the northern arm of the bay past thatched cottages, before turning left at the boarded up Huers Hut to follow the coast to Poltesco. National Trust signs reveal the latest coastal land management strategy, Shetland ponies.

Round Enys Head it is 820 yards (750 m) to Poltesco, a National Trust property. The path leading down to the bridge can be slippery in the wet due to the serpentine rocks that have been incorporated on their sides into the path. Descending the steps, go over the bridge. The next two paths off to the right lead to the Serpentine works and the beach, where ships used to take large slabs of Serpentine away that had been sliced and cut.

Continue uphill. At the top where the path veers left, there are three steps going up to your right and out to a small viewpoint. Returning to the path, beware again in wet weather of the shiny rocks set in the path. The path bears right around the back of Little Cove.

A golf course and caravan park occupy Thorny Cliff, where there are handy interpretation boards of the wildlife that might be encountered along this stretch of coast. Keeping seaward the path leads around the edges of the course onto the road leading down to Kennack Sands. If the seasonal cafés are open, stock up now as this is the last refreshment stop before Coverack. There are also toilet facilities and car parking here. Kennack is geologically unique with exposures of gneiss, gabbro, granite and basalt. The beach is littered with the story of the last 400 million years. The far beach is dog friendly and when the tide is out you can walk around the Caerverracks, the shiny red and black Serpentine outcrop, as opposed to taking the well signed path behind both beaches.

The Coast Path is the less obvious choice of the two paths at the end of the second beach, but nevertheless it is clearly signposted and follows the outline of the coast. You ascend up to the undulating land of the Eastern Cliff before crossing the promontory of what was a cliff castle at Carrick Luz. Follow the well signed path along the coastline, where it soon descends quite dramatically to Downas Cove.

Having made the ascent from Downas Cove there is a further but smaller descent after Beagles Point to Beagles Hole. Cross a bridge and the path cuts into the surrounding rock, making a very narrow climb, where you can use both hands to aid the effort of the ascent. Watch out for the sign on a rock on the ground that will indicate the direction to take. Turning right the path leads up along the cliffs to Black Head. There is a lookout building here, where inside, sightings of whales and seals are written by observers for all and sundry.

Descending gently over Chynalls Cliff the path presently leads down over very difficult terrain across wooden walkways to the seaward side of what was the Headland Hotel at Chynalls Point. If the vegetation is overgrown beware of your footing. The promontory of the Point is the official path and it continues hugging the coast to the clearly marked and well trodden path that leads into Coverack.

On reaching tarmac 55 yards (50 m) along, the official path veers right, above a children's playground that is right on the coast. There is no sign to indicate that you turn into the playground. Continue up and over the brow of a hill and again turn right, down some steep steps and then left squeezing between the coastal properties to the car park at the back of the pub. This is Dolor Point. Walk around the Paris public house to view Coverack and the inspiring coast that sweeps eastwards to Lowland Point, which is the furthest promontory that can be seen from Dolor Point. Lowland Point marks another northerly change in the path's direction on its way towards Porthoustock, just like Black Head to Coverack, a short while back.

41   Coverack to Helford (Ferry)   OS E103 (V) Coverack

Grading: Moderate			Distance -	21.1	523.3	13.1	325.1
Ascent:	663	19691	2175	64602			

Timing: 5.75 hours

See also our Coverack to Helford Path Description.

This distance includes the walk around Gillan Creek. If you arrive there at low tide and cross on the stepping stones, or indeed paddle, deduct 2 miles (3.2 km).

Note: evening meals may present a problem in Helford. At busy periods the Shipwright Arms (01326 231235) will only serve pre-booked meals. There is now a cafe at Helford Chapel, in the main car park, telephone 01326 231893. Along the way there are pubs in Porthallow and Manaccan.

In Coverack the Coast Path continues behind the harbour and the beach and continues along the road. Where the main road out of Coverack goes sharply uphill, go straight ahead onto a small tarmac road. There is a sign for the Porthgwara residential home. There are houses to the left and right. Once past the nursing home there are only a few houses seaward. At the top of the road a bench is reached, where there is also a path heading inland to St Keverne. The Coast Path continues ahead downhill. Very soon the Coast Path veers off right, just before the South West Water gate.

The path out to Lowland Point can be very wet and muddy in all seasons, but luckily the path is often just following the coast and there is always a choice of terrain. It is best to keep close to the shore going east all the way round the Point to Dean Quarry. Look out for the seals that often bask on the rocks just offshore and the birdlife.

The South West Coast Path Association fought hard to get a path through Dean Quarry - the alternative would have been a long diversion inland. The quarry closed in 2005 and there is a good path edged with large rocks and railings passing between the quarry and the coast. The route provides good views of the bleak disused workings, old jetty for loading ships and the size graded bunkers of gabbro - the unique stone quarried here.

Exit the quarry and head down on to the beach at Godrevy Cove. From the quarry exit above the beach look left up the fields to view the buildings of Rosenithon. Unfortunately the path does not continue around the coast here and you must access the path at the back of the beach, going uphill towards the buildings. Veer left to the back of the beach, having crossed half of it. The signs should be visible for you to walk through fields up a gravel track and sunken lane to Rosenithon. The path has been redirected around the property at the top and although it is often muddy, enjoy the elm trees, the horsetails and the fact that you don't have to enter a courtyard where others are staying. The sea is also in view from the path.

Walk up the tarmac road and at the T-Junction in Rosenithon, turn right and go up the hill. The road bears right and 5.5 yards (5 m) past this the Coast Path takes off left into a field: there is only an ivy covered path marker to alert you to the change in direction. Cross the first field to a Cornish stile, possibly the forerunner of the modern cattle grid, with four large granite stones to cross. Traverse two more fields in the same direction, aiming for the visible roof of a property, to a hidden stile overlooking a road.

Turn left on the road and then first right down into Porthoustock. There are toilet facilities here behind the excellent new Lottery-funded village hall. From Porthoustock to Porthallow the official route again goes inland to avoid the now unused quarries around Pencra Head and Porthkerris Point. However there is a path, which in contrast to the official path, does go along the coast.

Coastal Route
In Porthoustock keep right of the old red dilapidated telephone box, having passed the entrance to the beach. Passing in front of a thatched cottage you soon come to a metal gate. To access the path walk right, around the wall.

Continue along the track and take the left fork approximately 150 yards (137 m) beyond the northern end of a disused quarry, which leads to a steep uphill slope. 20 yards (18 m) beyond the top of the slope, fork right for the shorter route to Porthkerris beach, except around high water spring tides. The simpler route for any state of the tide is to proceed up along the track for a further 450 yards (410 m), and turn right onto another track through a field, which leads down to behind Porthkerris beach. Walk straight up the hill opposite, passing the way up to a restaurant on the left. (Should this latter track not be open, continue on to the MoD building and turn right along the road.)

Where the road bears left, carry straight on through two fields parallel to the coast, to a kissing gate. Proceed ahead up the path and then steeply down to the beach at Porthallow.

Official Route
You leave Porthoustock going up the hill but soon where the road bears right go ahead on a track. You pass thatched houses on your right and then the track ends. Go straight ahead and choose the path going immediately uphill and not straight along the long path at the bottom of the wood. The path rises sharply uphill into a field. From the middle of the field look up to the top of the field and there will be a break in the fencing. This follows a fence and is a path that goes up 10.9 yards (10 m) to a stile on the left that you have to raise the top bar to cross.

Entering another field look just right of straight ahead to a six bar gate. Depending on the crops, it is best to turn right and go up around the field to the other side, to the hidden cattle grid-type stile leading on to a road. Turn left and follow the road past a beige coloured house on the left and then left around the bend after more cottages to a T-junction. Trenance is to your left, which you ignore. Simply follow the main road uphill until reaching another T-junction. Look for the footpath ahead a few yards to your right - it goes down alongside a vineyard, through a set of barns at the bottom of the path, to join the road. Turn right down to Porthallow. A post office and store is available on the descent to the beach. The pub, Porthallow Arts, a seasonal eatery and toilet facilities border the beach.

The fact that Porthallow is exactly half way around the South West Coast Path (at 315 miles) inspired the Association to celebrate this with a large waymark at the top of the beach. It was completed in 2009 and the engraved wording gives an interesting insight to the history, flora and fauna of the area.

You leave Porthallow by following the back of the beach and up the steps that are in front of the homes overlooking the Cove. Good weather rewards you with fine views as one ascends and descends the narrow path out of Porthallow.

After a mile or so a stile is encountered announcing the National Trust area of Nare Head. Standing on top of the stile, four headlands are visible to St Mawes and beyond. At this stile make sure that the path diagonally descending the field is taken. There is a small sign 10.9 yards (10 m) downhill. Do not be tempted to walk straight on along the top of the field. Eventually you hug the coastline, having passed another short marker next to some light coloured rocks that are prominent over the brow of the field. Through the bracken on the edge of the coast, head to Nare Point; Pendennis Castle, Falmouth and St Mawes come into view as you round the promontory.

The disused MoD observation post at Nare Point has been converted to a National Coastwatch Institute lookout station. This point has excellent views to the Helford River, Roseland Peninsula and out to sea, and is an important place to monitor the safety of both pleasure craft and commercial shipping.

Follow the coast around into the Helford River. At the private slipway, go through the gate and over a small ravine on the footbridge. Descending many steps announces the closeness to Gillan. Look out for the weather vane on a flagpole. Go around the sheltered beach and cross the beach access road that leads up left. Bearing right, presently there is no sign to indicate that the path follows a very narrow way squeezing between houses.

Further on is another beach, Flushing Cove, and following the estuary, keeping the houses on the left, the path rises and continues for another 219 yards (200 m) before decision time arises.

If the tide is out then the river to St Anthony can be crossed by stones or paddling. Otherwise you have a longer but an extremely picturesque walk through Carne around to the sheltered Creek. You forget that it is actually road walking, whilst botanists will count on a good day in May or June up to fifty different plant species along the roads and around the estuarine beaches.

Gillan Creek walking round
Go up the grass centred concrete track to and along a made up road. At a left bend the Coast Path is signed to the right of a pebble-dashed house. The sign is on a pylon on the right just past the house named Dolton. Proceed along a short stretch of a narrow, possibly overgrown path into a field. Keep to the hedge on the left, to a six bar gate, then veer right diagonally up across the next field to, and over, another stile just left of another gate. Turn up the field to locate a ladder stile well to the right of a bungalow. Often there is livestock in this field, yet the landowner still makes provision for walkers, so crossing the field is easy. Climb over the ladder stile to the road and turn right down to Carne and right again beyond the creek head to St Anthony.

Gillan Creek Crossing (deduct 2 miles / 3.2 km)
It can usually be forded from one hour before to one hour after Low Tide. Predicted low water is 15 minutes earlier than shown in the tide tables. But do proceed with care.

There are two possible crossing places. Proceed until you can go no further along the path by the river, descend steps to the beach and paddle across towards two caravans on the far shore.

A little further upstream you can cross part way on stepping stones – take care as they could be slippery underfoot. If you do not use the stepping stones it is possible to paddle across here also.

Ferry

Sail Away	April 1st to Oct 31st
St Anthony	Anthony Jenkin offers a service.
Manaccan. TR12 6JW	It is not his main business and may
Tel: 01326 231357	not always be there. Worth a try though.

Coast Path continues
Once across turn right to pass in front of the church. Turn left up the hill. About 10 yards (9 m) past the last cottage, there is a churchyard on the left. Opposite there is a well signed path going off at a sharp angle high up to the right. This leads up to Dennis Head.

There is a rewarding circular route out around Dennis Head if you have time. To avoid the circular walk, turn left once through the gate, walking between the fence and the blackthorn hedge. To do the circular walk, turn right at the gate and left at the next stile. Then the path goes both left and straight. Either way, that is the ten minute circular walk. Carry on back to the gate and then between the fence and hedge heading up estuary. You pass through several fields and then there is a partially concealed right turn into the wood that encloses the path all the way to Helford.

After 1.5 miles (2 km) through small coves and woods of large oaks, sycamores and ash you come to an old railed hound enclosure. Go up the drive with grass in the centre. At the top turn right down the road and then turn left up steps just as you get to the drive of a house called Traeth Cottage. It is easy to miss and if you get to the shore you have missed it!

Go along the back of the car park down the road, crossing the first bridge over the creek. Turn right and go along past the Shipwright Arms to the ferry point.

There are all-year-round refreshments at the Church in the car park at Helford before you cross the bridge.

42 | Helford to Falmouth (Ferry Terminal)   OS E103 (V) Helford

Grading: Moderate   Distance -   16.1   539.4   10.0   335.1

Ascent: 358   20049   1175   65777

Timing: 4.5 hours

See also our Helford to Falmouth Path Description.

Helford to Helford Passage - use ferry, see details below. If the ferry is not running your alternatives are probably a taxi or a walk of 13 miles (21 km). This is mostly road but you can incorporate Frenchman's Creek. (Local taxi services - Autocabs 01326 573773 or Cove Cars 07980 - 814058).

Helford Passage (Helford River). Seasonal.   April 1st to October 31st. Between Helford
River Boats, Helford Passage,   Passage and Helford 10 am to 5 pm daily
Nr Falmouth Tel: Mawnan Smith   on demand.
01326 250770
e.mail: info@helford-river-boats.co.uk
Website: www.helford-river-boats.co.uk

We urge you to contact the ferry operator direct if you are relying on this service, particularly if you are anticipating a fairly late finish and need to confirm the time of its last run.

Helford to Helford Passage (Walking route) approx. 13 miles (21 km).

This moderate to easy route, on footpaths and minor roads, is as close to the Helford River as possible.

Take the path up the hill in front of the Shipwright Arms; you will pass houses on your right and come down to Penarvon Cove. Back at the west side of the cove you will need to turn inland. Follow this track up a road, where you turn right, then left, onto a farm track. This will lead you to the permissive path above Frenchman's Creek, eventually descending to continue alongside it through the woods. At the head of the creek you come to a definitive footpath. This is at the sign of the permissive path to Frenchman's Creek. Take the path on the right to Withan and Mudgeon past Frenchman's Pill cottage on the left, and across a footbridge over the river. Follow the waymarked route through the woods. When you get out of the woods, aim for the far left corner of the field and take the stile with the iron wheel gate on the left. Follow the boundary on the left and over the stiles past Withan Farm, from where you head in a westerly direction, until you reach a concrete-block stile to a farm lane, where you turn left. Pass Mudgeon Farm on your right. When you reach a crossroads, turn right towards Mawgan. After a short distance, the path goes downhill.

Proceed uphill and you will join the road from St Martin, where you turn right, passing the ancient settlement at Gear. Going downhill, you soon reach the narrow bridge over Mawgan Creek and on the next bend, you come to Bridge Farm. Turn left and proceed up the road. When you reach the main road, turn right. Just before the church turn left at the Gwarth-an-drea sign and left at the back of the bungalow called The Oaks. When you reach the road, turn right along Gweek Drive and follow this road until you meet a road on the left with a ford, and cross the bridge and follow the road to Gweek.

From Gweek, take the road opposite the Gweek Inn, past the post office and take the footpath on the right through a wooden gate, just before light industrial units. The path runs parallel to a stream and it is not very clear. You join a bridleway at the ruins of a building and need to turn right, passing Kestle Dee farm. You will meet the road at Carwythenack Chase and need to take the Constantine/Port Navas road. Follow the field edge and cross the corner of the field to the stile by the signpost. Follow the road, crossing a stream and take the footpath on the left after the stream. Follow the field edge and go over the stile in the corner of the field behind the hut. Follow the road to Nancenoy and Polwheveral. You will now have to climb uphill.

Descend from the footpath junction towards Polwheveral. At the crossroads, turn right into the

Port Navas road. After about 140 yards (128 m), take the left footpath into the corner of a field and cross the field to a stile left of the gate. Follow the field edge and cross the corner of the field to the stile by the signpost. Follow the road to Port Navas. We suggest you walk through Port Navas, exploring the creek and the quay. At Trenarth Bridge, by the post box, follow the Mawnan/Falmouth sign.

At the head of Port Navas Creek is a footpath on the left to Lower Penpol. Take the next footpath on the right, just past a turning to some houses. Cross the field to a stile left of a house. Continue right up the road past Budock Vean Golf and Country Club. Turn right at the road for Helford Passage. Turn right past Dring House. At the end of the road turn left onto a new definitive footpath before 'Ridifarne' and walk down to The Bar and turn left, following the coastal path to Helford Passage. You now reach the Ferryboat Inn at Helford Passage, where the ferry from Helford would have put you down had it been operating.

Coast Path continues
If you are standing on the beach looking at the Ferryboat Inn, head towards the steps to your right that lead through a kissing gate up the grassy hill; you are heading to the mouth of the Helford River. When you reach a concrete track veer right following it, heading for a kissing gate 55 yards (50 m) ahead. This takes you over Trebah beach at Polgwidden Cove. From this very beach in 1944 the Americans made their way over to Omaha Beach in Normandy for the D-Day landings. You can access Trebah Gardens via a path a short walk from the beach but not directly from it . Continue to Durgan, where you enter the village, turning sharply right downhill and head for the river front. Go up the road, reaching a grassed area with a bench on your right. A few yards after this there is a path on the right. Ignore it and continue to the brow of the hill where the road bears left. Go straight ahead over a granite stile on to the National Trust Bosloe property.

The next beach is Porth Saxon. Turn right down a steep stile onto the beach in front of the boathouse and head for the far side. Through a field, a gate placed on top of a lot of rocks accesses the next beach, Porthallack. This is due to the fact that it is often flooded and they become stepping-stones.

Round Toll Point, through a kissing gate, with the sea to the right, look left to view the whole of the upper reaches of the Helford River. You reach the wooded area of Mawnan Glebe. Keep to the lower path heading sharply downhill. Uphill you can make a detour up to Mawnan Church.

Passing the long beach of Prisk Cove, which is accessible, keep to the seaward path to go around Rosemullion Head. The path is very well worn and has magnificent views of the Roseland and Falmouth. Alternatively go up to sit on top of the Head. Again keeping seaward descend across a field, over a stile and through a small wood to find the Nansidwell House nestling amongst the trees.

Gatamala Cove and Bream Cove follow before reaching Maenporth Beach. Watch for traffic when walking the road around the back of the beach; you can stop for refreshments at the beach café. Turning right around the back of the café, head for Swanpool Beach via Pennance Point past the Falmouth golf course and enjoy the restricted views due to the high fence of a new property on the cliff's edge. Turn right at the road into Swanpool.

The path to follow is at the other end of the beach and takes you to Gyllyngvase Beach. It is now a stroll along the promenade for 0.6 mile (1 km). The Falmouth Hotel is the final one along this stretch. Follow the pavement of the road up to the T junction - do not follow the railings. Turn right along the road towards Pendennis Castle. At the no entry signs cross the road for the pavement. At the Pendennis Point car park there is a signed path, which is the official path, heading to Falmouth docks.

The path passes through woods and you cross the road and back again at Ships and Castles opposite the docks. Head downhill to a T junction, turn right and make your way over a roundabout, under the railway bridge and follow the road around to the left - this is Bar Road. Carry on with the Maritime Museum on your right and head into town. After about 0.6 mile (1 km) the Prince Of Wales Pier is just before Milletts, and is where you get the ferry to St Mawes.

Grading: Moderate   Distance -   0   539.4   0   335.1

Ascent: 0   20049   0   65777

See also our Falmouth to Portloe Path Description.

In season you can cross by using two ferries, see details below. The only point to watch is that depending on conditions, the first ferry takes 20 to 30 minutes for the passage.

The ferry from Falmouth to St Mawes runs the whole year round except for winter Sundays. The scarcity of public transport in winter on Sundays combined with the fact that it is a long hike, makes us advise anyone arriving in Falmouth in winter on a Sunday to take it as a day off!

The ferry from St Mawes to Place only runs in season. If you are a purist there is a reasonable walking route round of 8-9 miles (13-14 km), two sections of which are very good walking indeed, see below for details. There are about a couple of buses a day from St Mawes to Gerrans, except on Sundays, or you could consider a taxi. If the ferry is not in service you can always ask. We have heard from walkers who have been lucky enough to get a lift from local boat owners.

Falmouth/St Mawes
King Harry Ferry
2 Ferry Cottages, Feock, Truro, TR3 6QT
01326 313201 - Kiosk (Summer)
07855 438674 -

Ferries operate between Falmouth (Custom House Quay and Prince of Wales Pier [Prince of Wales Pier in winter only]) and St Mawes all year round. During the summer (from June to October inclusive) there are 3 ferries per hour. Coast Path walkers are advised to enquire about the weekend services.

The King Harry Ferry is prepared to land pre-organized parties of 20 or more at Place House. To do this they would need prior knowledge to lay on an extra boat. This is also dependent on the state of the tide and weather. For a map and timetable please go to www.falriverlinks.co.uk

St Mawes/Place Creek (St Anthony)
The King Harry Ferry (details above) also operates a seasonal ferry from St Mawes to Place Creek. This runs daily from Easter to 31st October between 1000 and 1645, every half hour.
Tel: 07791 283884
Website: www.kingharryscornwall.co.uk

We urge you to contact the ferry operator direct if you are relying on this service, particularly if you are anticipating a fairly late finish and need to confirm the time of its last run.

Ocean Aqua Cab
A service operates Easter-September, weather permitting, between 1200 and 1500. The service will carry you from Falmouth to St Mawes or to Place direct and vice versa. We have been told it would be best if you could telephone the day before you require the crossing. Tel: Brian Kneebone on 07970 242258 Website: www.aquacab.co.uk

Walking route around the Percuil River (approx. 9 miles / 14 km)
At St Mawes, on leaving the ferry from Falmouth, turn left along the road. As you approach the castle, take a minor road going left, the most prominent sign being 'St Mawes Castle car park'. If you look carefully there is also a small footpath sign amongst the clutter. Follow this minor road until you come to the National Trust's Newton Cliff, which you enter. The route follows a very scenic path along the Carrick Roads with superb views across to Falmouth and the far shore. Ignore two minor stiles on the left which lead down to small coves. You come out on a minor tarmac road to turn right. Continue along this road, bearing left at the junction to pass in front of a boatyard. Immediately after passing the boatyard buildings the path bears a few yards to the right to proceed along the bank above the shore.

You come to the gate leading to the churchyard with a large sign 'Dogs on Leads Please Consecrated Ground'. Go through this gate keeping left all the way to pass the church on your right. Ignore the turning right marked 'way out' but instead keep left through a lych-gate and pass a house called Lanzeague. After its second gate the path bears right up the hill. You go through a metal gate, where there is a public footpath sign 'St Just Lane' and continue uphill with views of the creek to your left. You go through another gate into a lane, in parts muddy, in parts green, to finally exit onto the road.

Turn left and walk along the road for about 150 yards (135 m), ignore the first footpath on the right immediately past a house, but take the second on the right shortly afterwards. For the first field you have the hedge on the right. For the second and third it is on your left, then for the fourth it is again on your right. Take care in this fourth field, as there is a temptation as you enter to turn right; do not do this but go straight ahead to continue with the hedge on the right. Look for the sharp right turn through the hedge a little before you come to the end of the field. Descend the bank to the road, where you turn right and proceed down to meet the main A3078 at Trethem Mill.

Turn left - this is on a bridge crossing the creek - and immediately turn right up some stone steps and ascend the footpath through a wood. Coming out of the wood, cross the field on a bearing of 110°. In the next field bear right on 140° and leave by a wooded track. At the top there is a stile; cross it and bear 137° diagonally across the field to a hedge and follow this to the road. Turn left down the road.

At the next junction follow the road curving round to the right past Polhendra Cottage. Here almost immediately turn left through the second gate, a metal one. There is a footpath sign if you look for it, but it is not readily apparent. Aim across on 123° to descend to the bottom of the hedge which you can see on the opposite side of the valley. Here you will find a bridge, cross it and proceed up the slope as close as possible to the hedge on your left. Skirt around the gorse near the top and look for the stone steps behind the gorse. At the top ascend the stone steps and cross the next two fields on 125°. On reaching the road turn right into Gerrans and walk down to the church.

At the church take the left fork (not left turn) into Treloan Lane. You walk via Treloan and Rosteague, at each junction keeping straight ahead. At the house just beyond Rosteague you pass through a pedestrian gate into a field. At the end of the hedge on your right, look for the Blue Arrow marker post and follow that across the open field to the opposite hedge to a stile. Cross over into an enclosed lane, eventually coming to the road at Porth Farm about 1.5 miles (2.4 km) from Gerrans.

The slightly quicker way is then to turn right along the road and left where there is a sign 'Footpath to Place by Percuil River' to cross a wooden bridge. The pleasanter alternative, a few yards longer, is to go ahead on the road to turn right through the gates of the Trust's Porth Farm, then turn right to come to the same bridge.

Over the bridge the path turns right to follow Porth Creek and then the Percuil River, down to the low tide landing point for the ferry and soon on to Place itself. This last stretch of walking is very scenic.

44 Place House to Portscatho (The Quay)   OS E105

Grading: Easy				Distance -	10.0	549.4	6.2	341.3
Ascent:	280	20329	919	66696				

Timing: 2.75 hours

See also our Falmouth to Portloe Path Description.

Starting at the ferry point, Place House dominates the locality. Walk past the gates of the property up the road. After 328 yards (300 m), look for the signpost to the right. Turn right to go through the churchyard of the magnificent St Anthony in Roseland Church (doors are open most of the time for a visit). Go up some steps to the left of the church into a wooded area, then descend the path to the creek. Follow the C road, watch for the sign next to the Cellars Plantation that leads you off the road and left up the side of the field to Amsterdam Point.

Once over the stile in the tall Cornish hedge the views of St Mawes are magnificent and whilst walking to Carricknath Point more and more of Falmouth comes into view. If the wind is up, whether a regular south-westerly or a northerly, it is at Carricknath Point that the full force of it will be felt for the first time, but not for the last. Heading towards St Anthony's Head you cross a footbridge. Do not go up the stairs to the left but follow the coast around to the right. Go through a large gate or over the stile, whichever you prefer, a sharp left up a concrete path to steep steps is imminent. This brings you out to the top of St Anthony's Head.

Magnificent views up the Carrick Roads to Feock and Truro are matched with all points east and west. There are toilet and picnicking facilities here. Heading to Portscatho you hug the coast to keep to the official path. There is a descent to Porthbeor Beach which affords a little shelter, as does Towan Beach. The Coast Path continues on from Towan past Greeb Point and Raven's Hole until you literally stumble on Portscatho without warning as it is sheltered from view.

45   Portscatho to Portloe (The Lugger Hotel)   OS E105 (V) Portscatho

Grading: Strenuous				Distance -	12.0	561.4	7.5	348.8

Ascent: 451   20780   1480   68176

Timing: 3.75 hours

See also our Falmouth to Portloe Path Description.

Walking into Portscatho, turn right before the Plume of Feathers pub following the signs. Head past the Harbour Club (toilet facilities can be found by taking a right turn before the Harbour Club to seaward). Continue out of the village. At the Porthcurnick National Trust sign climb the stairs and then turn right (carrying on up towards the stile brings you to the car park).

At Porthcurnick Beach, either go around the back of the beach, or go down and up the stairs and veer right past the seasonal café and down some steps to the back of the beach. Go up the jetty road and after 10.9 yards (10 m) turn right at the gate and along the top of the coastal edge.

There is a small wooded area and a descent to Porthbean Beach. Traverse 10.9 yards (10 m) at the back of the beach up some steps and then the path ascends. Keep to the seaward side and ignore any paths to the left, which lead to the hotel. Go through a wooded area and over a stile to a field, where you obtain great views of the (inevitably named) Gull Rock and Nare Head. After an undulating walk around the edges of a series of fields, a sign pronounces 1 mile to Pendower Beach or a walk inland to Curgurrell. It is now a gentle descent to the beach.

There is an inland section where you join the road and walk behind Pendower Court, go through the car parking area and descend to the Pendower Beach Hotel.

Keep to the back of the beach and look for the steps that lead left up to the toilet block. Turn right, ascending the hill. After 10.9 yards (10 m) around the bend, veer right to follow the Coast Path. On reaching the Nare Hotel, the path goes behind it, not through the tennis court. Turn right onto the road descending to Carne Beach. Go up the road for a further 10.9 yards (10 m) and turn right at the sign, up the steps to follow the coast.

For the next 3 miles (4.8 km) or so it is quite remote and only a map will reveal the road access points that are a 0.5 mile (800 m) or so away at various points. To reach Nare Head, a steep descent and ascent at Tregagle's Hole takes you past the derelict but preserved cottage on the way up. Views from Nare Head are amongst the best on the whole coast and require a short detour off the Coast Path (mobile phone reception is very good also).

Keep to the seaward path around Rosen Cliff. To reach Kiberick Cove, signs request that you stick to the official Coast Path around the back of the valley, although a direct down and up seems to be the easiest route.

At Blouth Point, go over the stile into an enormous field. Keep to the left for 22 yards (20 m) and then head downhill to the right towards the stile where a clump of trees meets the edge of the small Parc Caragloose Cove.

A National Trust sign indicates Broom Parc and the path twists and turns upwards and then takes you around Manare Point. On reaching The Jacka the roofs of Portloe are to the left. A strange anomaly occurs here where the path for a 5.5 yard (5 m) stretch requires very careful negotiation: there are no steps or obvious route – at the time of publication, this is under review by the South West Coast Path Team and the local parish council. The route then descends on a tarmac path passing the public toilets to bring you out in the centre of Portloe.

46   Portloe to East Portholland (Car Park)   OS E105

Grading: Strenuous   Distance -   3.8   565.2   2.4   351.2

Ascent: 181   20961   594   68770

Timing: 1.25 hours

See also our Portloe to Mevagissey Path Description.

Coming out of Portloe requires nerves of steel, only because it does not seem right that the path, once it climbs out of the village, is waymarked right, into a driveway: this is correct. Indeed you descend towards a private garage and squeeze between the garage on the left and the house on the right, and the path actually goes around the side of the house towards the sea - do not descend the steps at the end of the house. Turn immediately left with the sea on your right and ascend towards the end cottage on the row of houses. The path then ascends seaward to the right of the house, leading to a stile announcing the start of the National Trust Flagstaff area. The path goes around the old coastguard lookout.

There is a road between West and East Portholland. Do not be tempted by the sea wall linking the two settlements which can be very wet, slippery and strewn with obstacles; the road affords better views anyway and you turn right into East Portholland. There are toilets here on the left on the road into the village. A seasonal café/house with picnic tables is a welcoming sight in East Portholland.

47   East Portholland to Gorran Haven (Beach)   OS E105

Grading: Strenuous   Distance -   10.3   575.5   6.4   357.6

Ascent: 364   21325   1194   69964

Timing: 3 hours

See also our Portloe to Mevagissey Path Description.

From the quay follow the row of houses to the end of the village and ascend up the track for 22 yards (20 m). A sign for the Coast Path points to the right up an incline. At the end of this track you go through a new gate and instead of following the top of the next field, which seems the obvious direction to follow, you must descend quite sharply to the right towards the sea and edge around the field, through some new kissing gates, until reaching a stile at the edge of a field, which reveals a road that leads down to Porthluney Cove and Caerhays Castle.

Descending down the road to Porthluney Cove there is a car park with a sign to the coast. Ignore this and carry on along the road with the seasonal café on your right. After the car park entrance, and opposite the large metal gates of Caerhays Castle, there is a stile and gate on the right. Go through the gate and cross diagonally, heading for the trees and fenced area closest to the back of the café area. Pass through kissing gate, cross another field diagonally seaward to go through another kissing gate by a bench to join the cliff top path.

An ascent is made through woods past Lambsowden Cove and Greeb Point on the way to Hemmick Beach. The fields closer to Hemmick are not enclosed and the wandering livestock will get interested in any animals not on a lead. There is a steep ascent up to Dodman Point, which is one of the most archaeologically important headlands of the whole Coast Path; and an 18th century coastguard watch house has been maintained as a walkers' shelter, with an information board, just north of the Point. The cross at the top of Dodman Point allows for some wonderful views across to the Lizard and beyond in the west and towards Devon in the east - be aware that a certain sense of achievement might be forthcoming!

Bow or Vault Beach is a lengthy stretch of sand. There is car park access but this would entail another lengthy ascent/descent, which could prove tricky if laden with possessions. There is access at the far side closest to Gorran Haven, which itself is reached by continuing along the path past Little Sand Cove and Pen-a-maen or Maenease Point.

Coming into Gorran Haven on Foxhole Lane, at the T-junction, for the shops and toilets go uphill to your left, or for the beach and path, descend to the right. To leave Gorran Haven by the official Coast Path ascend Church Street, ignoring the signs on your right for the coast until the sign for Cliff Road is viewed 219 yards (200 m) up the hill. Turn right along Cliff Road.

Walkers intending to stay overnight in Gorran Haven in the winter should note there are very limited facilities to eat in the village.

48 Gorran Haven to Mevagissey (Harbour)   OS E105 (V) Gorran Haven

Grading: Easy   Distance -   5.7   581.2   3.5   361.1

Ascent: 179   21504   587   70551

Timing: 1.5 hours

See also our Portloe to Mevagissey Path Description.

Proceed along Cliff Road and pass to the left of the last house to an awkward stile. Once into the field turn right and follow the path around the crumbling cove of Great Perhaver Point. The path hugs the coastline from here to Turbot Point. Descending to Chapel Point and Colona Beach the course of the path is signposted past the extraordinary dwellings on Chapel Point at Bodrugan's Leap. Do not go up the hill to the left but cross the tarmac that follows the coastline.

Ascend gently up to the C road heading to Portmellon. Turn right past the sets of seats and turn right again down the main road into Portmellon. It is main road all the way until you get to the descent into Mevagissey. At the park gates on the right, as you descend into the village, there is a sign for the Coast Path that takes you into the park. This is all new so keep to the right hand path, zigzagging down to the outer harbour wall. Watch for the acorn signs on the blue viewing telescopes indicating the direction. There are new metal steps that lead from the park to the harbour (and you will pass the only all year round public toilets on the Coast Path until Pentewan). This new course of the path is much safer than walking along the road into the village. It also allows for much better views of the inner and outer harbour of Mevagissey.

49 Mevagissey to Charlestown (Harbour)   OS E105 & E107 (V) Mevagissey; (V) Pentewan

Grading: Strenuous   Distance -   11.6   592.8   7.2   368.3

Ascent: 620   22124   2034   72585

Timing: 4 hours

See also our Mevagissey to Charlestown Path Description.

Please note: *there have been major cliff falls near the Charlestown end of this section so at the time of going to print, there is currently about 2 miles (3 km) of road walking between Porthpean and Charlestown until a new cliff-top route can be negotiated with local property owners. Follow the signed diversion soon after you leave Porthpean Beach.*

In Mevagissey walk along the back of the harbour and turn right along the eastern side, looking out for the steep left fork signed 'Coast Path Pentewan 2¼ miles'. After passing the old coastguard station on your right, you come out into open playing fields. Go straight across, aiming for the seaward end of a terrace of large houses.

Continue along (avoiding the right turn down steps to Polstreath Beach). After descending to cross a footbridge, turn left uphill to Penare Point and continue on the well waymarked path, gradually descending again to walk behind the ruins of the old fish cellars at Portgiskey Cove. Ignore the next stile on the right but continue along the seaward field boundary uphill, following the signs until you reach a newly-created path parallel to the road. This excellent off-road route now avoids the traffic dangers of the busy road to St Austell. This path ends at the entrance to Pentewan Sands Holiday Park, where you now have to join the road (B3273) as there is currently no right of access through the caravan park. Continue along the pavement and take the first right turn, before the petrol station, signposted Pentewan.

Pentewan has a pub and shops; take the chance of refreshment here as you have a long tough section ahead.

You are then faced with a choice. You can either:

A. continue on the road through Pentewan, and up Pentewan Hill for about 100 yards (90 m), taking the first right turn (sharp right) signed "The Terrace" and "All Saints Church" to follow the official path, past a charming terrace of attractive houses.

B. take the Association's preferred route by turning right off the road into the harbour area just after the public toilets, and walking along the harbour to the end of the cottages where you will see a path immediately after the last cottage on your left, going steeply up through gardens to link up with the Coast Path. The path through the gardens is signed as a public footpath and does not look like a public right of way, but it is!

Back on the Coast Path put this book away; you will need your energies for other things! However take it out again in approximately 1¼ miles (2 km) when you have crossed a wooden bridge in a sizeable wood.

Having crossed the bridge, you soon cross another small stream and come to a T-junction. Turn right here and follow this path down towards Hallane Mill Beach, a lovely spot for a picnic, with a waterfall. Shortly before the beach you will come to another T-junction - turn left to continue on the Coast Path (right to visit the beach). You soon turn back to the right to start ascending towards Black Head, a superb diversionary viewpoint on a clear day. It was once a rifle range but was purchased by the National Trust, helped in a small way with a donation from this Association. If you wish to go out to Black Head, turn right at the memorial stone to A L Rowse, the Cornish poet and historian: to continue on the Coast Path, turn left.

The passage of the wood behind Ropehaven can give trouble if signing is not maintained. On entering the wood you turn right, taking care on this rocky path which can be slippery when damp, then left at the seat. Avoid the right fork down to a cottage and turn sharp left at the top into a narrow walled lane. Turn right on to the narrow road. The path leaves it to go into a field just beyond the little car park/lay by. After the long climb to Silvermine Point, keep to the fence, and don't be tempted to follow the better defined track inland.

At Porthpean Beach the sign forward can be misleading - you do in fact go down on to the promenade to walk along past toilets and a seasonal café. Continue to the end; it does not look likely, but there is a steep set of steps at the end to get you back on track. Once you are back on the top of the cliffs, you are likely to encounter the "Path closed" sign following two major cliff falls. Do not be tempted to continue past it, although a new path has now been created at the western end and it may appear from a distance that you can get through - you will only have to retrace your steps and take the road route as it becomes completely impassable near Charlestown. Cornwall Council is negotiating with the adjacent property owners to buy a strip of their gardens to recreate the path, but this is a long process. Follow the signed diversion inland (look for signs on lampposts and traffic signs) taking you into Charlestown along the road (1¼ miles 2 km).

50 Charlestown to Par Sands (Polmear)　　　　OS E107 (V) Charlestown

Grading: Easy				Distance -	7.0	599.8	4.3	372.6
Ascent:	89	22213	292	72877				

Timing: 1.5 hours

See also our Charlestown to Fowey Path Description.

The official path does not go across the dock gate at the mouth of the harbour, but provided the gate is closed most people will go that way.

Once on the east side of the harbour, take the seaward path to the right of a house called Salamander. The path is fenced here but the views are wonderful. Later you come out beside a road, walk a few yards along it to turn right and then fork left.

Ignoring small paths off to the right, continue walking on the seaward side of the large Carlyon Bay Hotel, until you come out by a big car park. Keep to the right of this and cross the beach road; take care here as there may be construction traffic. Developers are trying to build a resort and apartment complex on the beach below. The path continues along the cliff top, skirting the hotel golf course.

The china clay processing works are now in sight, giving you a glimpse of one of Cornwall's traditional industries. Turn sharp left at Spit Point to come inland, with the old clay works on your right. You will gradually be hemmed in between the main line railway and the clay works on a narrow and unattractive path. However, proposals to regenerate this former industrial site are now being discussed and may lead to significant improvement. Stay on this path until you reach the road and turn right to go past the entrance to Par Docks.

Continue on the pavement and go under a railway bridge to turn first right signposted A3082 Fowey, cross a level crossing and under another railway bridge. The road forks, and you should keep right on Par Green, a one-way road. You pass The Good Shepherd Church on your right and Welcome Home Inn on your left. (If your journey ends at Par and you need the railway station, keep walking along Par Green until the turn on your left for Eastcliffe Road, which you follow until you reach the station.)

Keep walking along Par Green, looking out for number 52, on your right. When you reach number 52, turn right, off the road, to follow the **new offical Coast Path route via Par Sands**, which cuts out a lot of road walking.

The new route should be well signed but, in case you need directions:

Bear left up the path from Par Green to cross a tidal river, cross the private 'haul road' used for china clay lorries, and when you reach another road, cross over, keeping to the left of the beach car park, and pick up the path along the back of the beach. At the far (eastern) end of the beach, where there is another big car park, you have the choice to continue towards Polkerris and The Gribbin (next section) or to seek out the Ship Inn for refreshment. For the Ship Inn at Polmear, go straight out through the car park exit. To continue on the Coast Path, go into the car park, but keep skirting the right-hand side, looking out for the Coast Path waymark, which signs you over a footbridge and stream and up onto the edge of The Gribbin.

51 | Par (Polmear) to Fowey (for ferry to Polruan)   OS E107 (T) Par (Trains)

Grading: Moderate		Distance -	9.6	609.4	6.0	378.6
Ascent:	341	22554	1119	73996		

Timing: 2.5 hours

See also our Mevagissey to Fowey Path Description.

It is a fine walk out from Par Sands or Polmear via Polkerris around Gribbin Head and on to Fowey. The availability of public transport from Par to Fowey makes this a very practical half day excursion with lovely views nearly all the way.

Starting at the main beach car park behind the Ship Inn at Polmear, look out for the Coast Path waymark and footbridge leading up to the cliff edge path towards Polkerris. Ignore the Saints Way path, which takes a more inland route to Fowey.

As you enter Polkerris, go towards the beach and turn left near the Rashleigh Inn, and up the ramp to join a zig-zag path to the top.

Follow the cliff top path onto the National Trust property, The Gribbin. The official route goes to the Daymark and then sets off downhill towards Polridmouth. But you can take a more seaward route around Gribbin Head if you wish, rejoining the official route as you head back down towards Polridmouth Bay.

The Daymark is owned by the National Trust and is open to visitors on some summer Sundays. Do take the opportunity to go up the tower if you can as the views from the top are memorable.

You come down towards Polridmouth (pronounced 'Pridmouth') Beach and walk around close behind it and across easy stepping stones. This is a lovely little stretch by the house and lake, and is the beach featured in Daphne du Maurier's 'Rebecca'. The path then goes steeply up, bearing right through woods at the other side.

After Allday's Fields (memorial stone on your left), you enter Covington Wood, then take the switchback path immediately on your right to follow the realigned Coast Path to St Catherine's Castle and superb views of Fowey. Then keep straight on to go down an increasingly rock cut lane, which has a very sharp elbow about two thirds of the way down.

The path comes out at Readymoney Cove and you follow the road to enter Fowey. However if you are continuing along the Coast Path in summer months, watch for the ferry point on your right before you get into the town. It is down steps just after Fowey Hotel's tea garden (if you are walking in low season, you may find that the ferry is operating from the Town Quay in Fowey itself).

(**BUS USERS, PLEASE NOTE**: you will pass a bus stop as you leave the Esplanade - buses for Par and St Austell no longer stop here. For these services (25 and 524), you need to go uphill towards the main car park at Hanson Drive. For daytime buses Monday to Saturday, you will find the bus stop in Hanson Drive. On Sundays and weekday evenings, the bus stops not far from there at the Safe Harbour Inn on Lostwithiel Street.

[A guide book to the Saints' Way, which cuts from north to south across mid-Cornwall (Padstow to Fowey) is available from Fowey TIC (see page 162).]

52 Fowey (& Polruan) to Polperro (Harbour)   OS E107 (T) Fowey; (V) Polruan

Grading: Strenuous		Distance -	11.5	620.9	7.1	385.7
Ascent:	491	23045	1611	75607		

Timing: 3.5 hours

See also our Fowey to Polperro Path Description.

This section is very good value for money in two senses of the word. Firstly there is a fine path all the way from Polruan to Polperro with magnificent sea views. Secondly, it is probably the toughest stretch of walking on the South Cornwall coast. (Leaving Fowey, if you have time on your side, you can go via the car ferry from Caffa Mill to Bodinnick and walk The Hall Walk via Pont Pill to Polruan [4 miles / 6 km].)

Foot Ferry Fowey/Polruan (River Fowey) All year round at 5-10 min intervals.
Polruan Ferry Co. Ltd   1st May - 30th Sept. Daily 0715 - 2300 hrs
Toms Yard   except Saturday 0730 start, Sunday 0900 start.
East Street   1st Oct - 30th Apr. Daily 0715 - 1900 hrs.
Polruan-by-Fowey   except Saturday 0730 start, Sunday
Cornwall   1000 - 1700hrs. Closed Xmas Day
PL23 1PB
Tel: 01726 870232

We urge you to contact the ferry operator direct if you are relying on this service, particularly if you are anticipating a fairly late finish and need to confirm the time of its last run.

From 1st October to 1st April and when the weather deteriorates, you will find that the ferry operates to and from the Town Quay at Fowey rather than from Whitehouse Quay lower down the harbour; there should be a sign up to this effect.

Landing from the ferry in Polruan, go along the quay and up Garrett Steps just beside The Lugger and at the top turn right along West Street and then left steeply up Battery Lane. The path comes out in a grassy area; keep with the wall on your left going round the corner. The path goes right, just after an earth bank and then you proceed ahead across another open area with a small ruin up on your left. It joins the road beside a school; continue ahead to turn sharp right just before the notice saying 'Furze Park'.

When you reach the National Trust money box on the path, take the right, downward path.

About 2 miles (3 km) after leaving Polruan there is a considerable hill behind Great Lantic Beach. You can go all the way to the top and turn right there. The route we recommend turns right about 30 yards (28 m) before the top, goes over a stile and drops down again. Ignore the first two turnings right as these are beach paths. Presently a wide path, the other route, joins from the left (there is a gate on your right).

Although a definitive right of way is shown below the Watch House, at the moment the practical route is the broad path above it. Assuming you are on this path, ignore the stile on your right which goes directly to the house. Just after this is another loop path right but it has little in views to compensate for the extra effort. After this you can either take the right turn, or keep to the upper path and then join the lower one to follow the path around the back of a cove. When you come to Lansallos Cove, turn inland for the Coast Path.

Later, as the first houses in Polperro come into view, there is a series of parallel paths all going to Polperro. You should take the rocky path on your right, this is the most seaward path and passes several seats and shelters to arrive at a rocky area overlooking the mouth of the harbour. From the rocky area turn left and the official route into Polperro is the first set of steps on the right.

53 | Polperro to Looe (Bridge)   OS E107 (V) Polperro

Grading: Moderate			Distance -	8.0	628.9	5.0	390.7
Ascent:	204	23249	669	76276			

Timing: 2.25 hours

See also our Polperro to Looe Path Description.

This next section is particularly well walked.

In Polperro you have to walk behind the harbour, crossing the Roman Bridge to turn right. Leaving Polperro there is a loop path right called Reuben's Walk. If you take this, turn left again just before the miniature lighthouse.

Just before the top of the hill, take the right fork at the junction of two well-defined paths where the National Trust's attractive stone marker indicates right for Talland.

Note the spectacularly sited War Memorial on Downend Point. A little way past this is another beach path right which you ignore.

There are seasonal refreshments at Talland. After the beach café go up the tarmac track, turn left to pass the toilets, and then right. Turn right at the Smugglers Rest café into a small car park to rejoin the path, a short, steep climb out of the bay. Steps constructed here only a few years ago have been undercut by coastal erosion so keep well away from the cliff edge.

The walk to Hannafore and West Looe is pleasant and quite easy. Do not be tempted to follow paths off to the right anywhere along this stretch as there is no way back up from the beach farther along.

On entering Looe at Hannafore, you have a choice. You can either follow the official path along the road, passing flower beds and a seasonal café, or you can take the first right to walk alongside the beach. Either route will bring you to a stretch of road with no pavement. This drops into a dip and watch for a battlemented look-out platform on your right. Just past this are steps down to the harbour area of the river; that is the best way to go. This has a double advantage; it keeps you away from the traffic and takes you past the tidal ferry to East Looe.

You will notice on the rocks close to the path a bronze statue of Nelson, the large one-eyed seal who was a frequent and much-loved visitor to Looe over some 25 years. Nelson died in 2003 and this statue was unveiled by Sir Robin Knox-Johnston in May 2008.

The ferry runs between West and East Looe and is dependent on both the weather and the tide.

If you are walking, simply keep to the quayside in West Looe, cross the bridge, and turn right into the main street, Fore Street, in East Looe. (For the railway station and trains to the main line at Liskeard, turn left after crossing the bridge).

54 | Looe to Portwrinkle (Quay)   OS E107 & E108 (T) Looe (Trains); (V) Downderry

Grading: Strenuous, moderate in parts			Distance -	12.2	641.1	7.6	398.3
Ascent:	551	23800	1808	78084			

Timing: 4.5 hours

See also our Looe to Portwrinkle Path Description.

You leave East Looe by turning up Castle Street, across a minor crossroads and continue up the hill. The road peters out becoming a pleasant high level path above the sea.

The path becomes a road again and at the first junction bear right into Plaidy Lane. Pass Plaidy Beach on your right, and continue on the road until just after it has veered left. Here a steep tarmac path takes off right just beyond a big electric cable post.

At the top of the path you come to a road again to continue ahead for a while until the road bears left but the path goes forward again between houses. Go down steps, do not turn left or right but continue nearly opposite to go ahead.

The path comes down to Millendreath: pass behind the beach to go up the cul-de-sac road the other side. The road becomes a path in a sunken lane and then emerges onto another road. About 150 yards (135 m) after you reach this road, turn right into the National Trust's Bodigga Cliff property. This beautiful place is now accessible for people of varying abilities, including wheelchair users.

To continue on the Coast Path, keep to the left of the picnic tables. Make the most of this next stretch - about 1¹/₂ miles (2¹/₂ km) of varied and enjoyable coast walking, before you reach the roads and houses of Seaton.

The path comes out on the road above Seaton, and you turn right down what is Looe Hill. Go down to the bottom and turn right into Bridge Road. The Official Coast Path is routed along the road from here and through Downderry - if you need to use this great care is necessary as it is a narrow and busy road, but depending on the tides an alternative route is available.

Alternative Beach Route
At low and mid tides, there is a much more pleasant alternative from Seaton to Downderry, using the path on top of the sea wall and then the beach but you *must first consider the time and height of the tide* (start by checking the tide tables on pages 21 & 22.) As you approach the outskirts of Downderry along the beach, you have a choice of routes into the village, depending on how fast and deep the streams are running across the beach. The first left turn by a stream will bring you into the centre of Downderry for shops, toilets and seasonal refreshments. The next will bring you to the Inn on the Shore. If you don't need any facilities, you should continue on to the next stream and turn left up some concrete steps; this latter option will lessen the amount of road walking. You come up beside a school to turn right along a road, and to rejoin the official route.

Continue with the road as it bears sharply inland at a hairpin bend. Take the waymarked turn off right, next to a house called Downderry Lodge, ignoring the right turn immediately after you have taken this path. The path zigzags uphill to come eventually into a field.

The long-awaited Coast Path here was officially opened in May 2002: this Association lobbied for more than 15 years for this. Thanks to the work of the then Cornwall County Council and the Port Eliot Estate, this wonderful path is easy to follow, if strenuous - enjoy your walk to Portwrinkle. Keep on the road through this quiet village.

(Please note: not many buses stop at Portwrinkle itself. The nearest alternative is Crafthole, a 10 minute walk uphill.) Take care if relying on a bus at Crafthole - apparently there are two bus stops, for different services, 150 yards apart and on different roads. If the obvious stop does not list the bus you want, go ahead at the crossroads, signed Liskeard, and turn left at the T-junction to find the other stop.

55   Portwrinkle to Cremyll (for Plymouth)   OS E108 (V) Cawsand/Kingsand

Grading: Moderate

		Distance -	21.4	662.5	13.3	411.6
Ascent:	594	24394	1949	80033		

Timing: 5.75 hours

See also our Portwrinkle to Plymouth Path Description.

From Portwrinkle village, the Coast Path takes the second path on the right, opposite the entrance to the golf club. It is currently well marked except right at the end of the course, where you need to aim for the pedestrian gate seen on top of a rise.

Permissive Path through the Tregantle Ranges
Thanks to the work of the Ministry of Defence (MoD) you can now take a fascinating walk through the Tregantle Ranges when there is no firing.

You will be able to obtain information up to a week or two in advance (or on the day) from the Range Office on 01752 822516 (Fax: 01752 823875). It seems that shooting at Tregantle is more flexible than Lulworth. If you draw near to the ranges and hear firing or see red flags, the gate will be locked, and sadly you will have to resign yourself to the long road-side route below.

Having passed a navigational beacon, you will see a gate on your right, which you take if the gate is unlocked. The path is well marked, has great sea views and omits 1½ miles (2½ km) of road walking. When you leave the Range path through a high gate, turn right to walk along the road to rejoin the official Coast Path; beware of traffic.

Official Coast Path (when permissive path is closed)
You come out to the road but the path for a while is just inside the hedge. This path ends by the road junction to Torpoint where you have to come down to the road and turn right along it. You are likely to meet quite a lot of traffic until you after you are past the Tregantle Fort entrance and you regain a true Coast Path on the National Trust land on top of the cliffs

Coast Path continues
Where the road bears left, a right turn leads you to a National Trust path, which was extended in 2005 to remove 328 yards (300 m) from this busy road. There may be further improvements along this stretch, so look out for signs. There is then another long stretch of road, until you see notices for Whitsand Bay Holiday Park on the left and the Coast Path starts again on the right. (At this point you may wish to detour a short distance down to the right to the welcoming Cliff Top Cafe, usually open all year round.) The Coast Path is now well marked as it twists and turns up and down past scattered holiday chalets and gardens, and is a great improvement over the road, despite two steep climbs.

The path continues to be well marked all the way to Rame Head, and includes gates donated by the South East Cornwall Tourism Association to commemorate the 25th anniversary of the Coast Path.

It is well worth taking the short detour up to the ruined chapel on Rame Head to enjoy splendid views out towards Eddystone Light.

Continue along the Coast Path with no more steep climbs, bearing left near Penlee Point (where you will find an interesting grotto just down some rocky steps on your right, giving more superb views, now towards Plymouth Sound.)

The path then joins a tarmac road with intermittent views ahead to Plymouth Sound Breakwater and presently, some 500 yards (400 m) later, takes off into the wood on the right - look out for the waymark post.

Through Cawsand/Kingsand the official and in fact easiest way is not straightforward and only some of it is signposted, so read the next paragraph carefully.

You enter Cawsand from Pier Lane; turn right through the square to pick up Garrett Street, passing the Cross Keys Inn on your left. As you come towards the end of this street look for the old 'Devon/Corn' boundary mark on a house on your right. Turn right in front of the post office. Soon you will approach a street called The Cleave. Just before you reach it, turn left. Then turn first right up what is Heavitree Road but you will not know this until you are a few yards up it. As you ascend you will see a sign for Lower Row on your left; turn right here and enter Mount Edgcumbe Country Park.

After about a mile through the Country Park, you come out on to a road at Hooe Lodge. Turn right, but look out for the path back into the Country Park on the left.

Bear right through the gate and follow the lower, waymarked path which climbs gradually up into the woods. There have been major landslips farther on and a new zig-zag path has been installed around them. It is quite well signposted although steep in places. As you start to descend again, with the landslip on your right, follow the path down to the foreshore, where you can again enjoy wonderful views across Plymouth Sound.

Ascend once more and continue past a stone folly on your left and through a high deer gate; you come out by a classical summer house and lake and you should keep along right to pick up a concrete driveway, and later right again, enjoying some excellent views towards Plymouth.

If you are not too pushed for time, a visit around the gardens of Mount Edgcumbe is worthwhile, and free. A charge will be made if you wish to visit the House (open in season).

Keeping just inside a high hedge, the path comes out by The Orangery café/restaurant, set in a fine Italianate garden. Go through an arch then go ahead to turn right through the park gates to the Edgcumbe Arms and the Cremyll ferry point for Plymouth.

56 | Cremyll (for Plymouth) to Mount Batten Point   OS E108 (T) Plymouth (Trains)

Grading: Easy   Distance -   12.0   674.5   7.5   419.1

Ascent: 124   24518   407   80440

Timing: 3.5 hours

See also our Plymouth to Wembury Path Description.

The distance includes the signed Coast Path route around to Mount Batten Point via Cattedown, Oreston, Hooe and Turnchapel. If you use the Mount Batten Ferry service, then deduct approximately 5 miles (8 km) but remember it is not the official route of the Coast Path.

Cremyll/Plymouth

All year round at 30 minute intervals, but no sailings at 0930, 1230 and 1530 from Mount Edgcumbe, and 0945, 1245 and 1545 from Plymouth.

Cremyll Ferry,
Cremyll Quay,
Cremyll,
Torpoint,
Cornwall. PL10 1HX
Tel: 01752 822105.
(Full timetable available - phone above no.)
www.tamarcruising.com
info@tamarcruising.com
The ferry operates depending on weather, tides and other circumstances permitting.

Summer service from 1st May to 18th Sept.
From Mt Edgcumbe Weekdays 0650 to 2015
Saturdays 0815 to 2100, Sundays 0900 to 2100
From Plymouth Weekdays 0715 to 2030
Saturdays 0845 to 2115, Sundays 0915 to 2115
Winter service from 19th September to 30th April
From Mt Edgcumbe Weekdays 0650 to 1815,
Saturdays 0815 to 1830, Sundays 1000 to 1700
From Plymouth Weekdays 0715 to 1830,
Saturdays 0845 to 1845, Sundays 1015 to 1715
Closed Xmas, Boxing & New Year's Days

We urge you to contact the ferry operator direct if you are relying on this service, particularly if you are anticipating a fairly late finish and need to confirm the time of its last run. Further information about the Cremyll ferry can be found at www.plymouth.gov.uk/cremyllferry.

Plymouth's Waterfront Walk is a treat. From stepping ashore at Admirals Hard, watch out for a variety of information plaques and pieces of artwork all relating to Plymouth's history - follow lamp posts with white bands edged with black on them. You will find many pavement direction signs. The first thing you will see is a blue marker which tells you it is 352 miles to Minehead. Those of you who have walked it will know it is really 411 miles.

On landing at Admirals Hard, walk up the road and turn first right then around the car park into Cremyll Street, and continue to the massive gates of the Royal William Yard. Pass them on your right and continue on out to Firestone Bay. At the sea wall you have a fine view to Drake's Island and beyond towards Wembury. A slight excursion could be made by turning right to walk out to Western King's Point and Devil's Point, for River Tamar views, but you will have to return.

From the sea wall turn inland to walk into Durnford Street, continue along it and walk past the Royal Marine Barracks, turning right immediately after them. This will bring you into Millbay Road where you continue, passing the Dock Gates (east). Then you turn right into West Hoe Road. Keep to this road. You are now in the West Hoe area and the streets surrounding you have numerous B&B establishments. Fork right into Great Western Road.

As you approach a terrace of three storey small hotels, watch out for a path on your right known as Rusty Anchor. This is a slight diversion from the main road and provides a shore line walk.

On regaining the main road, turn right and continue along the Hoe foreshore. You stay on this promenade all the way around to The Barbican and Sutton Harbour. However, you could achieve grand views over Plymouth Sound by climbing steps opposite the swimming pool up to the lighthouse, Smeaton's Tower, and passing that to cross The Hoe to have a look at Sir Francis Drake, still scanning the English Channel for the Armada.

Retrace your steps and continue your shore line walk to The Barbican. A small jetty on your right is of historic significance in that it is the site of the Mayflower Steps; of great interest to our US members. As you are about to walk onto Mayflower Steps jetty you will see on the right a new steel bridge and pontoon. This gives access to the Mount Batten ferry.

Whatever you decide upon, ferry or the official Coast Path, it is well worth exploring the ancient Barbican area before carrying on.

Sutton Harbour / Mount Batten

Mount Batten Ferry	All year round. Runs 15 and 45 minutes past the hour
07930 838614	from The Barbican, and on the hour and 30 minutes
www.mountbattenferry.com	past from Mount Batten Point. Ferry starts at 0745 from
info@soundcruising.com	The Barbican on weekdays, and from 0900 at weekends. Last ferry departs Mount Batten at 1815 in winter, and 2300 in summer.

We urge you to contact the ferry operator direct if you are relying on this service, particularly if you are anticipating a fairly late finish and need to confirm the time of its last run.

Walking Route to Mount Batten Point (Official Coast Path)

This section of the Coast Path is well marked with innovative signs and art work installed by Plymouth City Council.

Lock gates have now been installed at Sutton Harbour, so walk on across them into Teat's Hill Road. As you progress along Teat's Hill Road you will arrive at Breakwater Hill. Turn right here, but do not walk into the scrap yard unless you want to view vehicles being broken up. Carry on up the hill for a limestone, cliff top walk with views over the Cattewater. You will descend to the area of Cattedown Wharf. We will now just supply directions - continue on past warehouses into Maxwell Road, a road will take you direct to Laira Bridge, which you take to cross the River Plym. You now have pavements to walk upon. Watch out for the 'Poetry' Wall and the rhinoceros. At the first roundabout turn right. Stay on the right side of the road, passing busy traffic islands on the left.

It does seem our representations have paid off. We understand that, as we go to print, we have achieved our requested new route.

After passing the Oreston Rhinoceros you come upon Breakwater Road, turn right into it and continue along until you reach Yacht Haven and an aggregate company. A path has been created passing both onto Oreston Quay through a dinghy park. It may not be signed but walkers should try it.

If this route is not installed when you get there (and it should be) then carry on uphill passing Breakwater Road then bear right into Oreston Road. Continue along Oreston Road and take care because there are no pavements. Turn rightinto Rollis Park Road which leads to Oreston Quay, where you bear left.

Whichever way you have arrived at Oreston Quay (and we hope it is the new route) walk past the grassy area and then enter Marine Road. In 50 yards (46 m) turn left into Park Road and stay with it to the top of the hill. Tucked away in the left hand corner is the entrance to a path. Climb the ancient stone stile and continue along. You will cross Broad Park and into another footpath which leads down to Radford Lake.
(At Hooe Lake you can take the coast to coast walk to Lynmouth by using the Erme - Plym Trail, the Erme Valley Trail and the Two Moors Way. Guide books to all three routes are available from Ivybridge TIC (see page 162).

The 'castle' through which you walk was once the lodge to a large house, now no more. Turn right after the causeway on to a path alongside the southern shore of Hooe Lake. After walking round the sewage works, turn right along a path. You will join a narrow road which leads to Hooe Lake Road.

Walk straight across the grassy area keeping to the shore and turn right along Barton Road, and by staying with this road you will come into Boringdon Road, Turnchapel. Continue on and turn left on St. John's Road to a car park on your right. In the corner is a signed route to Mount Batten Point.

57 | Mount Batten Point to Wembury (Warren Point Ferry) OS E108 & OL20

Grading: Easy   Distance -   11.8   686.3   7.3   426.4

Ascent: 340   24858   1115   81555

Timing: 3 hours

See also our Plymouth to Wembury Path Description.

Due to the praiseworthy activities of Plymouth City Council you are about to step out onto welcome Coast Path realignments. Those who have walked this section before will be amazed at the difference and those who have been Association members for a while will realise that our efforts have been successful.

The path goes around Mount Batten Point then runs south climbing to Jennycliff, where there is a café.

Keep to the cliff edge and continue south, that is to the end of the grassy area, where you will find a signed path entering woodlands. The blue cast iron marker at Jennycliff shows that it is 175.5 miles to Poole – sorry about that but it is really 212!

This up and down new path is a delight and well below the dangerous road that we once had to walk. Within a 0.25 mile (400 m) this new path links in with the original Coast Path. Turn right for a scenic uncomplicated path to Fort Bovisand, one of the great forts that once defended Plymouth.

Those who have been this way before should now pause to reflect. Since Mount Batten Point you have not had to set foot upon a vehicular road! We congratulate all responsible for this improvement.

On the descent to a road the path can be seen ahead between hundreds of chalet/huts and the sea. At Heybrook Bay when you reach the road, turn right.

The path passes around Wembury Point in front of the site of HMS Cambridge, now demolished, the one-time gunnery school, which is now owned by the National Trust – the Association made a donation to the Trust's appeal.

Now follows a low cliff top walk to Wembury Beach. The path passes seaward of the church and climbs to a level path that leads into the estuary of the River Yealm. At a small house, The Rocket House, once used for the storage of life saving apparatus, the official path takes off downhill diagonally towards the river and the ferry point. We suggest you walk down to the ferry point, even if the ferry is not running or you do not intend to use it, because you can take advantage of a scenic short circular walk back to the Rocket House. Once the ferry steps have been reached, to return to Rocket House carry on for a few yards then take a wooden stepped path on the left that climbs to good views over Newton Ferrers and Noss Mayo.

(At Wembury you can take the coast to coast walk to Lynmouth by using the Erme - Plym Trail, the Erme Valley Trail and the Two Moors Way. Guide books to all three routes are available from Ivybridge TIC (see page 162).

58 | Wembury (Warren Point) to Bigbury-on-Sea (Car Park) OS OL20

Grading: Starts easy then strenuous   Distance -   21.8   708.1   13.5   439.9

Ascent: 705   25563   2313   83868

Timing: 5.75 hours

See also our Wembury (Warren Point) to Bigbury-on-Sea Path Description.

The first obstacle is crossing the River Yealm (see over)

Wembury (Warren Point) to Noss Mayo Ferry.

River Yealm
Bill Gregor,   Seasonal all week, on demand.
1 Underhaye,   29th March until end September
Yealmpton   1000 - 1200 and 1500 - 1600 hrs.
PL8 2JR.
Tel: 01752 880079 or 07817 132757

During fine weather and school holidays the ferry is operational between 1000 and 1600 daily - but please phone first. Mr Gregor is often there outside normal operating hours. There is a signal board to summon the ferryman by the steps at Warren Point or at the slipway at Noss Mayo. We suggest you might also telephone ahead to Mr Gregor to give him an idea of your estimated time of arrival.

If there is no ferry then this means a walk back to the Rocket House to follow the path described below into Knighton. There is an hourly bus service (number 48) to Plymstock and Plymouth, where there is available an infrequent service to Noss Mayo (number 94). For a quicker conveyance around the estuary there are reasonably priced taxis available:-

Wembury Cabs - John Pitcher 01752 862151

Walking route around the River Yealm.

This is about 9 miles (14.5 km) from ferry landing to ferry landing. We advise that you should not walk the A379 as a 'short cut' to the below-described route. From the Rocket House the track leads into a road. At the corner of the garden wall to 'Monckswood' a stile leads to a field and to the footpath junction. The path you want is the one to the right which runs alongside a high wall. Follow it to the end of the wall, where it goes through two successive kissing gates. It then bears left approximately 330° across fields and allotments towards Knighton. As you leave the fields it goes down a few steps. Turn left and then first right. This will bring you out onto the road. Turn left and the bus stop is a little further along on the other side of the road just before the pub. The distance from ferry point to bus stop is 1.5 miles (2.5 km). Before reaching the bus stop and opposite the shop there is a telephone box where you can call a taxi if you want.

Go across to a minor road opposite to descend and turn left and then right at the next road junction. Continue along the road for about 0.5 mile (800 m) ignoring all turnings and footpaths. At a major road turn left for a few yards to turn right on a footpath just by a bus stop. This is now a waymarked route, the Erme-Plym Trail. Stay with it down to Cofflete Creek and up the other side until you reach the main A379 road. Turn right and a mile of main road walking follows, the best pavement is at first on the left, then switches to the right leaving Brixton, then for a long stretch there is none at all but it restarts on the left. (There is a safer but longer alternative starting at Brixton Church, see below.) Turn right down the road signed Newton Ferrers 3 miles. Go down to Puslinch Bridge and bear right up the hill. Nearly at the top, a footpath goes right cutting the corner to Wrescombe. Emerging onto the road turn right to continue along to The Butts and down the main road to Newton Ferrers. If you arrive within approximately two hours of low tide you can bear right down Yealm Road and turn down Newton Hill, to cross a tidal causeway to Noss Mayo and another across the inlet at Noss. If you are not so fortunate turn left down the road to Bridgend and Noss Mayo, being sure to turn first right as you enter Noss. Here those who have come around will have a picturesque riverside walk out to where those who have been fortunate enough with the ferry will disembark.

Alternative route - Brixton to Puslinch Bridge

At Brixton Church go up Old Road and follow the waymarked Erme-Plym Trail signs until you arrive on a minor road in the outskirts of Yealmpton. Here turn right and continue down the road, ignoring the footpath left turn of the Erme-Plym Trail. At the main A379 road, cross over, turning left and immediately right into Stray Park. At the bottom bear right along a tarmac footpath. This comes to a road; turn left along a stony track. At the footpath sign continue ahead to pass the entrance to Kitley Caves. The path eventually emerges in a car park. Leave this and turn left on the road to reach Puslinch Bridge. From here on the route is as described above.

Coast Path continues

From the ferry, the Erme Estuary is about 9 miles (14 km) ahead. You are the best judge of how long that will take you to get there for low tide, so plan your Noss Mayo departure accordingly. The well-marked path climbs through woodlands to pick up Lord Revelstoke's nine-mile drive, made for the carriages of his guests at Membland Hall, since demolished.
At Battery Cottage, just as you are leaving the woodlands, look out for a path going off to the right. You can take this down to Cellars Beach, for a swim maybe. It continues on around the back of the beach then climbs along the cliff edge to a flagstaff and up to rejoin the Coast Path beyond Brakehill Plantation where you turn right onto Lord Revelstoke's drive.

There is a definitive seaward path at Stoke Down at 560460 just after passing a single stone gate post on the left. Use this if you wish to visit the historic Church of St Peter the Poor Fisherman; this will mean an uphill road walk to regain the Coast Path. If you do not divert then the path crosses the Stoke Beach road to continue along, passing the ruined 'Tea House'.

You are now in for a very steep descent and further on a steep climb up to St Anchorite's Rock and you pass Bugle Hole. The section then to Mothecombe Beach provides superb views to the Erme estuary. It has been fairly described as England's most unspoilt river estuary: we certainly believe it to be the most attractive. At the beach do not turn inland but take the seaward path in the woods at Owen's Hill.

At Mothecombe the Old Schoolhouse Café, just uphill from the slipway, is open every day from April to October between 1100 and 1700, and is often open after this.

(At Mothecombe you can take the coast to coast walk to Lynmouth by using the Erme - Plym Trail, the Erme Valley Trail and the Two Moors Way. Guide books to all three routes are available from Ivybridge TIC (see page 162).

River Erme   No ferry

Low water here is at about the same time as the Devonport Tide Table shown on pages 21 & 22.

It is usually possible to paddle across the river 1 hour each side of low water along the old ford and under normal conditions, at low tide the water is about knee deep and the river bed is pebbles. Great care should be taken because heavy rains or seas can make the crossing dangerous. On modern maps the old ford is not shown but this in fact ran from Ordnance survey map reference 614 476 to map reference 620 478. In other words, the old ford connected the road by the row of coastguard cottages with the end of the inland road to Wonwell Beach from Kingston.

Should you arrive at the River Erme at a time that promises a very long wait for low tide to enable you to wade across then there is an inland alternative. This alternative is of about 8 miles (5 km) with fairly steep up and down country lanes. You are the best judge of your rate of travel so the decision to wait for the tide or continue walking is yours. (There are taxi services which operate in this area – contact John Edwards on 01548 830859 or mobile 24 hrs 07967 374502. Alternatively contact Wembury Cabs - John Pitcher 01752 862151)

Walking route around the River Erme
If you follow the riverside paths shown on OS map OL20 you will be trespassing on a private estate so follow the narrow country lanes to Holbeton village. Then continue on a northerly route to Ford and Hole Farm. Soon after passing Hole Farm take off on a public footpath on your right. From here to the main A379 road is about 0.75 mile (1.2 km). Turn right to cross the River Erme at Sequer's Bridge. Off road paths have been created and signed on the other side of the road but you will still have to return to road walking. Stay on the A379 for about 0.5 mile (0.75 km) but take care as this is an extremely busy road. You will see a road on your right signposted to Orcheton. Follow this road south towards the village of Kingston but before you reach that village you will see road signs to Wonwell Beach. Just before the slipway on to the sands you have a choice. If the tide now permits you can continue south along the beach or take to the waymarked Coast Path in the woodlands on your left.

Beyond the Erme the walking becomes tougher but the all round views will compensate for the effort. The path passes Challaborough with its café and caravans to Bigbury-on-Sea, where the Bay Café is open all day and the only establishment for evening meals.

Burgh Island can be visited by walking across the sands or by a 'sea tractor' if the tide is in. The pub is very old, the hotel is fascinating art deco modern and the hut at the top of the island stands on the site of a chapel. This hut was used by the 'huers' - pilchard fishermen on the lookout for shoals of fish.

Grading: Moderate   Distance -   9.2   717.3   5.7   445.6

Ascent: 269   25832   883   84751

Timing: 2.75 hours

See also our Bigbury-on-Sea to Salcombe Path Description.

There are riverside footpaths along both west and east banks of the River Avon to Aveton Gifford. This makes the inland walking route from Bigbury-on-Sea to Bantham and vice versa about 8 miles (13 km) in total. The OS OL20 map shows the riverside paths. What you have to watch is that the road between the two words 'Ford' is tidal and therefore is at times submerged. This route is described below.

The official route turns right, off the road after you have left the large car park. This cliff top path offers splendid views across the estuary. It returns to the road. Immediately cross over it into a field and turn right. Thanks to Devon's Local Services Group there is no risk now of getting knocked down on the busy road as the Coast Path is up hill along the field edge.

Cross the road to walk through the yards of Mount Folly Farm to the signed Coast Path across fields to the ferry point at Cockleridge.

Bigbury/Bantham (River Avon)
Marsh Dawes,   Seasonal – Daily, except Sundays
The Boathouse,   from 1st April – 25th September
Bantham,   1000 – 1100 hrs and 1500 - 1600
Tel: 01548 561196
Mobile: 07837 361306

We urge you to contact the ferry operator direct if you are relying on this service, particularly if you are anticipating a fairly late finish and need to confirm the time of its last run.

The ferryman is generally around, and can be called by waving. Low water is about the same time as the Devonport Tide Table. It is possible at low tide, when not rough, or the river is not in flood, to wade the river. However, we strongly stress we are not advising this as a cheap method of avoiding the ferry crossing. When the ferry is working, you are strongly advised to use it because wading is not easy and you may get a lot wetter than you expect. You will most likely be up to your thighs in water and in no circumstances should the crossing be attempted if conditions are wrong. The two guide points are just below the ferry crossing. On the true right bank - the western side - there is a line of Christmas trees on a bank running north and south with a pine tree on the edge of the river bank. On the left bank - the eastern side - there is a castellated building with battlements and a little flag pole in the middle. However, if crossing from the true right to the left - in other words from west to east - take off at the hedge and wade towards the castle-like building. If going the other way, vice versa. Please note it is important that you do wade at this point. The river looks shallow in a number of other places but there are deeper channels and indeed soft sand patches which can make it extremely difficult. Further towards the sea, there is a considerable tidal ebb which can be exceedingly dangerous.

PLEASE NOTE WHEN THE FERRY IS NOT OPERATING A RECOMMENDED WAY TO REACH BANTHAM IS BY REASONABLY PRICED TAXIS:

Arrow Cars - Mr Kemp - Telephone: 01548 856120

John Edwards - Telephone: 01548 830859. Mobile 24 hrs 07967 374502

It should always be borne in mind that the depth of water at low tide and consequently safe passage across is affected by natural conditions inasmuch that strong south west or westerly winds tend to bank up water in the English Channel and, therefore, there will be a greater depth of water than expected. This will also happen if there is a lot of rain in the catchment areas of the rivers, with consequently more water coming down. Caution: although we know several who have waded the River Avon we do not recommend it; great care is required, especially by those with backpacks.

VERY IMPORTANT - PLEASE TAKE NOTE

EVEN AT LOW WATER WE STRESS THAT YOU MUST SERIOUSLY CONSIDER, EVEN AT LOW TIDES, WHETHER YOU SHOULD WADE THIS RIVER. IT IS VERY DIFFICULT AND CAN BE DANGEROUS EVEN FOR TALL AND STRONG ADULTS. MANY OF OUR MEMBERS, INCLUDING YOUR SECRETARY WILL NOT VENTURE ACROSS. THEIR OPINION BEING - 'WHEN THE FERRY IS NOT RUNNING THEN THE *ONLY ALTERNATIVE IS TO GO ROUND'*.

Inland Walking Route - approx. 8 miles (13 km)

Much of this route has been waymarked 'Avon Estuary Walk' with a heron motif in blue and white.

When the tide is not low (and we urge you to read again our advice about wading) and the ferry is not available, the only way to the other side is an inland walk to Aveton Gifford and around. This is a pleasant 8 mile (13 km) diversion as it is mostly along country paths. Walking through agricultural land in deep country makes a change from the coast. The paths are shown on OS OL20 and are quite well marked but they are little used and are not always easy to follow. Allow plenty of time for some heavy walking, for straying off route or for a possible delay at the tidal road near Aveton Gifford.

Disregard the Coast Path where it turns right through Mount Folly Farm and descends to the ferry point, but proceed towards Bigbury for 60 yards (55 m) to the next footpath sign. Turn right into the field over a stone stile and walk along the field edge. Over a wooden stile will bring you onto the golf course where, after a short distance, you meet a surfaced track. Go northwards along the track towards the clubhouse for 200 yards (185 m), turning right at an entrance between two huts going down a track to Hexdown Farm. Pass left of the farmhouse to bear immediately right and then left. Bear right before the next gate to continue downhill with the boundary on your left. Proceed along a track through a timber gate. Follow the footpath sign slightly left along a tarmac drive, into woodland, then through Lincombe and on to the B3392 on a corner. Proceed northwards towards Bigbury for 350 yards (320 m) (be careful of the traffic) and turn right at the footpath sign to Aveton Gifford (via tidal road). Cross the field to a post and wire fence and enter the top of Doctor's Wood. Re-emerge into a field and cross due east to a wooden stile. Proceed along a high level path (beautiful views) then walk downhill to the tidal road which will bring you to Aveton Gifford. There is a viable alternative if the tide is over the road by walking north-westward to Foxhole then north-eastward to Waterhead and Aveton Gifford. The whole path is adequately waymarked.

Cross the Avon on the roadbridge (A379) towards Kingsbridge, and turn right at the end of the bridge into a cul-de-sac named Bridge End. Continue to a gate at a signpost, and straight on to a metalled road, where you turn right at a signpost.

Bear left at the road fork, following the footpath sign to a gate; turn right here and follow a fence on the right, and through another gate into a field.

Turn half right down to the bottom of the valley, and bear right to a gate with a waymark 'to Stiddicombe Creek'. Cross this and enter the wood on the right. Work steadily uphill to the top corner and follow the waymark signs along the top of the field with a hedge on the left (watch for herons by the river) to a stile by a gate; over another stile and continue. Bear right and cross a farm track to a gate between walls. Cross the stream ahead with stepping stones, and go along to a stile and waymark signs, where you turn right and go straight on to Bantham. Turn right and go through the village, where you will see the ferry sign; here you would have stepped ashore had it been operating. The Coast Path is straight on towards the sea. Some of this walk is shown in the National Trail Guide.

Coast Path continues

You should take great care where the path proceeds along the seaward boundary of the Thurlestone Golf Course; watch out for golfers and where they hit the ball. We have had a report of a walker on this section who was hit in the mouth by a golf ball at close range, with resulting horrific damage to teeth and lips.

60 | Hope Cove, Inner Hope to Salcombe (Ferry)   OS OL20 (V) Hope Cove

Grading: Strenuous   Distance -   12.9   730.2   8.0   453.6

Ascent: 421   26253   1381   86132

Timing: 4 hours

See also our Bigbury-on-Sea to Salcombe Path Description.

Excellent coastal walking, some of the finest in South Devon. Before leaving Inner Hope you ought to walk along the inland road to look at The Square and its attractive thatched cottages. It is well marked out to Bolt Tail where the remains of an Iron Age fort are marked by a dry stone wall and the remains of a ditch.

The path is obvious to Bolberry Down (refreshments available - Port Light Hotel) and on to a viewpoint overlooking Soar Mill Cove. There is a steep descent to the cove but the climb out is easier. We have heard of walkers going wrong as they near the splendid rocky Bolt Head. The correct route is the coast route; do not divert inland anywhere until the headland is reached. The path then runs due north into and around Starehole Bay.

From the bay the path joins the Courtenay Way which was cut out under rocky pinnacles. The way ahead is through woodlands to the roadway below the National Trust's Overbecks House and Youth Hostel. Follow the road to South Sands where, in season, a ferry can be taken to the main ferry point in Salcombe. If it is not running or you are a purist, the way ahead to the town and ferry for East Portlemouth is along the most seaward roads ahead.

Watch out for the Ferry Hotel as the steps beside it lead you to the ferry itself.

Whilst in Salcombe you may like to visit Salcombe Embroiderers who stock Association clothing with the Coast Path logo. You will find them at Hannaford's Landing, Island Street, Salcombe, TQ8 8FE telephone: 01548 842115

61 | Salcombe to Torcross (Car Park)   OS OL20 (T) Salcombe; (V) Beesands

Grading: Strenuous   Distance -   20.8   751.0   12.9   466.5

Ascent: 642   26895   2106   88238

Timing: 6.75 hours

See also our Salcombe to Torcross Path Description.

This is first class walking, some of the best of the whole Coast Path.

Salcombe to East Portlemouth Ferry   All year round.
The Salcombe Ferry,   Winter - ¹/₂ hourly between 0800 - 1730 hrs.
Tel: 01548 842061/842053   Summer - Continuous service 0800 - 1900 hrs.
                                       (July & August)
                                       0830 hrs start weekends and bank holidays.

Please note that the ferry point is located at the steps from the Ferry Hotel.

We urge you to contact the ferry operator direct if you are relying on this service, particularly if you are anticipating a fairly late finish and need to confirm the time of its last run.

Having crossed the estuary the path goes off to the right along the narrow road. At the National Trust car park at Mill Bay the path goes up to the right through the trees. Between Easter and October there is a shop and café open in East Prawle, about 0.5 mile (800 m) from the path.

The official route is to the very end of Prawle Point, to the Coastguard lookout. There is also a path out to the point along the western side of the headland, which is a better route than the one on the top.

It is easy walking for a while along the edges of fields on what is a 'raised' beach. The path then becomes rocky and up and down prior to Lannacombe Beach. About 0.5 mile (800 m) before Lannacombe, try to find time to take the existing path that the National Trust has exposed and inmproved to the right, signposted to the previously hidden Woodcombe Sand beach. Until now the beach, a peaceful isolated spot, could only be reached through the grounds of Woodcombe House, and many people didn't even know it was there. The path twists and drops, and you have to come back the same way, but it is only about 100 yards (90 m) and well worth the effort.

The path is straightforward to Start Point and on to Torcross and has recently been rerouted following the purchase of land between Hallsands and Beesands by the National Trust - this is a distinct improvement. It is not currently possible to visit the old deserted village at Hallsands, which is deemed to be unsafe. You can, however, get a glimpse of the ruins by taking the path to the village as far as the closure notice, which will not take long and is a very moving experience.

62 Torcross to Dartmouth (Lower Ferry)   OS OL20 (V) Torcross; (V) Strete; (V) Stoke Fleming

Grading: Starts Easy then Strenuous			Distance -	16.4	767.4	10.2	476.7
Ascent:	448	27343	1470	89708			

Timing: 4.75 hours

See also our Torcross to Dartmouth Path Description.

The Coast Path runs along the length of the shingle bank. You can walk either side of the road; the top of the beach for sea views or alongside the Ley for bird watching.

Possible new route

After leaving the beach and before reaching the A379 another new section of Coast Path may have been installed. Watch out for a sign to the right that will take you on a new path through scrub and trees. It will bear left uphill through Asherne Gully to Strete village.

Normal route

If this has not yet been opened carry on up the lane to the A379. Now, be careful. WE CANNOT OVEREMPHASISE THE NEED FOR CAUTION ON THIS SECTION LEADING TO THE VILLAGE. IT IS ALONG A BUSY, NARROW, DANGEROUS ROAD.

Following years of lobbying, this notorious stretch of path is at last beginning to resemble a Coast Path with the opening of a stretch between Strete and Stoke Fleming. There is still a nasty stretch of road at the top of the path from Strete Gate, where you have to go through the village of Strete with extreme caution. Having passed through the village, continue along the road for approximately 450 yards (411 m) to a stile on the right, which takes you on to the new path and some breathtaking views. Follow the path through fields downhill to a marvellous wooden bridge.

The path then contours to the right and goes down into a steep valley and up the other side to the road. Again, take care, cross the road and walk to the right then up and over the hill and down to Blackpool Sands, passing over a new packhorse bridge. Cross the road again and into Blackpool Sands, where there are toilets and refreshments.

The path then runs parallel with the A379 for about 547 yards (500 m) where it is again necessary to cross the road further up the hill, following the old road into Stoke Fleming. This is the end of the realigned section.

It is then necessary to follow the signs around the village until you come out again on the A379 at the new village hall.

Across the road, a further section of road (approx. 0.6 mile - 1 km) follows until you reach the National Trust car park at Warren Point and back to the coast proper.

At Warren Point you reach National Trust land and, of course, an enjoyable coastal walk to Dartmouth Castle. Before setting forth look to the west and be hopeful that a new Coast Path could be there in a year or two.

Dartmouth Castle commands the mouth of the River Dart and should be visited, time permitting. In season there is a regular ferry from the castle to Dartmouth and this can be utilised for a pleasant river trip, instead of walking down the road – for the purist, stay on the path.

On approaching the town there is an interesting very short alternative to the signed path just before Warfleet (which can be seen through the trees). Turn right at the Coast Path sign and follow a path down to the creek head and then under a road bridge to emerge up some steps back onto the official route. The way from here follows the road, with views of the harbour, down to the town. Look out for the Coast Path sign at the head of some steps down to an old fort and Bayard's Wharf, an old cobbled corner of Dartmouth. The lower car ferry is immediately to your right but you may prefer to carry on to explore the town and take the ferry instead from old Dartmouth Station which was the only one in Britain without a railway.

63 | Dartmouth to Brixham   OS OL20 (T) Dartmouth; (V) Kingswear (Trains)
(King William of Orange Statue)

Grading: Strenuous				Distance -	17.3	784.7	10.8	487.5
Ascent:	880	28223	2887	92595				

Timing: 5.75 hours

See also our Dartmouth to Brixham Path Description.

Walkers will probably use the lower ferry to cross the River Dart but there are two other regular ferries which also run all year round. Nearby is the passenger ferry, which lands by the steam railway station, and which gives a more comfortable crossing, and if these two are not running then further up the river is the higher ferry taking pedestrians and vehicles. If you use the higher ferry you will then need to turn right along the railway line to the road, then turn right again and descend the hill to join the Coast Path by the lower ferry slipway.

Dartmouth/Kingswear   All year round (not Christmas Day), continuous
South Hams District Council, Lower Ferry,   between 0700 and 2300 hrs.
Lower Ferry Office, The Square,   Sundays start 0800 hrs.
Kingswear TQ6 OAA
Tel: 01803 752342
Fax: 01803 752227
Website: www.southhams.gov.uk/sp-dartmouthlowerferry

We urge you to contact the ferry operator direct if you are relying on this service, particularly if you are anticipating a fairly late finish and need to confirm the time of its last run.

On landing at Kingswear, by the lower ferry, pass through an arch on the right. Ascend Alma Steps then turn right along Beacon Road. In 1.25 miles (2 km) turn right down steps at Warren Woods. Much of the path in Warren Woods is on the estate which was owned by the late Lt. Col. Jones, the Falkland Islands VC, and has very properly been dedicated to his memory. Although you will catch a glimpse of Kingswear Castle, this is not accessible to the public.

When you reach the old Battery Buildings at Froward Point, do divert inland to see the Daymark navigation tower nearby if time permits, but then return to the Coast Path to continue. The sign here is 8.75 miles (14 km) to Brixham and the path descends steeply, going right from the back corner of the derelict look out building and then passes through the World War II gun and searchlight positions. Next at Pudcombe Cove you can obtain access to the National Trust gardens at Coleton Fishacre if they are open.

Walking on above Pudcombe Cove and Ivy Cove to Scabbacombe Head, you will see the Scabbacombe Sands, Long Sands, Man Sands, Southdown Cliff and Sharkham Point before reaching St Mary's Bay. Taken together, the strenuous grading of this section is well justified.

Now you have a pleasant walk to Berry Head Country Park, a Nature Reserve with much of interest - do spend time there if you can. The Northern Fort, one of the two Napoleonic Forts, contains the Berry Head lighthouse; next to it, the old Artillery Store houses an exhibition centre explaining 400 million years of Berry Head history, and the old guardhouse is now a café, open in the season and sometimes out of season as well.

When you leave Berry Head and go past the Berry Head Hotel, turn right through the public car park and follow the path past Shoalstone Beach and along the new promenade. (In wild weather it may be better to continue along the road until you are level with the breakwater, and then take the steps down to the promenade.) This follows the water's edge past the marina to the inner harbour.

64 **Brixham to Torquay Harbour**   **OS OL20 (T) Brixham; (T) Paignton (Trains)**

Grading: Moderate   Distance -   13.5   798.2   8.4   495.9

Ascent: 277   28500   909   93504

Timing: 4 hours

See also our Brixham to Torquay Path Description.

The path goes along the back of Broadsands, along the back of Goodrington Sands beach, around Roundham Head, along Paignton and Preston sea fronts and along the promenade at Torquay.

From Brixham to Elbury Cove the path is fair though not as scenic as one might hope. Thereafter it becomes more urbanised with the poorest section from Hollicombe to Torquay Harbour, where you usually have quite heavy traffic nearby. Remember, in case of need, there is a very frequent bus service from Brixham to Torquay via Paignton! There is also a regular Brixham/Torquay seasonal ferry service. In the built up areas of Torbay where the Coast Path is routed on pavements and other hard surfaces look out for the special waymarks used by Torbay Countryside Service. These are brass national trail logos (an acorn) set into the surface of the route.

When departing from Brixham leave by the new path running along the harbour, signposted Coastal Footpath to Oxen Cove and Freshwater Car Park. At the car park continue on past the Zeneca Brixham Environmental Laboratory and on to the Battery Gardens, where you follow the lower path to Fishcombe Cove. Ascend from the cove and at the road junction turn right, signposted Public Footpath to Churston Ferrers. (By the road junction, the Battery Heritage Centre, illustrating the importance of the site from the Napoleonic Wars to D-Day, is well worth a visit if it is open.)

At the far end of Elberry Cove ignore the more obvious path going inland and leave the beach by ascending the steps. Walk along Broadsands Beach to the end - do not follow the path up the cliff but turn left instead, up the wide tarmac path, pass under the railway viaduct and then turn immediately right where the Coast Path is signposted.

At Goodrington turn right under a railway bridge, follow the promenade round and just before the end a zigzag path takes you up, through ornamental gardens on to Roundham Head.

At Hollicombe Head you can turn right and go through the delightful park that was once the gas works. Bear left to emerge through the main gate onto the road. Then turn right for Torquay and continue along its sea front.

65 **Torquay Harbour to Shaldon (Ferry)**   **OS E110 (T) Torquay (Trains)**

Grading: Strenuous   Distance -   17.3   815.5   10.8   506.7

Ascent: 894   29394   2933   96437

Timing: 5.75 hours

See also our Torquay to Shaldon Path Description.

At Torquay harbour go across the new pedestrian bridge between the inner and outer harbours. Go up Beacon Hill, passing the Living Coasts Centre (with penguins and puffins visible under a vast netting tent) until you reach the Imperial Hotel. Turn in right here to pass in front of the main entrance to the hotel and then follow the scenic path to the grassy plateau of Daddyhole Plain, which you cross to find the path descending to Meadfoot Beach.

At the far end of Meadfoot Beach turn right through a small car park and ascend to Marine Drive, where you turn right. Shortly, turn right at a signpost for the Coast Path, going round Thatcher Point. The path eventually emerges onto the road. At the road turn right and shortly find a path above the left hand side of the road (the path down on the right offers an interesting detour around Hope's Nose), and at the end of this, cross the road and take the Bishop's Walk path signposted to Anstey's Cove.

As you join the road by the car park above Anstey's Cove you can, time and energy permitting, take the steep path down to the picturesque cove; however, you'll have to return the same way, as following repeated rock falls the adjacent Redgate Beach has been sealed off indefinitely by Torbay Borough Council, and it is no longer possible to cross the two beaches and regain the official route by the path up the cliffs. Instead, about 50 yards (46 m) beyond the turning down to Anstey's, take the path through the woods to the right signposted 'To Babbacombe & St Marychurch over the Downs', which takes you up to Walls Hill.

From Walls Hill the path will take you to the road descending to Babbacombe Beach, at the far end of which you traverse a wooden bridge structure to Oddicombe beach, where the path bears upwards just before the lower station of the Babbacombe Cliff Railway. Shortly you pass under the railway and then take care to turn right downwards at the start of a pleasant path leading to a grassy picnic area where you bear left uphill. Because of a landslip, the path is now diverted inland: signs direct you up the grassy hill to the road. Turn right along the road, go down Petitor Road and turn left at the end to rejoin the track to Watcombe.

At the valley road linking the main Torquay/Teignmouth Road to Watcombe Beach, turn left and immediately right, signposted Maidencombe 0.75 mile (1 km) and follow a wooded path. There are two places along this route where 'alternative inland' routes are signed, but you are recommended to keep to the lower, more coastal routes. From the car park at Maidencombe, go a few yards up the road and turn right.

From here there are some quite stiff gradients until you reach the road at Labrador where you turn right and in a few yards leave the pavement to take a sunken path on your right and shortly enter a field on your right via a stile by a field gate.

You will get superb views now as you descend along the coastal side of the field system, then take the path round The Ness to Shaldon.

---

66 Shaldon to Exmouth (Ferry)

OS E110 (V) Shaldon; (T) Teignmouth (Trains); (T) Dawlish (Trains); (V) Dawlish Warren (Trains); (V) Starcross (Trains)

Grading: Easy				Distance -	12.7	828.2	7.9	514.6
Ascent:	173	29567	568	97005				

Timing: 3 hours

See also our Shaldon to Exmouth Path Description.

The above figures relate to the distance involved when the Starcross ferry is operating. If not, the walking route around the Exe is described below, and you should add approximately 10.6 miles (17 km).

This is a section where you may have problems depending on the time of year and state of the tide.

At the time of going to print the Shaldon/Teignmouth ferry service is suspended, and it is hoped the service will resume at Easter. Up-to-date information can be obtained from Steve Reading, Teignbridge District Council, telephone: 01626 215609.

If the ferry is not working, your walking route around is to continue along riverside roads from the ferry point and cross Shaldon Bridge. Immediately after crossing the railway line, exit from the bridge into Milford Park. Walk beside the railway line, through Bitton Sports Ground into Park Hill, cross into Bitton Avenue at Clay Lane, then turn right into Willow Street. At the end bear left, then right, which will bring you into Quay Road, into Osmond Street and then straight on to Harbour Beach and the ferry. Keep going on out onto 'The Point', turn north east and once more you are upon the Coast Path.

Shaldon/Teignmouth Ferry (River Teign)

If the ferry service has resumed by the time you arrive in Shaldon the operating schedule should be available at the ferry operating point on the beach.

Coast Path continues

After crossing from Shaldon by ferry, follow the promenade past the pier and shortly you reach Eastcliff Walk forking up on your left and there you must make your first decision. The true route is ahead along the sea wall but at certain states of the high tide and particularly in bad weather it may be impossible after a 2 mile (3.2 km) walk to pass under the railway line at the end of the wall, and if this appears likely a detour is needed. However the steps are only unavailable for about one hour either side of high tide. You should refer to the tide tables (see pages 21 & 22) and calculate the time of high water from the two times given for low water. You should ascend Eastcliff Walk, which soon becomes a track and will eventually lead you to the A379, where you turn right and rejoin the Coast Path at the top of Smugglers Lane.

If conditions look right, enjoy the walk along the sea wall and at the end pass under the railway line and ascend Smugglers Lane to the A379. Now you have a short walk on this busy main road, although there is a footpath on the left hand side, and after about 150 yards (135 m) turn right into Windward Lane, then immediately left and take the path on your left. After a field section you are back on the road but immediately follow the Old Teignmouth Road on your right, until you reach the main road yet agai n. Turn right and shortly, by some railings, turn right and follow the path which soon zigzags down to the boat cove, then follow the sea wall to Dawlish Station.

From here it is possible at low tide to walk along the sea wall to Dawlish Warren, then at the start of the new promenade cross the railway by a footbridge, turn right, and cross the car park to the main road and reach the main road. If the tide is high you must take the alternative route by turning left opposite the Railway Station and in 30 yards (27 m) turning right through an arch and ascending the steps. Continue forward, passing a new housing development on your left, and after passing through another two arches, you emerge onto the A379 road and continue forward. Shortly after passing the new Rockstone Flats turn right on the road signposted Dawlish Warren 0.75 mile (1 km) and immediately take the coastal footpath signed on your right to follow the Ladies Mile to Dawlish Warren. (You can in fact take a footpath immediately before the Rockstone Flats, although this is not signposted, then take the left fork to join the Coast Path.)

There is no official path along the Warren but if time and energy permit you can enjoy a circular walk round this sandy Nature Reserve.

Watch out for vehicles whilst walking around the harbour at Cockwood - there are no pavements. Thanks to Devon County Council there is a new cycle/walkway from Cockwood Harbour to Starcross. Watch for the direction sign.

You are now faced with crossing the River Exe and in the summer months there is a ferry from Starcross to Exmouth reached by walking along the road from Dawlish Warren.

Starcross/Exmouth (River Exe) Mid April - end October.
Mr B Rackley, Hourly, 7 days a week.
Starcross Pier & Pleasure Company From Starcross Pier
26 Marine Parade, on the hour from 1010 until 1710 hrs.
Dawlish, EX7 9DL From Exmouth, Ferry Steps.
Tel: 01626 862452 / 01626 774770 on the half-hour from 1040 until 1740 hrs.
www.exe2sea.co.uk

Last Ferry	From Starcross	From Exmouth
end March, Oct	1610	1640
mid May, June to mid Sept	1710	1740
August	1810	1840

We urge you to contact the ferry operator direct if you are relying on this service, particularly if you are anticipating a fairly late finish and need to confirm the time of its last run.

Alternative routes around the River Exe

1. Exeplorer Water Taxis (1st April to 4th September. Runs daily from 0845 to 1800, weather permitting) will pick up passengers from the north-west end of Warren Point and take them to Exmouth. Please telephone 07970 918418 before relying on this service.

2. Turf/Topsham Ferry Daily, 7 days a week Easter Holiday; Mid May -
Steve Garrett mid September; Weekends April - October. From Turf 1145 –1600
Tel: 07778 370582 From Topsham 1130 - 1515.
E-mail: seadreamferry@btinternet.com Website: www.topshamtoturfferry.co.uk
(There is a train station at Topsham, with services running to Exmouth and Exeter.)

3. Topsham Ferry (River Exe) Apr. - Sept. Daily except Tuesdays, from 1100 to
Exeter City Council Canals & Rivers Dept. 1730 hrs. Oct - Mar. Saturdays, Sundays and
Tel: 01392 274306 (Office) Bank Holidays 1100 to 1700 hrs or sunset.
Tel: 0780 120 3338 (Ferryman) Wave at, or phone ferry to call service.

Between April and September this ferry may be available outside these hours, weather and tides permitting.

We urge you to contact the ferry operator direct, particularly if you are anticipating a fairly late finish and need to confirm the time of its last run.

(There is a train station at Topsham, with services running to Exmouth and Exeter.)

4. You can use the frequent bus services, changing routes at either Countess Wear or in Exeter.

5. You can catch a train at Dawlish Warren, changing at Exeter and going back down to Exmouth.

Once across the river you have to get to Exmouth and we are inclined to suggest the frequent bus service, but failing this the walk as far as Lympstone will be on the road except for a small footpath section between Clyst Bridge and Ebford. From Lympstone there is a riverside path to Exmouth, now part of the East Devon Way - look for the mauve markers featuring a foxglove.

67 Exmouth to Budleigh Salterton (River Otter Car Park) OS E115 (T) Exmouth (Trains)

Grading: Moderate				Distance -	9.9	838.1	6.2	520.8
Ascent:	230	29797	755	97760				

Timing: 3 hours

See also our Exmouth to Sidmouth Path Description.

No real problems here for walkers but keep inland of the range at Straight Point. Please keep to the waymarked route through Sandy Bay caravan site. Climbing to a point just south of West Down Beacon, the path then borders the golf course on the left. After gently descending for about 1000 yards (1 km), the Coast Path turns sharp left inland and, almost immediately, branches off to the right away from the footpath down into the town. The Coast Path runs alongside the cliff edge and down onto the esplanade until it reaches the car park at the eastern end.

68 Budleigh Salterton to Sidmouth (River Sid) OS E115 (T) Budleigh Salterton

Grading: Moderate then strenuous				Distance -	11.1	849.2	6.9	527.7
Ascent:	301	30098	988	98748				

Timing: 3.5 hours

See also our Exmouth to Sidmouth Path Description.

The Coast Path leaves Budleigh Salterton from the north-east corner of the large car park at the eastern end of the esplanade. It follows a raised path inland to the River Otter Bridge at South Farm, then a riverside path back to the coast.

The path around High Peak is well marked but it does not go over the top as you, and many others in the past, obviously expected. If you do battle your way to the top you will certainly not be disappointed with the views. The path on the top of Peak Hill immediately west of Sidmouth has been improved to give better seaward views.

The descent from Peak Hill towards Sidmouth takes you down through a wood and out on to the road. Turn right and keep to the right hand side of the road to pass through two kissing gates, then bear right through a gap in the hedge on to parkland for the descent into Sidmouth. At the bottom of the lawn, make your way onto the zigzag path which leads down between beach huts onto the small esplanade. Turn left and continue at sea level on the Clifton Walkway to the main esplanade.

69 | Sidmouth to Seaton (River Axe) OS E115 & E116 (T) Sidmouth

Grading: Severe then strenuous Distance -   16.7   865.9   10.4   538.1

Ascent: 643   30741   2110   100858

Timing: 5.5 hours

See also our Sidmouth to Lyme Regis Path Description.

Please note that there are a number of quite considerable ascents and descents on this section, so do not judge the effort required purely on the distance. There are one or two places in this stretch where it is easy to come off the route but you are not likely to come to any severe harm. Landslips have caused diversions on this stretch, but the temporary route and the proposed alignments are well signed, and for the most part, enjoyable.

On leaving Sidmouth, dramatic cliff falls are the cause of a diversion. Heading east, the Coast Path crosses the river Sid via Alma Bridge, climbs a zig-zag path and then is diverted on public roads (Cliff Road and Laskeys Lane). The diversion is well marked. At the top of Laskeys Lane, where the path turns south towards the sea, it crosses through the middle of a field and then re-joins the Coast Path at the start of the woods before rising to the Salcombe Hill cliff top.

After Branscombe Mouth there are alternative paths. The one over Hooken Cliffs gives superb views and is probably easier to walk. The undercliff path, apart from the beginning among the holiday chalets, is scenically better and we would recommend this if the weather is good. You have the interesting undercliff itself, the massive cliffs to the left, interesting rock formations ahead, and good views to seaward. At most states of the tide it is possible to walk along the beach from Seaton Hole to Seaton, avoiding some road work.

WATCH THE TIDE - YOU CAN GET CUT OFF

70 | Seaton to Lyme Regis (Town Car Park) OS E116 (T) Seaton

Grading: Moderate Distance -   11.0   876.9   6.8   544.9

Ascent: 372   31113   1220   102078

Timing: 3.25 hours

See also our Sidmouth to Lyme Regis Path Description.

You leave Seaton across its bridge over the River Axe and have to turn inland. Go up the road to the golf course, then walk due east across the fairway into a lane, which you go along, turning to the coast in less than 0.25 mile (400 m).

The section through the Landslip is in a National Nature Reserve and can be very rewarding to some but extremely frustrating to others. Views are extremely limited and the path in places puts on a fair imitation of a corkscrew or helter-skelter; you are unlikely to get lost but most unlikely to know where you are. Small piles of brushwood have been placed on the former worn path to allow eroded areas to regenerate, but obvious alternative routes have been cleared. The time to walk the Landslip does vary depending on the walker. We have received reports from some who have taken about 4 hours whilst others report 2 hours. We thought you would like to be aware of this.

The path into Lyme Regis has now been improved and you can take a path directly down to The Cobb without having to come into the car park, and then down the road.

LANDSLIDES / SLIPPAGES ON THE DORSET COAST

From Lyme Regis to Studland the geology is such that the cliffs are very vulnerable to slippage, particularly at the western end of the county. During the very wet winter of 2000/01 a number of considerable cliff falls and landslips occurred on the Dorset section. These resulted in some major temporary diversions having to be put in place. In 2006 a new section of Coast Path was opened east of Charmouth and the long diversion up Stonebarrow Lane was lifted. However a short section of this new path has already slipped and regrettably the diversion via

Stonebarrow Lane is again in force. In addition, a landslide below Lyme Regis Golf Course has raised safety issues in using the Right of Way along the beach from Lyme Regis to Charmouth and this alternative is now closed.

We have no clear information on when solutions will be found on the two diversions between Lyme Regis and Charmouth or the more minor diversion at Seatown. The passage of the Marine and Coastal Access Bill has stalled negotiations on alternative or replacement routes until the full implications of the new legislation are known. Regrettably it is looking very much as if those diversions will still be in place for 2010 with little prospect of the Coast Path being reinstated. In this year's edition we have again included the details of both the coastal route and the temporary diversions. The diversions described start at the points in the text marked by a bold letter 'D' and a number e.g. **(D2)**. However at the time of writing we still do not know what further damage could occur during the winter of 2009/10 so you will need to be on the lookout for possible diversions not mentioned in this Guide. When walking the path the best advice we can give is to follow the signed route and any official notices or signs. For up to date details of temporary diversions you should visit the Association's website.

Leaflets about the Lyme Regis to Charmouth diversions can be obtained from the TIC in Lyme Regis or from the Heritage Coast Centre at Charmouth.

---

71 | Lyme Regis to Charmouth (River Char)   OS E116 (T) Lyme Regis

---

Grading: Moderate   Distance -   4.4   **881.3**   2.7   **547.6**

Ascent: 214   31327   702   102780

Timing: 1.25 hours

See also our Lyme Regis to West Bay Path Description.

From Lyme Regis town centre take Church Street and Charmouth Road (A3052) until you reach Lyme Regis Football Club on the right, beyond which you will find a gate at the corner of a lane and take the footpath across fields to a lane where you turn left (yes west!) for 100 yards (90 m). At a finger post sign turn right up through the wood and near the top **[D1]** turn right onto the path that runs between the cliff edge and the golf course. Take the track downhill to Charmouth and at the first junction (with Old Lyme Hill) turn sharp right and follow the signposted route back to the cliff edge **[D2]**.

The alternative route along the beach to Charmouth mentioned in earlier editions of this Guide is currently no longer available, as it is closed following a landslide.

D1. Diversion 1 - Lyme Regis Golf Course. The diversion starts at the path junction in the wood at GR 3456 9330. Turn west on a path for 130 yards (120 m) to a junction with a road named Timber Hill. Turn north on this road, passing the golf course club house, to join the A3052 road. Continue north on this road for about 110 yards (100 m) and turn eastwards onto a public footpath (signposted to Fern Hill) across the golf course and bear north-east down through woods to rejoin the A3052 road. Turn south-east down this road for some 550 yards (500 m) to the roundabout with the main A35 road. Take the right hand fork, which is the local road into Charmouth, and follow it south-south-east downhill into the village for about 760 yards (700 m) to the second road junction. Here turn right into Higher Sea Lane (which later becomes a footpath) and proceed south-east for about 650 yards (600 m) to rejoin the Coast Path at Grid Ref 3640 9305.

Some very helpful maps of the diversion have been provided along the route at the principal junctions.

The diversion described above is the official Dorset County Council route. However we think there is a better route on the approach to Charmouth that we have called **D1A**. It also has the advantage of being a route that overcomes the next temporary path closure at Raffey's Ledge and this section is called **D2A** (see D2 below). Our recommended route is as follows.

D1A. Charmouth West (Alternative)
At the roundabout at the junction of the A3052 and A35 follow the Coast Path diversion signs to take the local road towards Charmouth village. Shortly after this junction, by another Coast Path diversion sign (that you should ignore), take the steps on the right to a stile and public footpath. Follow the waymarked direction up the field to Lily Farm. Look for, and cross, a stile hidden in a corner, at the left hand side of the stone gable wall of the central farm building. Pass

between the farm building and the Dutch barn on the left and after the buildings bear up to the right to pass through a field gate. Continue across a field, where you come to a tarmac lane known as Old Lyme Hill. Turn right and within 90 yards (80 m) turn left (where you rejoin the original route of the Coast Path) to shortly come to a minor road (Old Lyme Road).

D2A. Raffey's Ledge (Alternative)
Here the Coast Path goes forward to the cliff edge and has suffered a landslip, so there is another (this time more minor) diversion. This is above the area shown on maps as Raffey's Ledge. Turn left down Old Lyme Road and in 80 yards (70 m) turn right into a private road named Westcliffe Road. This road descends steeply for over 330 yards (300 m) to a junction with a road named Five Acres. Turn right and at the end of the cul-de-sac take a footpath going forward into a narrow lane. Shortly you will reach a wider road (Higher Sea Lane). Turn right and immediately ignore a sign to the left indicating to Lower Sea Lane and the Coast Path. Continue along the road and in about 100 yards (90 m) ignore a signpost to The Beach and bear right. In 50 yards (45 m) ignore yet another footpath sign to the left and keep right around the bend in the lane that rises for some 130 yards (120 m) to an oak signpost on the left. Here you can finally leave the lane through a metal gate to shortly rejoin the Coast Path proper. Turn left down the grassy slopes to the Heritage Coast Centre at Charmouth Beach.

D2. Diversion 2 - Charmouth (Raffey's Ledge).
If Diversion 1 has been lifted there is still the possibility of a further diversion on this section. This is the official Dorset County Council diversion. From the end of the track (Grid Ref 3580 9345) at the west end of the road called Old Lyme Hill continue north-eastwards on the road to reach the main road through the village. Turn right down this road and in 110 yards (100 m) turn right into Higher Sea Lane (which later becomes a footpath) and proceed south-east for about 650 yards (600 m) to rejoin the Coast Path at Grid Ref 3640 9305.

| 72 | Charmouth to West Bay (Bridport Arms) | OS E116 1 mile to (V) Charmouth |

Grading: Strenuous				Distance -	11.2	892.5	7.0	554.6
Ascent:	605	31932	1985	104765				

Timing: 3.75 hours

See also our Lyme Regis to West Bay Path Description.

Having now reached (by whatever route) the coast again at Charmouth turn left up the narrow road past the pub and toilets and turn right onto a footpath leading over an arched timber footbridge. Then take the obvious green swathe of the new Coast Path up the hill ahead.

As mentioned on page 91 this section is again closed and the diversion D3 needs to be followed.

D3. Diversion 3 - Charmouth (Stonebarrow)
From Lower Sea Lane west of the footbrige over the River Char at Grid Ref 3652 9320 turn north east along a tarmac lane called River Way and at the end continue along a gravel footpath to reach Bridge Road. Carry on northwards up this road to the junction with the main village road, The Street. Turn eastwards along The Street to Newlands Bridge and fork right into Stonebarrow Lane. Continue up this narrow lane for nearly three quarters of a mile (1150 m) taking care of the traffic. At the top of this lane a car park is reached. Immediately turn sharp right to find a four directional signpost. Take a grassy track as signed and go generally south-westwards to rejoin the Coast Path at Grid Ref 3803 9301. This diversion is also provided with the helpful maps mentioned in D1 above.

This is a section of interesting walking with spectacular views from Golden Cap, the highest mainland point on the south coast of England, and later from Thorncombe Beacon. However, be warned, your good views are not obtained without effort!

When you get to what looks like the top of Golden Cap you have to turn left and go a little higher to the trig. point to find your way down, which starts at the north end before later bearing east again. **[D4]** There is a car park and a pub at Seatown.

D4. Diversion 4 - Seatown
A minor diversion occurs on the western approach to Seatown. At the path junction at Grid Ref 4158 9197 follow the signed diversion north-east and then easterly down to a road (Sea Hill Lane). Here turn southwards down the road to rejoin the Coast Path at Grid Ref 4199 9175.

73 | West Bay to Abbotsbury (Swannery Car Park)   OS OL15 (V) West Bay; (V) Abbotsbury

					Distance -	15.2	907.7	9.4	564.0

Grading: Moderate

Ascent: 203   32135   666   105431

Timing: 4.25 hours

See also our West Bay to Abbotsbury Path Description.

SEE SECTION 80 FOR DETAILS OF THE ALTERNATIVE INLAND COAST PATH FROM WEST BEXINGTON TO OSMINGTON MILLS.

After you have walked round the back of West Bay harbour, pass to the right of St John's Church and ahead to the West Bay Public House, opposite which is the Coast Path sign pointing across to the foot of surprisingly steep cliffs.

Watch out for the inland loop at Burton Freshwater which is still shown on older OS maps. This has been changed and an improved route running between the caravan park and the beach has been installed and is well signed.

At Burton Beach, just east of the hotel, there is a café/toilet (open all year).

At Burton Mere, unless you are particularly interested in maritime flowers, the definitive route goes inland of the Mere, rather than going along the seaward side: you will get quite enough pebbles later.

There is a fair weather café and all year round toilets at West Bexington, and further on seasonal snack wagons in the car park, where the road turns inland past Abbotsbury Gardens. Coast Path walkers, however, should continue along the back of the beach for another 200 yards (185 m) before the route turns inland.

An alternative for the tough walker who wishes to stay on the coast all the way to Ferry Bridge, avoiding all of section 74, is to use the Chesil Bank; you can do this by going onto the beach where the path turns inland at Abbotsbury but note you cannot 'get off' again until you reach the causeway from Wyke Regis to Portland. This is only a walk for the fit and not one to be attempted at times of severe gale! Please note that the Chesil Bank is closed to visitors from 1st May-31st August for the Schedule 1 bird nesting season.

WARNING: If you intend to walk the whole length of Chesil Bank rather than going to Abbotsbury and along the edge of the Fleet (Section 74), you should telephone Major Hazard on 01305 783456 ext. 8132, to check whether the bank is safe to walk. There may be some firing at Chickerell Rifle Range and it is not unknown for the odd bullet to mis-target, and travel as far as the Bank. As a result, walkers will be sent back despite having walked half this gruelling hike.

The official route of the Coast Path runs to the south and east of Chapel Hill but avoiding Abbotsbury village. There is a short cut using a permissive path that leads to the Swannery car park.

There are refreshments, shops, toilets and B&Bs in Abbotsbury. If you have time, the climb up to St Catherine's Chapel is worth the effort.

74 | Abbotsbury to Ferry Bridge (Wyke Regis)   OS OL15

					Distance -	17.5	925.2	10.9	574.9

Grading: Easy. Chesil Beach: Strenuous

Ascent: 281   32416   922   106353

Timing: 4 hours (Official Route)

See also our Abbotsbury to Ferry Bridge Path Description.

The Coast Path does not actually go into Abbotsbury. However if you visited the village the best route back to the coast is to leave by the path that you entered the village. That is the path going south from the B3157 (West Street) adjacent to Chapel Lane Stores. At a path junction in 220 yards (200 m) continue south to Nunnery Grove to rejoin the Coast Path.

The Coast Path now goes inland but is well marked and enjoyable to walk; part of it goes along a ridge and has some good views. You do not get back to the shores of the Fleet until Rodden Hive.

On the outskirts of Abbotsbury, after Horsepool Farm, keep going up the ridge; beguiling, much better tracks go round the hill to the right, but they will not bring you to the stile you need at the top. In about 1 mile (1.5 km) turn south off to the ridge and after Hodder's Coppice turn sharp left. A track goes forward, but this is NOT the one you want. After you have crossed a minor road, the official path follows the field headland east and then south to the north-east corner of Wyke Wood as signposted, and not in a direct line as shown on some older maps. Take particular care as you approach Rodden Hive - the path suddenly dives through a hedge on your left. There is an apparent track that might make you think that the path goes to the right of the stream, but it does not.

At Tidmoor Point, follow the red and white posts, unless you have to divert as firing on the range is in progress across the coastal route. Near Wyke Regis the Coast Path deviates slightly inland around a MOD Bridging Hard.

75 | The Isle of Portland   OS OL15 (T) Portland

Grading: Moderate				Distance -	21.3	946.5	13.2	588.1
Ascent:	333	32749	1093	107446				

Timing: 6 hours

See also our Isle of Portland Path Description.

The total distance includes walking Portland Beach Road (A354) twice (there and back).

In June 2003 the route in this section was officially designated as part of the SWCP National Trail. The circuit of the Isle of Portland is well worth the effort and should not be omitted, although it is easy to do so. It is a fine walk, and while not beautiful it is rugged, spectacular, particularly in rough weather, and full of interest. The Island and Royal Manor of Portland still quarries its famous limestone, still 'hosts' HM Prison Services, but is replacing the Ministry of Defence with new port and tourism facilities. The opening of the Osprey Quay development on former MoD land beside Portland Harbour has presented the opportunity for a new coastal route to be formed for the Coast Path. Although it is not yet officially recognised by the Authorities we have included it in our alternative route in this area of Portland. There now remains just a small but vital gap of approx. 437 yards (400 m) in the public rights of way needed to complete the Association's objective of a true Coast Path around the north-east corner of the Isle of Portland. Agreement has been reached on a new section of path at this location and it is hoped that the improvements will be installed before too long.

From Ferry Bridge you have a number of choices, none of them of much merit, for the first two miles (3 km). Using the shared footway/cycleway beside the busy A354 road; crossing over the car park beyond the Chesil Beach Centre, to slog along the pebbles of Chesil Beach; or catching a bus to the south end of the causeway, to alight at the two new roundabouts at Victoria Square at Chiswell. Fourth, and probably best, is to cross the bridge to beyond the boatyard and on the eastern bank, walk along the raised bed of the old railway to near the end of the causeway at the roundabout for the access road to Osprey Quay, before returning to the footway/cycleway on the A354 to come to Victoria Square. From the southern roundabout take the main road southwards and shortly turn right into Pebble Lane, and then turn left just before the public toilets. Continue to the Cove House Inn and bear right up onto the promenade. About halfway along, at the floodgates, cut back sharp left and then right, following Coast Path signs up a steep tarmac path, past the school and up the steep path in the grass incline, to the steps to the terraced path that was the old A354 road (that has been realigned).

Bear off right onto the Coast Path running between old quarry banks and the cliff face. Then follows 3 miles (5 km) of spectacular and airy cliff top walking to Portland Bill.

On reaching Portland Bill, with its lighthouse, obelisk, cafés, toilets and Pulpit Rock, continue around the end of the low headland. Then head northwards and pass to the seaward of wooden chalets, to follow a winding path along the top of low cliffs, to join a road above Freshwater Bay after about 1.5 miles (2.5 km).

Turn right up the road (taking the footway on the west side of the road) for 600 yards (550 m), past Cheyne Weares car park to a finger post on the right. Follow the zigzag path down into the rugged undercliff area, and follow the waymarks through the disued quarry workings down to Church Ope Cove.

From this point there is the choice of two routes.

Designated Route
The designated route is signed and waymarked to run along the cliffs to the prison road, then through disused quarries, before returning to the west side of the 'island', where the A354 road reaches the top of the hill. The route then retraces its outward route to Chiswell and onward to Ferry Bridge.

However we think our preferred alternative route is better and is recommended until such time as route improvements are made on northeast Portland. This route is described below. If following our route, ignore other Coast Path signs and waymarks, as the two routes do connect in two locations.

Alternative Route
From Church Ope Cove before the 'West Cliff' and 'Coast Path' signs, turn right through a gap in the hedge with a 'Crown Estate' sign on to the undercliff path. Continue to seaward along the narrow rugged path to Durdle Pier and bear up left to turn right onto a wide firm path (old track bed of the former Weymouth to Easton railway line). Continue along the track for 550 yards (500 m) to a public footpath sign on the left and turn left over a bank to follow a rocky path that climbs up the cliffs to what appears to be an isolated chimney seen above on the skyline. A word of warning here - although the track continues northwards and appears to be well used, do not be tempted to continue, as the way forward is eventually blocked by the perimeter security fence of the former MoD establishment and there is no other route up the high cliffs.

Our preferred route is to turn sharp right at the chimney to go along a prison road, and follows a tarmac road northwards through a gap in a high wall. At the next road turn right and bear downhill toward the gates of the former MoD establishment, but shortly go left at a fork on an access road to compounds. Continue forward to a left hand bend, and carry on ahead on a grassy path towards a large pinnacle of rock (Nichodemus Knob) after which, at the 'rock falls' sign, bear left steeply up on to the higher escarpment, heading for a large communications mast. At the high wire perimeter fence turn left and follow the fence along and then around to the north, to reach the south entrance of Verne Prison. Take a path through a little gap to the left of the entrance, passing beside railings and down steep steps. Bear right along a path that traverses under the grassy banks.

The path then drops downhill towards houses, to a waymark post but ignore the left fork down to the road and continue again on the level, on a grass path, to pass through a stone and concrete underpass below a road. The path then descends steeply down the Castletown Incline (a former quarry tramway), crossing two footpaths and a road. Near the bottom pass under a footbridge and through another underpass to reach the access road to the former HMS Osprey premises and turn left to a roundabout. Continue westwards on the road for some 30 yards (27 m) and then cross to turn right down Liberty Road (signposted for Portland Castle). Go past the entrance to the castle and at the castle car park turn right towards the harbour, heading for five black posts. Here join the new segregated footpath/cycleway (footpath on red brick pavers) to follow the harbour-side until the boundary fence of the new Weymouth and Portland National Sailing Academy is reached.

This is to be the venue of the sailing events of the 2012 London Olympics. Although the path follows (now alongside a cul-de-sac access road) around the perimeter of the academy, the fencing is of an open design so that the views and coastal amenities are not unduly marred. Continue on the footpath/cycleway to reach the roundabout at the main A354 road. Here you rejoin the official route of the Coast Path, however the worst section of walking on the footpath of the A354 has been avoided and you can take the Association's favoured option of walking on the track-bed of the former railway line as far as the boatyard before Ferry Bridge.

Grading: This section runs from easy to moderate to strenuous. Distance - 22.7   969.2   14.1   602.2

Ascent: 766   33515   2513   109959

Timing: 6.25 hours

See also our Ferry Bridge to Lulworth Cove Path Description.

SEE SECTION 80 FOR DETAILS OF THE ALTERNATIVE INLAND COAST PATH FROM WEST BEXINGTON TO OSMINGTON MILLS.

Although the signposting of the route of the Coast Path through Weymouth has been much improved in the last year or so, we have retained much of the detail of the route in this guide.

A footpath sign shows you where to continue on to Weymouth, using the track-bed of the old railway line from Portland (but take care as this is also a cycleway). After passing behind the sailing centre cut down to the right to continue into Old Castle Road. Opposite some new three-storey houses ignore a footpath sign pointing towards the coast. This now only leads to the beach and the continuing coastal footpath (known as Underbarn Walk), shown on most maps above Western Ledges, has been permanently closed as a result of a landslip. The Coast Path is now unfortunately routed along residential roads. In 260 yards (240 m) from the footpath sign turn right into Belle Vue Road. Continue for about 600 yards (560 m) to a crossroads and turn right into Redcliff View. At the end of this road a path leads across a grassed area back onto the Coast Path at Grid Ref 6815 7814. (Westbound walkers should follow the path worn across the grassed area to the northern leg of Redcliff View, to then follow the eastbound route in reverse.) Continue on the path close to the coast to Nothe Fort and bear sharp left and then turn down steps on the right to the harbourside. This is followed to the Town Bridge, which is crossed and the opposite side of the harbour is followed back to the Pavilion Complex. Here bear left to join The Esplanade. In summer a little ferry may run across the harbour to shorten the route.

Weymouth Harbour

Weymouth & Portland Borough Council,	Rowing Boat, Easter – June 1100 - 1500
Harbour Master's Office,	July 0930 – 1700
3 Custom House Quay,	August 0930 – 1900
Weymouth, DT4 8BG	September – October 1100 – 1500
Tel: 01305 838423	Weather permitting

Leave Weymouth along the new promenade and at Overcombe, go up the minor road to Bowleaze Cove. However, after passing the Spyglass Inn it is best to bear right to cross the grass public open space and follow the cliff edge to the Beachside Centre. From this point most maps show the Coast Path taking a route through the Beachside Centre and to the south of the Riviera Hotel (large white building). However, because of cliff falls, the route of the Coast Path now continues along the road to the north of the hotel. At the end of the road follow the signed Coast Path route back to the cliff edge near Redcliff Point. Beyond a former holiday camp, now an education and adventure centre, follow the signed and waymarked route of a re-established section of Coast Path that avoids landslips.

On the downhill approach to Osmington Mills the route avoiding a further landslide bears away from the cliff edge over a stile and down the right hand side of a field. At the bottom it joins the Inland Route just before it crosses two stiles to meet the narrow road that is followed down to the coast.

At Ringstead you are taken slightly inland, because the path shown on maps seaward of the houses does not exist. At the old coastguard cottages at White Nothe, be careful to take the left fork of the two yellow arrows, that being the correct route. From White Nothe onwards you will find that there are some quite severe gradients to be traversed before you reach Lulworth. Some older maps show the Coast Path turning south from Hambury Tout. This is not correct and the route (that is not a right of way) can no longer be used.

West of Lulworth Cove a stone-pitched path will lead you down through the car park and past the Heritage Centre. However, lower down and just before the main car park, there is a signed route to the south, that joins a minor road and is more convenient if you wish to avoid the traffic and crowds in this area. However some people turn further inland than they need. Some signposts indicate 'Youth Hostel - Coast Path' and contain the acorn logo. These signs are intended to indicate the route to the Youth Hostel at West Lulworth and are not the continuation of the Coast Path.

The official Coast Path now turns right at the Lulworth Heritage Centre, to join the route from the minor road and turns along the cliff to take in the view into Stair Hole, with its spectacular upturned rock formations. When the commemorative stone marking the inauguration of the Jurassic Coast is passed, turn down towards the cove and pass in front of the boathouse. The onward route leaves from behind the café.

77 | Lulworth Cove to Kimmeridge, Gaulter Gap (Beach car park)OS OL15 (V) Lulworth

Grading: Severe
609.5

Distance -   11.8   981.0   7.3

Ascent: 641   34156   2103   112062

Timing: 4 hours

See also our Lulworth to Kimmeridge Path Description.

The coastal path through the Army ranges is open at the times shown below, and is a very fine walk indeed, but a tough one. If the section is closed when you plan your walk, we recommend you rearrange your schedule so that you walk it when open, then resume your walk where you left off. Many do this - it is worth it. If closed, two alternative routes are shown below and on the next page.

The path behind the beach café is now open again. Higher up, follow a short signed alternative to avoid an eroded area close to the cliff edge. Tide permitting, the beach route avoids a considerable ascent and descent. At most states of the tide, it is perfectly possible to walk along the pebble beach at Lulworth Cove, going up the path which rises diagonally on the far side of the beach. At the top of the steep ascent off the beach, the best route proceeds seawards and there the path turns south eastwards along the coast to the beginning of the Army Ranges, just by the Fossil Forest.

The village of Tyneham, church, school and historical information are worth going inland 0.5 mile (800 m) to see, between 1000 - 1600 hrs.

The route onwards is straight forward – just follow the yellow topped posts through the ranges to arrive at Kimmeridge Bay passing the 'nodding donkey' oil pump.

RAC Gunnery School Lulworth Ranges: No Firing and Firing Periods

1. *NON FIRING PERIOD.* The Range Walks will be open to the public during the following holiday periods, all dates are inclusive:

EASTER 2010	2 – 11 APR 2010
MAY BANK HOLIDAY 2010	1 – 3 MAY 2010
SPRING 2010	29 MAY - 6 JUNE 2010
SUMMER 2010	31 JUL – 30 AUG 2010
CHRISTMAS/NEW YEAR 2010/2011	18 DEC 2010 – 3 JAN 2011

2. *FIRING PERIODS.* The Range Walks are normally open to the public every Saturday and Sunday except for some weekends in the year. For this year they have reserved the following six weekends for firing:

FIRST	23 - 24 JAN 2010
SECOND	13 - 14 MAR 2010
THIRD	17 - 18 APR 2010
FOURTH	12 - 13 JUN 2010
FIFTH	2 - 3 OCT 2010
SIXTH	13 - 14 NOV 2010

3. Experience has shown that it is sometimes possible to avoid firing on some of these

reserved weekends and if this is the case, the Range Walks will be opened. Should this occur this year we will make every effort to publicise the fact.

4. Tyneham Church and the School are normally open for viewing 1000 hrs - 1600 hrs when the walks are open.

5. Information is also available by ringing 01929 404819, which is a 24 hour answering service.

Alternative Routes when Lulworth Range Coast Path is unavailable: Lulworth Cove to Kimmeridge, Gaulter Gap.

Option 1 - approx. 13.5 miles (22 km) on a safer, quieter but more strenuous route, using mainly rights of way, and permissive paths through Lulworth Park (pre-plotting of given grid refs onto a map will assist navigation).

Leave the Cove and take the second road on the left, by a bus shelter (Grid Ref 825 807), and in 100 yards (90 m) turn right steeply uphill on a footpath that leads north for 0.75 mile (1.2 km); turn right (east) and after 100 yards (90 m) turn left (north) to pass Belhuish Coppice and Belhuish Farm, and then cross the B3071 at Grid Ref 835 832.

At the eastern boundary of Burngate Wood (Grid Ref 845 828), use the permissive (blue) path north-east past Park Lodge, and go across the road (Grid Ref 855 832) onto a bridleway.

Continue north-east along the bridleway to Grid Ref 865 839, where it veers north, and later north-east through the Highwood to meet the road at Grid Ref 872 862. Walk east along the road and then fork right (signposted Stoborough) at Grid Ref 882 855. Go over the crossroads with the B3070 at Grid Ref 886 855 and walk east for a further 1.5 miles (2.4 km) along Holme Lane to Grid Ref 911 854.

(*) Turn right just before a railway bridge onto Dorey Farm bridleway at Grid Ref 911 854. After 1.25 miles (2 km) turn right onto Creech Road, leading south-south-west towards the Purbeck Ridge. After another 1.5 miles (2.4 km) of road, walk up a steep gradient to a viewpoint car park. Beyond the car park at Grid Ref 902 815, take the left road that turns back and down over the ridge to Corfe. (A short cut bridleway at Grid Ref 905 817 zigzags down to meet the same road.) As the road levels out, at a left hand bend at Grid Ref 907 812, take the bridleway ahead that leads out south through Steeple Leaze Farm.

200 yards (185 m) south of the farm, a footpath leads south crossing another ridge bridleway, down a steep path, and across a field to Higher Stonehips, and on to Gaulter Gap, the easterly point of the range walks.

Option 2 - approx. 12 miles (19 km).

This route is mainly road walking, and care is needed on narrow bends. Leave the Cove to West Lulworth on the B3070, and then turn right to East Lulworth at 835 816 to continue on the B3070. After 3 miles (5 km), turn right (east), at Grid Ref 886 855, along Holme Lane, and then continue from * above, at Grid Ref 911 854.

Taxi operators Mike Whittle, Silver Cars, 01929 400409 (mobile: 07811 328281) and Adrian, Valley Taxis, 01929 480507 offers their services in the Lulworth/Wool/ Kimmeridge area.

78 Kimmeridge, Gaulter Gap to Swanage (The Pier)   OS OL15

Grading: Severe and then moderate			Distance -	21.4	1002.4	13.3	622.8

Ascent: 701   34857   2300   114362

Timing: 7.25 hours

See also our Kimmeridge to South Haven Point Path Description.

From Gaulter Gap, Kimmeridge, the path is straightforward, although care may be needed where small sections have slipped, cracked or may be close to the cliff top. The Clavell Tower has been relocated 27 yards (25 m) inland and an improved Coast Path installed. After descending Hounstout the official route turns inland to avoid dangerous, wet and unstable ground, on what appears to be the direct route to St Aldhelm's Head. Do not be tempted into trying to find a route that connects to what looks like a new zigzag path on the side of the hill ahead. Take care to follow the signed and waymarked route even though it seems to be heading in the wrong direction, to go inland to Hill Bottom cottages, where the path turns south again, and beyond the gate climbs left up to a high level route which is well signposted. The climb up West Hill is away from the views, but as you gain height along Emmett's Hill, the views back along the Dorset coast are very good. The Royal Marines memorial is just to the left of the path.

From St Aldhelm's Head, there is fine high level walking all the way to Durlston Head, but not much accommodation along this stretch.

There is only minimal signing in the Durlston Country Park but improvements have been promised. However, you keep on the low level path all the way round Durlston Head but as you come up on the north side of it you take the second turning right, not the first, which is a dead end into a quarry.

As we go to print we have just received information about the commencement of the Durlston Project. Building work is due to commence on the conversion of Durlston Castle into a Jurassic Coast Centre and this will mean that part of the Coast Path between Tilly Whim Caves (SZ 032 770) around the headland to the woodlands to the north east of the castle (SZ 033 773) will have to be temporarily closed for periods throughout 2010. An alternative footpath route will be signposted. We have been assured that the Coast Path will only be closed when it is absolutely necessary for safety reasons.

The Lookout Cafe at Durlston Castle has now been closed. Some temporary catering will be provided at the Durlston Country Park Visitor Centre until the refurbishment work is complete in 2011.

For up-to-date information please see the Association's website.

After leaving Durlston Castle follow the broad stony Coast Path north through the woods above Durlston Bay for some 760 yards (700 m) to reach a barrier and sign. From this point the Coast Path has been permanently diverted following a massive cliff fall. Turn left on a good path for some 125 yards (115 m) to reach Durlston Road at a kissing gate. Turn right and in about 185 yards (170 m) turn right again into Belle Vue Road. Just before a block of flats called Durlston Cliff, the original Coast Path rejoined the road (the current path at this location now only leads to the foreshore). Follow the road north-eastwards, to the grassed open space leading down to Peveril Point. In bad weather or high tides the route along the foreshore from the Point should be avoided in favour of the roadway and then cut down the footpath at the town end of the coastal buildings.

The section of the Coast Path through Swanage is now provided with signposting, some of it quite subtle. Continue along the sea front promenade.

79 Swanage to Sandbanks (South Haven Point)   OS OL15 (T) Swanage;(V)Studland

Grading: Moderate				Distance -	12.2	1014.6	7.6	630.4
Ascent:	173	35030	568	114930				

Timing: 3.5 hours

See also our Kimmeridge to South Haven Point Path Description.

At the telephone box at the north end of Swanage Sea Front, the official route takes the main road (Ulwell Road) and where it bears left into a one-way system, continue ahead into Redcliffe Road. At a shop and post box turn sharp right into Ballard Way and at the end do not be put off by the signs 'Ballard Private Estate'. Carry forward into the chalet estate and follow signs for the Coast Path, to emerge on to a grassed area on the cliff edge. However at the seafront telephone box, except at very high tide or in severe weather, you may wish to keep along the quite narrow promenade. At the end then walk 200 yards (185 m) along the beach, which has recently been replenished with coarse sand built up over the pebbles, and turn up some rough steps to join the official route in a little valley.

From Ballard Down the path is obvious all the way to Handfast Point and the much photographed rocks of Old Harry. On the approach to Studland village look out for a superb new section of Coast Path, installed by the National Trust, that avoids the narrow road walking though the village but also the pub. If you are seeking refreshment, continue until you reach a road by a public toilet and turn up the road to the Bankes Arms. A nearby signpost will direct you back on to the Coast Path.

Alternative Coast Path – South Beach

From the track on the outskirts of the village turn east at a fingerpost sign marked Coast Path and descend the stony path to South Beach. On reaching the shore, turn north along a terrace in front of beach huts above the beach, to a seasonal café. Then continue northwards along the beach for some 90 yards (82 m) and look for a Purbeck Stone tombstone sign between beach huts numbered 59 and 60B, to find a narrow path that ascends steeply up the low cliff. At the top, at another sign, turn right (or straight on for the Bankes Arms) and follow the cliff edge around past Fort Henry (stop to read the historical notes) to join the Middle Beach access road by a barrier. Turn sharp right down to the beach and go left by another café.

The final few miles are on the sandy beach. When the tide is out, this is firm, but when it is in more effort will be required. Further up the beach, maybe we should mention there is a naturist beach, so you must not be put off if you find that on this last lap that you are the only one wearing clothes! The National Trust has also provided an alternative route, The Heather Walk, through the dunes, and this is marked by yellow-topped posts, however the naturist area is still partially in view and the soft sand underfoot is tiring at the end of a long walk.

Despite any notices you may see, dogs on leads may accompany Coast Path walkers along the shore line, but be sure to clean up after your dog if necessary.

Until the Autumn of 2002, the official finish of the path at the ferry road was undistinguished. Following years of pressure from this Association, there is now an impressive marker incorporating a steel mast and sail and a floor compass. Thanks are due to the efforts of the South West Coast Path Team and the generous donations made by our Association members and others.

At the South Haven Point Ferry you leave the South West Coast Path. You may meet someone about to start to walk the other way round. We know, from those who complete the Coast Path, their feelings of delight and disappointment, so how about planning your 'other way round' walk?

Shell Bay/Sandbanks (Mouth of Poole Harbour) Bournemouth-Swanage Motor Road & Ferry Company, Shell Bay, Studland. BH19 3BA.
Tel: 01929 450203. Fax: 01929 450498.
Website: www.sandbanksferry.co.uk

All year round. Daily every 20 mins.
Sandbanks 0700 - 2300 hrs
Shell Bay 0710 - 2310 hrs
Christmas Day every half hour.

In November, the Shell Bay/Sandbanks ferry is often suspended for a couple of weeks for maintenance. For full details of this closure period, contact the ferry company and/or look at its website.

Alfred Wainwright, at the end of his work on the Pennine Way said; 'You have completed a mission and achieved an ambition. You have walked the Pennine Way, as you dreamed of doing. This will be a very satisfying moment in your life. You will be tired and hungry and travel stained. But you will feel great, just great.' Dear reader, just substitute the South West Coast Path for the Pennine Way. We will add whether you have been lucky enough to walk the whole way from Minehead at one go, or simply, as most of us have, in bits and pieces over a period, nonetheless you will be glad you walked and have just finished Britain's longest and finest footpath. It's a longer step than most take in their lifetime!

If you are continuing to walk eastwards from Sandbanks see the notes following section 80 on page 104.

80 Alternative Inland Coast Path - South Dorset Ridgeway
West Bexington to Osmington Mills OS OL15

Grading: Moderate				Distance - 27.0	16.8

Ascent:	698	698	2290	2290

See also our alternative Inland Route Path Description.

Although this is certainly not a coastal path it is an enjoyable walk along well-marked paths with good views seaward from the ridges. Because it is inland a more detailed route description is given. When walking this section bear in mind that we found no place on the route for obtaining refreshments between the start of the walk, where there is a café, and the village of Osmington.

There is currently a signpost replacement scheme taking place on the Inland Route/South Dorset Ridgeway and it is likely that the names of some of the intermediate locations and/or distances will have been revised from those shown in this section. However it is unlikely that you will have any difficulty in following the route.

At West Bexington car park turn inland up the road signposted 'Inland Route - Coast Path', and where the road turns left, continue forward up the stony track, signposted 'For Hardy Monument'. At the top of the hill the footpath briefly joins the main road but you immediately leave it again over the stile on the right, to go through a field, signposted 'Hardy Monument'. Take care, as the way across this field is not clear and you should, at first, keep parallel to the road and then bear right to a waymarked post. After you have crossed a wall, you can start to bear upwards to the left to the further signpost near the road, marked with the acorn symbol and the words 'Inland Route'. After about 300 yards (275 m) continuing through the field and by the corner of a wall, there is a further signpost 'Hardy Monument'. Continue forward, very shortly emerging on to the B3157 road that you cross and leave through a gate, signposted again 'For Hardy Monument'.

You now approach Abbotsbury Castle (hill fort) and where the path in front divides, take the upper, slightly right-hand fork along the top of the southern earthwork of the fort, past the trig point, from where you can get superb views in all directions. You should be able to see the Hardy Monument clearly in the distance. Proceed eastwards and cross a minor road and go forward, signposted 'For Hardy Monument'.

Proceed in an approximate easterly direction along the ridge of Wears Hill and the crest of White Hill for about 2 miles (3.2 km), following the signposts and waymarks. However be careful not to follow signs (with the acorn symbol incorrectly shown) that indicate routes down to the village of Abbotsbury lying in the valley below, with the old chapel clearly visible. At the east end of White Hill bear north-east as signposted and leave in the inland corner through a gate on to a minor road. Turn left along this road for approximately 50 yards (46 m) and then turn right, signposted 'Inland Route - Hardy Monument'.

Follow the bridleway, marked with blue arrows, along the wire fence above the scrub to a path junction; where the bridleway carries on forward take the yellow waymarked footpath to the left and cross a stile. At the far side of the field the track then leads approximately 50 yards (46 m) to a further gate with a stile and waymark. Immediately adjacent to this gate is a stone circle, which is an ancient monument and there is a sign to this effect

You now continue forward, leaving a small wood to the left, to reach the road from Portesham to Winterbourne Steepleton. Turn left along the road for approximately 60 yards (55 m) and then turn right into a field over a stile, signposted 'For Hardy Monument'. On the far side of the field proceed forward, signposted 'Hardy Monument'. At this point there is a signpost forking right to Hellstone only, with a return possible on a different path.

At Blackdown Barn turn left to climb up through the woods, signposted 'Hardy Monument'. At the monument you will find a small signpost 'Inland Route-Osmington Mills 11 miles' with a blue arrow indicating the way forward. In season and on other days you may be fortunate enough to find a mobile refreshment van at this location. Cross the road to a further signpost with the acorn symbol and now descend through the bracken.

You reach the road again. Turn left and in a few yards ignore the signpost on the right, cutting back, indicating 'Bridleway to Coast Path' and continue forward, (signposted 'Coast Path East') and in another 100 yards (90 m) turn right, signposted 'Inland Route to Corton Hill'. Now there is a good ridgeway path without navigational problems for some 3 miles (4.8 km) and good views to seaward in the distance. At a radio mast look out for a minor diversion where a second underground reservoir is being built for the Weymouth area and shortly you come to the B3159 road, marked by the Borough of Weymouth boundary stone and continue across, as signposted and towards the A354 road.

During 2010 major road construction is taking place to bypass the existing A354 road where it crosses Ridgeway Hill and other areas to the south. Dorset County Council has assured us that the National Trail will remain open throughout the works. However from time to time this will mean temporary diversions that will be signed and which must be followed. At certain stages of the work this will mean some extra road walking along the road leading to Came Wood and Broadmayne. However this road becomes a cul-de-sac as a result of the works and the new road and will have a much reduced level of traffic. Continue with the route of the South Dorset Ridgeway from the corner of Came Wood in the paragraph below.

If you have been able to use the official route of the path east of the new road then follow the text from this point.

Before the farm, with its adjacent radio mast, take care to go through the gate on the right, marked with a blue arrow. After crossing the field, leaving two tumuli to your left, you reach a metalled road. Turn right and at the next junction at the corner of Came Wood, you turn right at the signpost 'Bridleway to Bincombe'. At the end of the path join a metalled lane and at the road junction turn left, signposted 'Inland Route East'.

Drop down the road into the village of Bincombe and where the road turns right take the track forward leaving a small church on your right. Where the path splits take the left hand fork, signposted again with a blue arrow and the acorn symbol. After the overhead high-voltage power lines, pass through a small signposted wooden gate and then proceed forward through one field, into the next to a footpath sign. Here turn left and then you have a choice of routes, we describe the one with least road walking.

At a waymark post turn sharp right down a steep grassy slope to a stile at a road ahead. Cross the road to go over another stile to follow a grassy path that contours around the west and south sides of Green Hill. When you reach a road at a gate and stile turn left and in 50 yards (46 m) turn right through a gate, signposted 'White Horse Hill - Osmington Mills'. The path now is easy to follow with extensive views to seaward over Weymouth and Portland. On passing a ruined building on your left you reach a broad track and turn right, signposted 'For Osmington' and after about 200 yards (185 m) go through a gate, signposted 'Inland Route Osmington'. You will shortly pass a trig point on your right and at the next field gate bear left and follow the field boundary along White Horse Hill. Just beyond the next gate fork right, signposted 'For Osmington'.

Descend to the village of Osmington and follow the signs through the village. When you reach the main Weymouth road near the Sun Ray Inn turn left and in about 250 yards (230 m) turn right at a signpost, over a stile and footbridge. Follow the field boundary on the left through two fields and at the top look back to see the Hardy Monument in the distance and also the white horse on the hillside. Go over the stile to the footpath sign, then turn half right to cross the field at an angle, to a further stile. Cross it and turn left along the hedge side to the bottom. At the end of the field there is a very short length of enclosed footpath to the road; turn right along it, descending to Osmington Mills.

FOR THOSE WHO WISH TO CONTINUE TO WALK EASTWARDS

The South West Coast Path from Plymouth to South Haven Point (Poole Harbour entrance) is now also part of the British section of European Route E9. The British section continues to Dover and is predominantly a coastal walk as far as Portsmouth. The so-called Bournemouth Coast Path and then the Solent Way provide an onward coastal walk across the remainder of Dorset and all of Hampshire to the Sussex Border at Emsworth. The E9 route follows these two paths as far as Portsmouth, where it turns inland.

After many years of being out of print a new edition of the guidebook to the Bournemouth Coast Path has been published. This book covers the coastal route between the South West Coast Path and the Solent Way at Milford-on-Sea. Entitled *Exploring the Bournemouth Coast Path* it is written by Leigh Hatts and published by Countryside Books at £7.99. ISBN 1 85306 9086. A revised guide to the Solent Way was published in 2003 and the linear route is included in *Pub Walks Along the Solent Way* by Anne-Marie Edwards and published by Countryside at £7.95ISBN 1 853067385.

ACCOMMODATION

This list of accommodation has been prepared in path order.

The majority of our B&B addresses have been **recommended by Coast Path walkers**. The fact that they are included in this book does not indicate a recommendation by The South West Coast Path Association. Their inclusion is merely for information purposes; they are there, if you want them. We cannot, for financial and practical reasons, introduce vetting, inspection or any form of `Star' rating. We do have a system whereby addresses can be removed from the list.

The following letter code is used.

Facilities

O	=	Open All Year	D =	Drying facilities for wet clothes
EM	=	Evening Meal	PL =	Packed Lunches
CP	=	Car Parking	LSP =	Long Stay Parking
DW	=	Dogs Welcome	KT =	Kit Transfer
PD	=	Pick Up/Drop Service	LT =	Luxury Tent

Room Codes

D	=	Double	T =	Twin
S	=	Single	F =	Family
ES	=	En Suite		

Please note:

The figure in brackets denotes the number of en-suite rooms e.g. 4D[2] = 4 double rooms, two of which are en-suite.

KT - Kit Transfer.

A service being offered by some of our accommodation providers is to transfer your kit to your next accommodation. This could prove useful to you. Naturally a fee may be levied for this service. Please request this service at the time of booking. Please ensure that the accommodation to which your kit is to be sent is aware of the arrangements you have made. See also the information on pages 17 and 18 about kit transfer.

PD - Pick Up/Drop.

This code appears following the distance from the path and denotes a facility whereby your host is prepared to collect and return you to the Coast Path within reasonable distance. No fee should be charged for this service.

Where this facility is offered, you may consider booking for two or three nights and asking them to collect you from your finishing point and return you there for your start the next day. This way the B&B gets you for more than one night and you can get to walk for a day or more with a lighter day sack. Again no fee should be charged for this service.

Distance from Path.

Please remember these are only approximate and may not be accurate.

LT - Luxury Tent.

Due to accommodation problems in the St Austell Bay area, some providers have installed superb tents in their gardens/paddocks. You will not need sleeping bags or any camping out gear.

Addresses.

The part of the address in CAPITALS is an aid to location; it does not signify the postal town. The extreme left-hand column refers to the appropriate section in the 'Trail Description'; we feel it may help you to find addresses quickly. The amount quoted gives an **indication of the starting rate** for bed and breakfast, and may well rise. If working on a tight budget, it is best to ask first.

Tourist Information Centres can be an additional source of accommodation addresses. We have provided a list of TICs along the Coast Path for your use on page 162.

Most of the B&B providers operate from their own private homes so do not expect plenty of staff as there are in hotels and large guesthouses. They work hard to make you comfortable, welcome, dry you out and make you feel like one of the family.

A few of our accommodation providers are not very near to eating establishments, and the last thing walkers want is a long walk after a hard day on the Coast Path. If your chosen address does not supply evening meals you should ask, when booking, how far it is to your evening meal – you can then decide if you want to stay there.

We wish to develop this list especially for many 'sparse' areas. Suggestions for inclusion in our next list will be welcome. Details of any new accommodation should be addressed to the Administrator. Our list is not comprehensive and walkers will find many B&Bs in towns and villages along the Coast Path that are not recorded in this book.

It would not be out of place here to add a word of thanks from those who walk, to those who kindly board. How many times have we been thankful for a friendly welcome and good 'digs'? Maybe a note we had from one of our accommodation addresses puts it well. 'We have had quite a lot of walkers this year and we have usually managed to dry them out - and feed them up.'

Although there are a lot of addresses that state they are 'open all the year', some of these close for the Christmas period. Walkers should remember that during the holiday season many of our accommodation addresses could be fully booked up in advance by holidaymakers staying for a week or two. Conversely a walker could book for one night only in good time, thus preventing a guest house proprietor from taking a week or more booking later on. Accommodation problems can be frustrating to all parties concerned so bear these facts in mind when bed hunting **for one night only.**

Important

1. If having booked ahead, and for any reason you are unable to get to your accommodation address, please telephone and explain your absence to your intended host. We have known instances where the host has become so worried about the non-appearance of walkers that they have informed the emergency services. The last thing we want is Police, Coastguards and Royal Navy helicopters out on a wild goose chase.

2. All the contract information in the following pages has been supplied by the accommodation providers themselves.

Sect.	Name and Address	Tel. No. Fax. No. Web / Email	Map Reference Opening Times	Distance from Path Starting Price Facilities Accommodation
1	Mr A Brunt The Yarn Market Hotel High Street DUNSTER TA24 6SF	01643 821425 as phone hotel@yarnmarkethotel.co.uk www.yarnmarkethotel.co.uk	993 438	4 km PD £40 O D EM PL CP DW KT PD 12D 4T 3S 4F ALL ES
1	Mr & Mrs P McKeon Dunkery Lodge Townsend Road MINEHEAD TA24 5RQ	01643 706170 stay@dunkery-lodge.co.uk www.dunkery-lodge.co.uk	969 457	300 mts £34.00 O D EM PL CP LSP DW KT PD 2D 1D/T ALL ES EM & DW by prior arrangement single supplement
1	Mr E Moulder Montrose Guest House 14 Tregonwell Road MINEHEAD TA24 5DU	01643 706473 montroseminehead@btinternet.com www.montroseminehead.co.uk	972 460	900 mts £27.50 O D CP KT 4D 1T ALL ES
1	Mrs L Pearse The Quay Inn Quay Street MINEHEAD TA24 5UJ	01643 707323 info@quay-inn.co.uk www.quay-inn.co.uk	971 467	30 mts £40.00 O D EM PL CP DW 2D 2F ALL ES £10 single supplement
1	Mr & Mrs S Poingdestre Kenella House 7 Tregonwell Road MINEHEAD TA24 5DT	01643 703128 kenellahouse@fsmail.net www.kenellahouse.co.uk	972 462	500 mts £32.50 O D EM PL CP LSP KT 4D 2T ALL ES Price based on two sharing
1	Mr & Mrs G Hayes Tigoni The Ball MINEHEAD TA24 5JJ	01643 708852 g_w_hayes@yahoo.co.uk	967 466	400 mts £25.00 O D CP LSP DW KT 1D[1] 1T 1S
1	Mr F O'Neill Tudor Cottage BOSSINGTON TA24 8HQ	01643 862255 mobile: 07831 211144 oneill@tudorcottage.net www.tudorcottage.net	898 479	100 mts £32.50 O D EM PL CP LSP KT 2D[1] 1T
1	Mr R G Steer Myrtle Cottage High Street PORLOCK TA24 8PU	01643 862978 As Phone bob.steer@virgin.net www.myrtleporlock.co.uk	885 467 Mar-Jan 10	1 km £27.50 D CP DW KT 4D/T/S/F ALL ES Single supplement
1	Mr & Mrs M Ley Reines House Parson Street PORLOCK TA24 8QJ	01643 862913 reineshousebandb@aol.com www.reineshouse.co.uk	885 465	1 km £27.00 O D PL KT 3D[3] 1T[1] 1S 2F[2]
2	Mrs Jan Richards Silcombe Farm PORLOCK WEIR TA24 8JN	01643 862248	833 482	750 mts PD £25.00 O D EM PL CP LSP DW KT PD 2D[2] 1T 1S

Sect.	Name and Address	Tel. No. Fax. No. Web / Email	Map Reference Opening Times	Distance from Path Starting Price Facilities Accommodation
2	Mrs J E Richards Ash Farm PORLOCK WEIR TA24 8JN	01643 862414	842 478 Apr-Nov	750 mts £25.00 D PL CP LSP KT 1D 1T 1S
2	Mrs S Pile Coombe Farm COUNTISBURY EX36 6NF	01598 741236 robert.pile@btconnect.com brendonvalley.co.uk/coombe_farm.htm	766 488 Mar-Nov	1.5 km £26.00 D PL CP LSP KT 1D[1] 1T[1] 1S 2F[2]
2	Mr L Allen & Rachel Williams The Bath Hotel LYNMOUTH EX35 6EL	01598 752238 01598 753894 info@bathhotellynmouth.co.uk www.bathhotellynmouth.co.uk	722 495 Feb-Nov	100 mts £35.00 D EM PL DW KT PD 10D 6T 1S 3F ALL ES single supplement
2	Mr & Mrs C Parker Tregonwell The Old Sea Captain's House 1 Tors Road LYNMOUTH EX35 6ET	01598 753369 thecaptainshouse@btinternet.com www.thecaptainshouseinlynmouth.co.uk	727 494	50 mts £28.00 O D PL CP LSP DW KT PD 5D 1T 1S 1F ALL ES DW by prior arrangement
2	Mr & Mrs A Francis Glenville House 2 Tors Road LYNMOUTH EX35 6ET	01598 752202 tricia@glenvillelynmouth.co.uk www.glenvillelynmouth.co.uk	727 494 March-Nov	200 mts £29.00 D PL 4D[3] 1T
2	Mrs S Hobbs Lorna Doone House 4 Tors Road LYNMOUTH EX35 6ET	01598 753354 info@lornadoonehouse.co.uk www.lornadoonehouse.co.uk	726 493 Feb-Nov	500 mts £34.00 D EM PL CP DW KT PD 4D 1T 1F ALL ES
2	Mr J Batch Bonnicott House 10 Watersmeet Road LYNMOUTH EX35 6EP	01598 753346 stay@bonnicott.com www.bonnicott.com	725 493	180 mts £30.00 O D PL EM PD KT 7D[6] 1T[1]
2	Miss D Smith Hillside House 22 Watersmeet Road LYNMOUTH EX35 6EP	01598 753836 gjbanfield@aol.com www.hillside-lynmouth.co.uk	725 493	200 mts £27.00 O D PL DW KT 4D[3] 1T[1] 1S
2	Mrs C Sheppard River Lyn View 26 Watersmeet Road LYNMOUTH EX35 6EP	01598 753501 riverlynview@aol.com www.riverlynview.com	725 493	150 mts £27.00 O D PL CP DW KT 3D 1T ALL ES seasonal supplement
2	Mrs B Jackson East Lyn House Hotel Watersmeet Road LYNMOUTH EX35 6EP	01598 752540 bookings@eastlynhouse.co.uk www.eastlynhouse.co.uk	725 493	150 mts £30.00 O D EM PL CP DW 7D 1T ALL ES

Sect.	Name and Address	Tel. No. Fax. No. Web / Email	Map Reference Opening Times	Distance from Path Starting Price Facilities Accommodation
2	Mr P Hood Woodlands Lynbridge Road LYNTON EX35 6AX	01598 752324 info@woodlandsguesthouse.co.uk www.woodlandsguesthouse.co.uk	720 487	500 mts £30.00 O D PL CP LSP 5D 2S ALL ES
2	Mr & Mrs J McGowan The Denes Longmead LYNTON EX35 6DQ	01598 753573 j.e.mcgowan@btinternet.com www.thedenes.com	715 494	400mts PD £30.00 O D EM PL CP KT PD 5D[4] 2T[2] 2S[2] 2F[2]
2	Mr & Mrs C Wilkins Sinai House Lynway LYNTON EX35 6AY	01598 753227 01598 752633 enquires@sinaihouse.co.uk www.sinaihouse.co.uk	721 492 Feb-Nov	400 mts £28.00 D PL CP LSP KT 5D[5] 1T[1] 2S
2	Miss P Lippett Castle Hill Guest House Castle Hill LYNTON EX35 6JA	01598 752291 info@castlehillhotel.co.uk www.castlehillhotel.co.uk	720 493 Apr-Oct	50 mts £30.00 D PL LSP DW KT PD 4D 2T 1S ALL ES Long breaks offered
2	Mrs M Roper Southview 23 Lee Road LYNTON EX35 6BP	01598 752289 maureenroper@hotmail.com www.southview-lynton.co.uk	717 494 Mar-Nov	250 mts £32.00 D PL CP KT 3D 2T ALL ES KT low season only
2	Mr & Mrs T Ley 29 Lee Road LYNTON EX35 6BS	01598 753418 trevor.e.s.ley@btinternet.com	717 494	300 mts £18.00 O D PL LSP DW KT 1D 1T DW by prior arrangement
2	Mrs A Wilford Gable Lodge 35 Lee Road LYNTON EX35 6BS	01598 752367 gablelodge@btconnect.com www.gablelodgelynton.co.uk	717 495	400 mts PD £26.00 O D EM PL CP KT PD 4D 1T 1F ALL ES LSP low season
2	Mr & Mrs J Hodges Chough's Nest Hotel North Walk LYNTON EX35 6HJ	01598 753315 relax@choughsnesthotel.co.uk www.choughsnesthotel.co.uk	718 497	on path £42.00 O D EM PL CP KT PD 4D 4T ALL ES
3	Mrs Dallyn Mannacott Farm Nr Hunters Inn MARTINHOE EX31 4QS	01598 763227	662 481 Apr-Nov	800 mts £25.00 D CP 1D[1] 1T
3	Mrs R Brown Blair Lodge Moory Meadow COMBE MARTIN EX34 0DG	01271 882294 as phone info@blairlodge.co.uk www.blairlodge.co.uk	579 473	on path £27.50 O D EM PL CP LSP KT PD 5D[5] 2T[2] 1S 1F[1]

Sect.	Name and Address	Tel. No. / Fax. No. / Web / Email	Map Reference / Opening Times	Distance from Path / Starting Price / Facilities / Accommodation
3	Mr & Mrs C Seddon Mellstock House Woodlands COMBE MARTIN EX34 0AR	01271 882592 enquiries@mellstockhouse.co.uk www.mellstockhouse.co.uk	573 472	on path £40.00 O D PL CP KT PD 4D 1T ALL ES
3	Mrs L Leyland Channel Vista Woodlands COMBE MARTIN EX34 0AT	01271 883514 channelvista@btconnect.com www.channelvista.co.uk	574 470	100 mts £28.00 O D EM PL CP LSP DW KT 4D 3T 2S 2F ALL ES LSP by prior arrangement
3	Mr & Mrs M J Lethaby The Royal Marine Public House Seaside COMBE MARTIN EX34 0AW	01271 882470 01271 889198 theroyal.marine@btconnect.com www.theroyalmarine.co.uk	576 472	200 mts £35.00 O D EM PL KT PD 3D 2T 1F ALL ES Also self catering apartments, free KT
3	Mrs R Irwin Trenode House High Street COMBE MARTIN EX34 0EQ	01271 883681	583 467 Apr-Oct	350 mts £22.50 D PL CP KT PD 1D[1] 1T 1F
3	Mrs D Middleton Hillside Nutcombe Hill COMBE MARTIN EX34 0PQ	01271 882736 middletonhome@tiscali.co.uk www.visithillside.co.uk	611 462 Feb-Nov	3 km PD £25.00 D EM PL CP LSP DW KT PD 1D[1] 1T 1S
3	Mrs L Miller Brooklands Buzzacott Lane COMBE MARTIN EX34 0NL	01271 883578 lindam1@operamail.com www.visitcombemartin.co.uk	598 459	1500 mts PD £25.00 O D PL CP LSP KT PD 1D 1T 1S
3	Mrs S Davey Fontenay Woodlands COMBE MARTIN EX34 0AT	01271 889368 daveysarah@tiscali.co.uk www.visitfontenay.co.uk	575 470	200 mts £24.00 O D PL CP KT 1D 1T 1S PL by prior arrangement
3	Mrs L Heard Park View Sunnyside COMBE MARTIN EX34 0JH	01271 883006 luzia.heard@yahoo.co.uk www.parkview-bandb.com	587 464	800 mts PD £23.00 O D PL CP KT PD 1D 1D/T/F ALL ES
3	Mr & Mrs D Payne Saffron House King Street COMBE MARTIN EX34 0BX	01271 883521 stay@saffronhousehotel.co.uk www.saffronhousehotel.co.uk	581 469 Mar-Oct	300 mts £25.00 D EM PL CP LSP DW KT 3D 2T 2S 2F ALL ES

Sect.	Name and Address	Tel. No. Fax. No. Web / Email	Map Reference Opening Times	Distance from Path Starting Price Facilities Accommodation
4	Mr & Mrs D Jenkins Avalon 6 Capstone Crescent ILFRACOMBE EX34 9BT	01271 863325 01271 866543 ann_dudley_avalon@yahoo.co.uk www.avalon-hotel.co.uk	523 478	200 mts £27.00 O D EM PL CP LSP 5D 3T 1S 3F ALL ES EM & LSP low season only
4	Mr & Mrs G Pannell Sherborne Lodge Hotel Torrs Park ILFRACOMBE EX34 8AY	01271 862297 visit@sherborne-lodge.co.uk www.sherborne-lodge.co.uk	514 475 Mar-Oct	200 mts £26.00 D EM PL CP LSP DW KT 3D[3] 2T[1] 1S[1] 4F[4]
5	Mr & Mrs J Brown Avoncourt Hotel Torrs Walk Avenue ILFRACOMBE EX34 8AU	01271 862543 01271 879408 johnbrown735@btinternet.com www.avoncourtilfracombe.co.uk	513 476	on path £30.00 O D EM PL CP LSP DW KTPD 6D 2S ALL ES
5	Mr & Mrs C Burley Rosedale Bed & Breakfast 33 St Brannocks Road ILFRACOMBE EX34 8EQ	01271 855550 gillybee@hotmail.com www.rosedalebandb.co.uk guided walking holidays Combe Martin to Woolacombe	515 468	800 mts £28.00 O D PL CP LSP KT PD 2D[1] 1T 1S
5	Mrs C Pearson Lyncott House 56 St Brannocks Road ILFRACOMBE EX34 8EQ	01271 862425 www.lyncotthouse.co.uk	515 468	1 km £35.00 O D EM PL CP 4D 1T 1F ALL ES
5	Mr & Mrs D Furmston The Collingdale 13 Larkstone Terrace ILFRACOMBE EX34 9NU	01271 863770 stay@thecollingdale.co.uk www.thecollingdale.co.uk	526 475 Mar-Oct	30 mts £32.50 D EM PL CP LSP KT 3D[2] 3T[3] 3F[3] single supplement EM by prior arrangement
5	Ms A Tappenden Ocean Backpackers 29 St James Place ILFRACOMBE EX34 9BJ	01271 867835 info@oceanbackpackers.co.uk www.oceanbackpackers.co.uk	522 478	25 mts £9.00 O D CP 1D[1] 6 DORMS[5] kitchen for self-catering
5	Ms J Waghorn Grey Cottage LEE Ilfracombe EX34 8LN	01271 864360 julia@greycottage.co.uk www.greycottage.co.uk	494 461	500 mts £35.00 O D EM PL CP DW KT PD 1D[1] 2T/D[1] 1F[1]
5	Mrs J Jackson Pensport Rock LINCOMBE LEE Ilfracombe EX34 8LL	01271 863419 mobile: 07977 243026 pensport_rock@talktalk.net www.pensportrock.com	498 459 Mar-Oct	1 km £30.00 D EM PL CP KT PD 2D[2]

Sect.	Name and Address	Tel. No. Fax. No. Web / Email	Map Reference Opening Times	Distance from Path Starting Price Facilities Accommodation
6	Mr & Mrs M Lambert The Rocks Hotel Beach Road WOOLACOMBE EX34 7BT	01271 870361 enquiries@therockshotel.co.uk www.therockshotel.co.uk	460 438 Mar-Dec	500 mts £45.00 D PL CP KT PD 4D 3T 1S 1F ALL ES
6	Mrs J Penman Bellacombe Western Rise WOOLACOMBE EX34 7AG	01271 870324 Mobile: 07967 049829 bellacombedevon@tiscali.co.uk www.bellacombe.co.uk	465 438	750 mts £35.00 O D EM PL CP LSP KT PD 2D 1T ALL ES
7	Mrs G Adams Combas Farm PUTSBOROUGH EX33 1PH	01271 890398 combasfarm@hotmail.co.uk www.combasfarm.co.uk	449 396	900 mts £29.00 O D PL CP LSP KT 2D[2] 1T[1] 1S 1F[1]
7	Mrs V Learmonth Chapel Farm Guest House Hobbs Hill CROYDE EX33 1NE	01271 890429 vall52@yahoo.co.uk www.chapelfarmcroyde.co.uk	444 390	1 km £30.00 O D CP KT 2D 1T 2F ALL ES PL & PD by prior arrangement, also self catering
7	Mrs R Littlewood Sundown Moor Lane CROYDE BAY Braunton EX33 1PA	01271 890066	431 397	on path £30.00 O D EM KT PD 1D 1S
7	Mr M Cotton Baggy Lodge CROYDE BAY Barnstaple, Devon EX33 1PA	01271 890078 michael@yarner.net www.baggys.co.uk	430 398	on path £25.00 O D CP KT 4D 3DORMS
7	Mr & Mrs F Cannock Sandbourne Down End CROYDE EX33 1QE	01271 890536 fredcannock@tiscali.co.uk	436 386	300 mts £30.00 O D PL CP KT PD 4D[2] 1T[1] 4-bed Self-catering chalet available
8	Mrs J Watkins North Cottage 14 North Street BRAUNTON EX33 1AJ	01271 812703 north_cottage@hotmail.com	485 367	750 mts £27.50 O D PL CP DW KT 1D 1D/T ALL ES
8	Mr & Mrs J Benning The Firs Higher Park Road BRAUNTON EX33 2LG	01271 814358 sales@jbenning.co.uk www.bennings.co.uk	498 364	2 km PD £30.00 O D PL CP LSP DW KT PD 1D 1T ALL ES
8	Mrs M Metcalf Silver Cottage 14 Silver Street BRAUNTON EX33 2EN	01271 814165 www.silvercottagebraunton.co.uk	487 367	400 mts PD £30.00 D PL 2D

Sect.	Name and Address	Tel. No. Fax. No. Web / Email	Map Reference Opening Times	Distance from Path Starting Price Facilities Accommodation
8	Mr C Brookes & Ms J Middle The Brookfield South Street BRAUNTON EX33 2AN	01271 812382 info@thebrookfield.co.uk www.thebrookfield.co.uk	487 362 Feb-Dec	400 mts £31.50 D PL CP LSP KT 5D 4T 4S 1F ALL ES
8	Mr J Moran The George Hotel Exeter Road BRAUNTON EX33 2JJ	01271 812029 georgehoteldevon@btconnect.com www.thegeorgehotel-braunton.co.uk	488 365	1 km £33.00 O EM PL CP LSP DW 2D[2] 4T[2] 1S PL by prior arrangement
8	Mr & Mrs P J Davis Cresta Guest House Sticklepath Hill BARNSTAPLE EX31 2BU	01271 374022 peterdavis170@virgin.net www.crestaguesthouse.co.uk	548 324	800 mts £25.00 O D PL CP KT 2D[2] 2T[2] 2S 2F[2]
8	Mrs J Manning Herton Guesthouse Lake Hill BARNSTAPLE EX31 3HS	01271 323302 janice@janicemanning93.wanadoo.co.uk www.herton-guesthouse.co.uk	554 322	500 mts £27.00 O D PL CP LSP KT 3D[2] 1T[1] 1F[1]
8	Mr P Chappell Yeo Dale Hotel Pilton Bridge BARNSTAPLE EX31 1PG	01271 342954 01271 344530 stay@yeodalehotel.co.uk www.yeodalehotel.co.uk	557 338	600 mts £40.00 O D EM PL CP LSP KT 7D[7] 2T[2] 3S[2] 2F[2] EM & LSP by prior arrangement
8	Mrs G Gaglione Carlyn 53 West Yelland BARNSTAPLE EX31 3HG	01271 860672 gaglione@talktalk.net	484 315	1 km £25.00 O D PL CP LSP DW KT PD 3D[1] 2T 2S 1F[1] £5 single supplement, DW by prior arrangement
9	Mr P Day Lower Yelland Farm FREMINGTON Barnstaple EX31 3EN	01271 860101 peterday@loweryellandfarm.co.uk www.loweryellandfarm.co.uk	492 322	200 mts £25.00 O D CP LSP DW 3D 2T 2S 1F ALL ES
9	Mrs S Pilarz Sunnymeade 26 Yelland Road FREMINGTON EX31 3BU	01271 346757 brianpilarz@hotmail.co.uk www.sunnymeade-bb.co.uk	507 324	500 mts £27.50 O D CP KT 1D[1] 1T[1] 1F
9	Mrs A Grigg Lovistone Cottage 3 Lyndale Terrace INSTOW Near Bideford EX39 4HS	01271 860676 martinandangela@lovistone.co.uk	475 305	80 mts £30.00 O D CP KT 3D Single supplement

Sect.	Name and Address	Tel. No. Fax. No. Web / Email	Map Reference Opening Times	Distance from Path Starting Price Facilities Accommodation
9	Ms V Ashford 54 Grove Cottages West Yelland INSTOW Barnstaple EX31 3HF	01271 861598 grovecottage@instow.net www.smoothhound.co.uk/hotels/oaktree	484 316	300 mts £25.00 O CP DW 2T[2] £10 single supplement
9	Mrs S Chapman Orchard Cottage Old Barnstaple Road BIDEFORD EX39 4ND	01237 422427 sfc_orchard@yahoo.co.uk www.orchard-cottage-website.orange.co.uk	463 267	200 mts £35.00 O D CP 1F[1]
9	Mrs H Laugharne Mount Hotel Northdown Road BIDEFORD EX39 3LP	01237 473748 01271 373813 andrew@themountbideford.co.uk www.themountbideford.co.uk	449 269	600 mts £35.00 D PL CP KT PD 2D 2T 2S 2F ALL ES
9	Mrs S Wright Old Barn Heywood Road BIDEFORD EX39 3QB	01237 478704 sue@oldbarnbideford.co.uk www.oldbarnbideford.co.uk	449 282	800 mts £25.00 O D PL CP LSP KT PD 1D £5 single supplement
9	Ms P Lucraft 19 Bude Street APPLEDORE EX39 1PS	01237 477127 peejay87@hotmail.com	464 304	75 mts £25.00 O D DW KT 2D 1T ALL ES single supplement
9	Mrs S Clegg Mayfield Avon Lane WESTWARD HO! EX39 1LR	01237 477128 mayfieldbandb@hotmail.co.uk www.mayfieldbandb.co.uk	435 291	100 mts £28.00 O D PL CP LSP KT PD 4D 2T ALL ES
9	Mr & Mrs P Snowball Brockenhurst 11 Atlantic Way WESTWARD HO! EX39 1HX	01237 423346 as phone info@brockenhurstindevon.co.uk www.brockenhurstindevon.co.uk	432 290	200 mts £35.00 O D CP KT 2D 1T ALL ES single supplement
9	Ms L O'Reilly Manorville Youth Hostel 1 Manorville Kingsley Road WESTWARD HO! EX39 1JA	01237 479766 manorville@talktalk.net www.manorvillehostel.com	432 290 Easter-Nov	250 mts £13.50 D CP LSP KT 1D[1] 1T 4DORMS[4] KT by prior arrangement
9	Mr & Mrs G Panayiotou Broomhayes Manor 78 Atlantic Way WESTWARD HO! EX39 1JG	01237 477716 as phone sue@broomhayes-manor.fsnet.co.uk www.broomhayesmanor.co.uk	440 291	1 km PD £30.00 O D PL CP KT PD 1D[1] 1T[1] 1S[1] 1F
9	Mrs L Batten Penkenna House 11 Nelson Road WESTWARD HO! EX39 1LF	01237 470990 penkenna@hotmail.co.uk www.penkennahouse.com	431 291	400 mts £28.00 O D PL CP 1D 1T 1F

Sect.	Name and Address	Tel. No. / Fax. No. / Web / Email	Map Reference / Opening Times	Distance from Path / Starting Price / Facilities / Accommodation
10	Mrs S Park Lower Worthygate GAUTER POOL, Horns Cross Bideford EX39 5EA	01237 451246 www.lowerworthygatefarm.co.uk	367 232	500 mts £25.00 O D CP DW KT 2D 1T
10	Mr & Mrs T D Curtis Fuchsia Cottage Burscott Lane HIGHER CLOVELLY EX39 5RR	01237 431398 tom@clovelly-holidays.co.uk www.clovelly-holidays.co.uk	313 242	1km PD £27.00 O D PL CP LSP KT PD 1D[1] 1T[1] 1S
10	Mr C West Pillowery Park Burscott HIGHER CLOVELLY EX39 5RR	01237 431668 as phone info@clovellyaccommodation.com www.clovellyaccommodation.com	312 241	1.5 km £24.00 O D PL CP LSP KT PD 1D[1] 2T 25-30% single supplement
10	Mrs M McColl 1 Southdown Cottage HIGHER CLOVELLY EX39 5SA	01237 431504 maryfmcoll@hotmail.com	297 236	3 km PD £25.00 D EM PL CP LSP DW KT PD 1D 1T ALL ES PD Barnstaple to Bude, EM by prior arrangement
10	Mr & Mrs M Dunn 55 The Quay CLOVELLY EX39 5TF	01237 431436 pmdunn@mac.com www.artistscottagebythesea.com	318 248	300 mts £30.00 O D PL CP LSP KT PD 1D 1T ALL ES
10	Mrs K Stuart The New Inn High Street CLOVELLY EX39 5TQ	01237 431303 01237 431636 newinn@clovelly.co.uk www.clovelly.co.uk	317 248	250 mts £28.50 O EM PL CP LSP 10D 6T 1S 3F ALL ES some rooms in annexe CP & LSP free in main car park
11	Mr & Mrs J W George Gawlish Farm GAWLISH Hartland EX39 6AT	01237 441320 as phone	256 263	300 mts PD £27.00 O D EM PL CP LSP KT PD 2D 2T ALL ES single supplement
11	Mrs Y Heard West Titchberry Farm WEST TITCHBERRY Hartland Point EX39 6AU	01237 441287 as phone	242 272	250 mts PD £24.00 O D EM PL CP LSP KT PD 1D 1T 1F[1] Closed Xmas
11	Mrs W Currington Cheristow Cottages Cheristow HARTLAND EX39 6DA	01237 441522 as phone info@cheristow-cottages.co.uk www.cheristow-cottages.co.uk	253 255	2.8 km £30.00 O D EM PL CP KT PD 5D 4T ALL ES Cottage accommodation

Sect.	Name and Address	Tel. No. Fax. No. Web / Email	Map Reference Opening Times	Distance from Path Starting Price Facilities Accommodation
11	Mr & Mrs C Johns Hartland Quay Hotel HARTLAND QUAY EX39 6DU	01237 441218 01237 441371 hartlandquayhotel@supanet.com www.hartlandquayhotel.com	223 248	On Path £40.00 D EM PL CP LSP KT 4D[3] 2T[2] 1S[1] 6F[6]
11	Mrs T Goaman Elmscott Farm HARTLAND EX39 6ES	01237 441276 01237 441076 john.goa@virgin.net www.elmscott.org.uk YHA Elmscott winter bookings available	231 215	400 mts PD £32.00 O D EM PL CP LSP KT PD 2D 1T ALL ES
11	Mrs J Yeates 7 Goaman Park HARTLAND EX39 6DF	01237 440005 richard.yeates@tiscali.co.uk	267 241	3.5 km £25.00 O D PL CP LSP KT PD 1D[1] PL by prior arrangement
11	Mrs F Greenslade Tree View STOKE Hartland EX39 6DU	01237 441752 fiona@treeviewstoke.co.uk www.treeviewstoke.co.uk	235 247	1.5 km £55.00 O D PL CP LSP DW KT 1D 1T price per room, single £35
11	Mrs A Dart 1 Coastguard Cottages STOKE Hartland EX39 6DU	01237 441011 dartstoke@tiscali.co.uk www.coastguardcottagestoke.com	235 246	1.5 km £25.00 O D PL CP KT 1D 1F
12	Mr T Neville Ley Park Mead WELCOMBE EX39 6HH	01288 331498 timten@btinternet.com www.leyparkfarm.com	222 176	750 mts £30.00 O D PL CP KT 2D[2]
12	Mrs Heywood Cornakey Farm CORNAKEY Morwenstow EX23 9SS	01288 331260	208 160 Mar-Dec	500 mts £30.00 D EM PL CP LSP KT 1D 1F ALL ES
12	Mrs J Hudson Little Bryaton MORWENSTOW Bude EX23 9SU	01288 331755 little.bryaton@dial.pipex.com www.littlebryaton.co.uk	221 156	1.2 km £32.00 O D CP KT 2D[2] Single supplement
12	Mrs E Cole Jays WOOLLEY Morwenstow EX23 9PP	01288 331540 cole.jays@talk21.com www.martincoleguitars.co.uk/jaysbarn.html	254 168	4 km PD £30.00 O D EM PL CP LSP DW KTPD 1D 2S
12	Mrs C White Trelawney Crosstown MORWENSTOW Bude EX23 9SR	01288 331453	208 150	800 mts £30.00 O D PL CP KT 1D 1T

Sect.	Name and Address	Tel. No. Fax. No. Web / Email	Map Reference Opening Times	Distance from Path Starting Price Facilities Accommodation
12	Mr R Tape The Bush Inn Crosstown MORWENSTOW EX23 9ST	01288 331242 www.thebushinnmorwenstow	208 151	600 mts £39.50 O D EM PL CP LSP DW KT 1D 2T ALL ES £45 single charge, KT by prior arrangement. Also self catering
12	Mr & Mrs Bramhill West Point CRIMP Morwenstow EX23 9PB	01288 331594 bramhill@supanet.com www.north-cornwall.co.uk/client/west-point	255 155 2 Jan-22 Dec	5.5 kms PD £30.00 D PL CP LSP KT PD 1D 1T ALL ES
12	Mrs B Dunstan Strands STIBB Bude EX23 9HW	01288 353514 Mobile 07896 483078 brendadunstanbude@yahoo.co.uk	217 107 Jan-Nov	2.5 km PD £22.00 D PL CP KT PD 1D 1F ALL ES
12	Mrs T Berrett Scadghill Farm STIBB Bude EX23 9HN	01288 352373 01288 354357 scadghillfarm@btconnect.com www.scadghillfarm.co.uk	224 104	3 km £28.00 O D EM PL CP LSP KT PD 2D[2]
12	Mrs M Skinner Stratton Gardens Hotel Cot Hill, Stratton BUDE EX23 9DN	01288 352500 moira@stratton-gardens.co.uk www.stratton-gardens.co.uk	231 065	1.5 km £34.00 O D EM PL CP LSP 3D[3] 3T[3] 1S
12	Mr M E Payne Pencarrol Guest House 21 Downs View BUDE EX23 8RF	01288 352478 pencarrolbude@aol.com	209 070 Mar-Oct	300 mts £30.00 D PL CP LSP KT PD 2D[2] 1S 2F[2]
12	Mr & Mrs M Fly Fairway Guest House 8 Downs View BUDE EX23 8RF	01288 355059 enquiries@fairwayguesthouse.co.uk www.fairwayguesthouse.co.uk	209 070 Feb-Nov	300 mts £25.00 D PL CP KT 6D[2] 3T[2] 2S[1] 1F[1] PL by prior arrangement
13	Mr & Mrs R Downes Tee-side Guest House 2 Burn View BUDE EX23 8BY	01288 352351 As phone rayandjune@tee-side.co.uk www.tee-side.co.uk	208 066	400 mts £28.00 O D PL CP LSP KT 2D 3T 1S ALL ES Single supplement £5 low season, £10 high season
13	Mr R Kelly Links Side 7 Burn View BUDE EX23 8BY	01288 352410 As phone linksidebude@hotmail.com www.linkssidebude.co.uk	208 067	400 mts £25.00 O D PL CP LSP KT 5D[4] 1T[1] 2S[2] 1F[1]
13	Mr M Safdar-Wallace Sea Jade 15 Burn View BUDE EX23 8BZ	01288 353404 seajadeguesthouse@yahoo.co.uk www.seajadeguesthouse.co.uk	209 065	450 mts £29.00 O D EM PL CP LSP KT PD 8D 4T 3S 4F ALL ES

Sect.	Name and Address	Tel. No. Fax. No. Web / Email	Map Reference Opening Times	Distance from Path Starting Price Facilities Accommodation
13	Mr & Mrs D Simmons Palms Guesthouse 17 Burn View Road BUDE EX23 8BZ	01288 353962 palmsguesthouse@tiscali.co.uk www.palms-bude.co.uk	210 066 Mar-Nov	500 mts £25.00 D PL CP LSP KT 1D 2T 1S 1F ALL ES
13	Mrs C Norlund Bossiney House B&B 1 Flexbury Park Road BUDE EX23 8HP	01288 353356 info@bossineyhousebandb.co.uk www.bossineyhousebandb.co.uk	211 067	800 mts £25.00 O D PL CP LSP KT 2D[1] 1T 1F[1] PL by prior arrangement
13	Mr R Steel Elements Hotel & Bistro Marine Drive BUDE EX23 0LZ	01288 352386 thechough@btconnect.com	200 045	10 mts £45.00 O D EM CP LSP KT 5D[5] 2T[2] 1S 3F[3]
13	Mrs S Trewin Harefield Cottage UPTON Bude EX23 0LY	01288 352350 01288 352712 sally@coast-countryside.co.uk www.coast-countryside.co.uk	203 048 Feb-Nov	220 mts £25.00 D EM PL CP LSP DW KT PD 3D 2T ALL ES
13	Mr & Mrs R Holmes Bears & Boxes Penrose DIZZARD, St Gennys EX23 0NX	01840 230318 rwfrh@btinternet.com www.bearsandboxes.com	173 986	500 mts PD £33.50 O D EM PL CP LSP DW KT PD 3D[3] 1T
13	Mr & Mrs G Symmons Dizzard Farmhouse ST GENNYS Near Bude EX23 0NX	01840 230277 symdizzard@msn.com www.dizzardfarmhouse.co.uk	168 984	200 mts PD £25.00 O D PL CP LSP KT PD 2D 1T ALL ES £5 single supplement
13	Mr & Mrs F Mussell Trewartha ST GENNYS EX23 0NN	01840 230420 As phone francismussell@btinternet.com	150 967	750 mts £26.00 O D EM PL CP LSP DW KT PD 4D[3]
13	Mr & Mrs C Morgan Coombe Barton Inn CRACKINGTON HAVEN EX23 0JG	01840 230345 01840 230788 jc.combebartoninn@btconnect.com	144 967 Feb-Oct	On path £28.00 D EM PL CP LSP KT 5D[3] 1F/T[1] limited LSP
13	Mrs G Lowe Gunnedah House CRACKINGTON HAVEN EX23 0JZ	01840 230265 as phone glowe@hotmail.co.uk	144 966	200 mts £30.00 O D PL KT 1D
13	Mrs S Bennett The Lodge CRACKINGTON HAVEN EX23 0JW	01840 230347 c.haven@tiscali.co.uk	158 958	2 km £30.00 O D EM PL CP KT PD 1D[1] EM & PL by prior arrangement singles accepted

Sect.	Name and Address	Tel. No. Fax. No. Web / Email	Map Reference Opening Times	Distance from Path Starting Price Facilities Accommodation
13	Mrs M Kirkwood 6 Penkenna Close CRACKINGTON HAVEN EX23 0PF	01840 230911 margaretkw@gmail.com	155 959	1.6 km £25.00 O CP LSP KT PD 2D
14	Mr & Mrs J Tillinghast The Valency Bed & Breakfast Penally Hill BOSCASTLE PL35 0HF	01840 250397 tillinghast@btinternet.com www.valencybandb.com	101 914 Mar-Oct	100 mts PD £37.50 D PL CP KT PD 3D 1T ALL ES self catering available
14	Mr & Mrs P Templar The Riverside The Bridge BOSCASTLE PL35 0HE	01840 250216 01840 250860 reception@hotelriverside.co.uk www.hotelriverside.co.uk	099 912	250 mts O EM PL CP LSP KT 10D 10T 2S 4F ALL ES
14	Mr & Mrs G Barratt Orchard Lodge Gunpool Lane BOSCASTLE PL35 0AT	01840 250418 orchardlodge@fsmail.net www.orchardlodgeboscastle.co.uk	906 099 Feb-Nov	500 mts £34.50 D PL CP LSP KT PD 3D[2] 2T[2]
14	Mrs J Horwell The Old Coach House Tintagel Road BOSCASTLE PL35 0AS	01840 250398 stay@old-coach.co.uk www.old-coach.co.uk	098 906	400 mts £32.00 O D PL CP DW 3D 3T 2F ALL ES
14	Mrs C Nicholls Trerosewill Farm Paradise BOSCASTLE PL35 0BL	01840 250545 01840 250727 enquiries@trerosewill.co.uk www.trerosewill.co.uk	098 904 mid Feb-Oct	1 km £37.50 D PL CP LSP KT PD 4D 2T 3F ALL ES single supplement
14	Mr N Reed Pendragon Country House DAVIDSTOW Camelford PL32 9XR	01840 261131 enquiries@pendragoncountryhouse.com www.pendragoncountryhouse.com	142 869	8 km PD £35.00 O D EM PL CP LSP DW KT PD 1D 2T 1S 3F ALL ES PD Bude-Padstow free to SWCP Assoc. members
15	Mrs A Jones Grange Cottage BOSSINEY Tintagel PL34 0AX	01840 770487	066 888 Mar-Oct	200 mts £28.00 D PL CP KT 1D[1] 1T[1] 1S 1F
15	Mrs P Tinney Bossinney Cottage BOSSINEY Tintagel PL34 0AY	01840 770327 bossiney@tinney.org	066 888	200 mts £25.00 O D EM PL CP 1D 1T 1S 1F
15	Mr & Mrs N Chamberlain Westcote House BOSSINEY Tintagel PL34 0AX	01840 779194 as phone stay@westcotehouse.co.uk www.westcotehouse.co.uk	064 888	450 mts £26.50 O D PL CP KT 1D 1T ALL ES price based on 2 sharing

Sect.	Name and Address	Tel. No. Fax. No. Web / Email	Map Reference Opening Times	Distance from Path Starting Price Facilities Accommodation
15	Mr & Mrs K Walker Bosayne Guest House Atlantic Road TINTAGEL PL34 0DE	01840 770514 enquiries@bosayne.co.uk www.bosayne.co.uk	050 890	300 mts £25.00 O D PL CP KT 2D[2] 1T[1] 3S 2F[1]
16	Mr & Mrs B Nutt Hillscroft TREKNOW Tintagel PL34 0EN	01840 770551 pat@bascastle.fsnet.co.uk	056 866	800 mts PD £27.00 O D PL CP LSP DW KT PD 2D[2] single supplement high season
16	Mrs M Andrews Hathaway Bed and Breakfast Roscarrock Hill PORT ISAAC PL29 3RG	01208 880416 marion.andrews1@btopenworld.com www.cornwall-online.co.uk/hathaway	995 807 Easter-Oct	50 mts £36.00 CP 2D 1T ALL ES
16	Mrs L Monk Lane End Farm Pendoggett PORT ISAAC PL30 3HH	01208 880013 nabmonk@tiscali.co.uk www.laneendcornwall.co.uk	026 793 Jan-mid Dec	2.5 km PD £30.00 D PL CP LSP KT PD 1D 1D/T 1S ALL ES single supplement also self catering
17	Mrs P White Seaways POLZEATH PL27 6SU	01208 862382 pauline@seaways99.freeserve.co.uk www.seawaysguesthouse.co.uk	939 788	350 mts £38.00 O D CP LSP KT 1D 1T 1S ALL ES
17	Mr G Beresford Endsleigh WHITECROSS Wadebridge PL27 7JD	01208 814477 georgeberesford@gmail.com	967 723	8 km PD £40.00 O D EM PL CP PD 3D[3] 2T[1]
18	Mr P A Tamblin Hemingford House 21 Grenville Road PADSTOW PL28 8EX	01841 532806 peter@tamblin21.fsnet.co.uk www.padstow-bb.co.uk	913 751	1km £35.00 D PL CP KT 2D[1]
18	Mr & Mrs P Cullinan 4 Riverside PADSTOW PL28 8BY	01841 532383 cullinan@madasafish.com www.padstow-bb.co.uk	919 754 Apr-Feb	190 mts £30.00 DW KT 2D[1] 1S £15 single supplement
18	Mrs A Crowley Trealaw Guest House & Tea Room 22 Duke Street PADSTOW PL28 8AB	01841 533161 as phone www.trealaw.com	918 754	300 mts £35.00 O EM PL KT 2D/T 1S ALL ES EM seasonal
18	Mr S Reevely Kellacott 29 Church Street PADSTOW PL28 8BG	01841 532851 kellacott@rocketmail.com www.padstow-paradise.co.uk	916 754	500 mts £25.00 O 2D[2]

Sect.	Name and Address	Tel. No. Fax. No. Web / Email	Map Reference Opening Times	Distance from Path Starting Price Facilities Accommodation
18	Mr J Lloyd Little Pentyre 6 Moyle Road PADSTOW PL28 8DG	01841 532246 as phone jujulloyd@aol.com	921 748	500 mts £27.50 O D CP DW KT 1D 1T ALL ES
18	Miss S Howells Damara House 1 Grenville Road PADSTOW PL28 8EX	01841 532653 info@sianhowells.com www.sianhowells.com	912 749	1 km £35.00 O D CP 1D[1] 2D/T[2] 2S
18	Mrs J Clinton Little Tregonna B&B Little Petherick PADSTOW PL27 7QT	01841 540446 enquiries@littletregonna.co.uk www.littletregonna.co.uk	915 721	3 km PD £30.00 O D EM PL CP LSP DW KT PD 2D 1D/T 1F ALL ES DW by prior arrangement, on Saints Way
18	Mrs L Hawkins The Slipway South Quay PADSTOW PL28 8BY	01841 532036 www.theslipwaypadstow.co.uk	919 753	on path £70.00 price per room O D DW KT PD 1D[1] PD by prior arrangement
19	Mrs J Ball Mordros Homer Park Road TREVONE PL28 8QU	01841 520769	894 757	300 mts £35.00 O D PL CP LSP 2D[1] 1T[1]
19	Mr & Mrs R Mills Well Parc Hotel TREVONE Nr Padstow PL28 8QN	01841 520318 sally@wellparc.co.uk www.wellparc.co.uk	893 755	400 mts PD £38.00 O D EM PL CP LSP KT PD 4D[2] 1T 1S 4F[4] £42 high season
20	Mr N Harradine Trevemedar Cottage PORTHCOTHAN BAY PL27 7UT	01841 520185 noel.harradine1@virgin.net	856 710 Easter-Sept	800 mts £25.00 D PL CP LSP KT PD 2D/T 2S
20	Mrs N Neale Penlan PORTHCOTHAN BAY PL28 8LP	01841 520440 as phone mobile: 07525 940404 mary@idenna.com www.porthcothanbay.co.uk	859 719	150 mts £25.00 O D PL CP LSP DW KT 1D[1] 1T
20	Mr & Mrs J Nederpel Old MacDonald's Farm PORTHCOTHAN BAY PL28 8LW	01841 540829 enquiries@oldmacdonalds.co.uk www.oldmacdonalds.co.uk	867 877	1 km £35.00 O PL CP LSP KT 1T 2F ALL ES Also camping, single charge £50, EM by prior arrangement
20	Mrs P Mcowen Greylands Treburrick St Eval PORTHCOTHAN PL27 7UR	01841 540451 pam.mcowen@btopenworld.com	862 707	500 mts PD £30.00 O D EM PL CP LSP DW KT PD 1D[1] Price based on 2 sharing, PL by prior arrangement

Sect.	Name and Address	Tel. No. Fax. No. Web / Email	Map Reference Opening Times	Distance from Path Starting Price Facilities Accommodation
21	Mr & Mrs J McLuskie Blue Bay Hotel TRENANCE Mawgan Porth TR8 4DA	01637 860324 as phone hotel@bluebaycornwall.co.uk www.bluebaycornwall.co.uk	851 679	300 mts £33.00 O D EM PL CP LSP DW KT PD 8D 1F ALL ES
21	Mrs K Alexander Seavista Hotel MAWGAN PORTH TR8 4AL	01637 860276 enquiries@seavista.co.uk www.seavista.co.uk	849 668	50 mts £35.00 O EM PL CP KT 4D 2S 1F ALL ES
21	Mr & Mrs T Bonici Trevarrian Lodge TREVARRIAN Mawgan Porth TR8 4AW	01637 860156 trevarrian @aol.com www.trevarrianlodge.com	850 661	400 mts £30.00 O D PL CP LSP KT PD 3D[3] 1T[1] 2S 2F [2]
21	Mrs S R Harper Chichester Interest Walking Holidays & Accommodation 14 Bay View Terrace NEWQUAY TR7 2LR	01637 874216 sheila.harper@virgin.net www.freespace.virgin.net/sheila.harper	813 614 Mar-Oct	750 mts £25.00 D PL CP 5D[4] 1T 1S[1] most rooms with shower
21	Mrs P Williams Roma Guest House 1 Atlantic Road NEWQUAY TR7 1QJ	01637 875085 romaghnewquay@aol.com www.romaguesthouse.co.uk	803 616	500 mts £30.00 O D PL CP KT 2D[2] 1T[1] 1S 2F[2]
21	Mr G Dolan The Three Tees Hotel 21 Carminow Way NEWQUAY TR7 3AY	01637 872055 greg@3tees.co.uk www.3tees.co.uk	824 621 Apr-Oct	250 mts £30.00 PL CP LSP DW KT 4D[4] 1T[1] 4F[3]
21	Mrs M Dewolfreys Dewolf Guesthouse 100 Henver Road NEWQUAY TR7 3BL	01637 874746 holidays@dewolfguesthouse.com www.dewolfguesthouse.com	828 620	500 mts £30.00 O PL CP DW 2D 2S 2F ALL ES PL by prior arrangement
21	Mr & Mrs G Brown Trevellis Guest House 21 Trebarwith Crescent NEWQUAY TR7 1DX	01637 874338 seasurfer@talktalk.net www.trevellisguesthouse.co.uk	812 617 Mar-Oct	50 mts £25.00 D 3D[3] 1T[1] 3S 1F[1]
22	Mr & Mrs I R Smithurst Sandbanks Beach Road CRANTOCK TR8 5RE	01637 830130 alisonsmithurst@hotmail.com www.sandbankscrantock.co.uk	790 604 Mar-Oct	500 mts £27.50 D CP 2D[1] 1T
22	Mr & Mrs B Clark Carden Cottage Halwyn Hill CRANTOCK TR8 5RR	01637 830806 cardencottage@btinternet.com www.members.lycos.co.uk/crantock2	791 603	500 mts £34.00 O D CP KT 2D 1T ALL ES closed Christmas

Sect.	Name and Address	Tel. No. Fax. No. Web / Email	Map Reference Opening Times	Distance from Path Starting Price Facilities Accommodation
23	Mrs W Woodcock Chy An Kerensa Cliff Road PERRANPORTH TR6 0DR	01872 572470 As Phone wendychy@aol.com	755 543	20 mts £20.00 O D PL CP DW KT 2D[1] 1T[1] 3S[1] 3F[3] DW - one dog only
23	Mrs M Burch Cliffside Hotel Cliff Road PERRANPORTH TR6 0DR	01872 573297 www.cliffsideperranporth.co.uk	754 544	On path £24.00 O D CP DW 2D[2] 2T[2] 2S 2F[2]
23	Mrs S Stirling & Mrs Sue Lawrie St George's Country Hotel St George's Hill PERRANPORTH TR6 0ED	01872 572184 info@stgeorgescountryhouse.co.uk www.stgeorgescountryhouse.co.uk	746 533	400 mts PD £35.00 O D EM PL CP LSP DW KT PD 5D 1T 1F ALL ES DW by arrangement
24	Mrs L Treseder Driftwood Spars Trevaunance Cove ST AGNES TR5 0RT	01872 552428 01872 553701 info@driftwoodspars.com www.driftwoodspars.com	721 513	on path £45.00 O EM PL CP LSP DW 9D 1T 1S 4F ALL ES LSP by prior arrangement
25	Mrs V Parkinson Buzby View Forthvean Road PORTHTOWAN TR4 8AY	01209 891178 As Phone buzbyview@freenet.co.uk	691 473 Easter-Oct	500 mts £27.00 D PL CP KT 2D 2T 1S
25	Mrs S Hardwick The Beach Hotel PORTHTOWAN TR4 8AE	01209 890228 As Phone rooms@thebeachhotel.net www.thebeachhotel.net	691 478	On Path £28.00 O D PL CP KT 4D 2T 1S 2F ALL ES single supplement
25	Mrs M Urban Moor House Bridge Moor REDRUTH TR16 4QA	01209 843120 maria.urban@earthlink.net www.moor-house-uk.com	667 449	80 mts £40.00 O D PL CP LSP KT PD 2D 1S
26	Mrs S Austin Portreath Arms Hotel The Square PORTREATH TR16 4LA	01209 842259 portreatharms@aol.com	657 452	100 mts £37.50 O D EM PL CP DW KT 2D[2] 5T[3]
26	Mr & Mrs S Haywood Cliff House The Square PORTREATH TR16 4LB	01209 843847 simon.viv.haywood@gmail.com www.cliffhouseportreath.com	656 455	on path £31.50 O D PL CP DW KT PD 2D[2] 2T[2] 2S[1] 1F[1] single supplement
26	Ms E Wherry & Mr D Berriman Dolphin House Cliff Terrace PORTREATH TR16 4LE	01209 842936 dolphinhouse@me.com www.dolphinhouse.me	656 453	on path £35.00 O D PL CP LSP DW KT PD 2D 1F DW by prior arrangement

Sect.	Name and Address	Tel. No. Fax. No. Web / Email	Map Reference Opening Times	Distance from Path Starting Price Facilities Accommodation
27	Mr T Greenaway Godrevy House GWITHIAN St Ives Bay TR27 5BW	01736 755493 as phone enquiries@gwithianholidays.com www.gwithianholidays.com	588 409	1 km £30.00 O D PL CP LSP DW KT 2D 2F ALL ES
27	Mrs L Davies Nanterrow Farm GWITHIAN St Ives Bay TR27 5BP	01209 712282 nanterrow@hotmail.com www.nanterrowfarm.co.uk	599 412 Feb-Nov	1.5km PD £29.00 D PL CP LSP KT PD 1D 1T/F £4 single supplement
27	Mrs P Ellis The Mad Hatter 73 Fore Street HAYLE TR27 4DX	01736 754241 paulineellis-madhatter.org@tesco.net www.cornwallonline.co.uk/madhatter	566 378	1 km £25.00 O D EM PL CP LSP DW KT PD 2D[2] 2T[2] 1S 1F
27	Mrs A Cooper 54 Penpol Terrace HAYLE TR27 4BQ	01736 752855 as phone jacoop@talktalk.net	558 374 Jan-Nov	on path £30.00 D PL CP LSP 1T 1S
27	Mr & Mrs M Reffold Fernleigh 26 Commercial Road HAYLE TR27 4DG	01736 752166 mikelynreffold@fernleigh.fsbusiness.co.uk www.fernleighhayle.com.uk	562 377	750 mts £30.00 O D PL CP LSP KT 2D 1T ALL ES £35 single occupancy
27	Mrs J McLeod Wheal Merth, Heather Lane CANONSTOWN Hayle TR27 6NQ	01736 740553 jean.mcleod@virgin.net	531 355	1.5 km PD £28.00 O D PL CP LSP DW KT PD 2D 1S
28	Mr & Mrs D O'Sullivan Hindon Hall LELANT St Ives TR26 3EN	01736 753046 As Phone enquiries@hindonhall.co.uk www.hindonhall.co.uk	543 369 Mar-Nov	on path £40.00 D PL CP LSP 3D[3]
28	Mr & Mrs M Laywood Halwell Fore Street LELANT TR26 3EL	01736 752003 jmlaywood@aol.com www.halwell.com	544 370	on path £35.00 O D PL CP LSP 3D 1T ALL ES PL by prior arrangement
28	Mr K R Weston The Grey Mullet 2 Bunkers Hill ST IVES TR26 1LJ	01736 796635 01793 834016 greymulletguesthouse@lineone.net www.touristnetuk.com/sw/greymullet	517 408	25 mts £30.00 O D PL 5D 1T 1S ALL ES
28	Mr C England The Anchorage 5 Bunkers Hill ST IVES TR26 1LJ	01736 797135 info@anchoragestives.co.uk www.anchoragestives.co.uk	517 407	on path £35.00 O D PL 4D[3] 1T[1] 1S

Sect.	Name and Address	Tel. No. Fax. No. Web / Email	Map Reference Opening Times	Distance from Path Starting Price Facilities Accommodation
28	Mrs L Bowden Carlill 9 Porthminster Terrace ST IVES TR26 2DQ	01736 796738 carlill@vodafoneemail.co.uk www.carlillguesthouse.co.uk	517 402	250 mts £40.00 O PL CP LSP KT 3D 1T 1S 1F ALL ES
28	Mrs S Martin 8 Ayr Lane ST IVES TR26 1JL	01736 793172	517 405 Apr-Sept	100 mts £25.00 D PL 1T 1S ALL ES
28	Mrs J Rowe Nancherrow Cottage 7 Fish Street ST IVES TR26 1LT	01736 798496 peterjean@nancherrowcottage.fsnet.co.uk www.nancherrow-cottage.co.uk	519 408 Feb-Nov	500 mts £40.00 D PL CP LSP KT 2D 1T ALL ES
28	Mr A Biss & Ms A Pascoe Primrose Valley Hotel Primrose Valley Porthminster Beach ST IVES TR26 2ED	01736 794939 info@primroseonline.co.uk www.primroseonline.co.uk	519 399 Feb-Dec	50 mts £50.00 price per room D PL CP 7D 2T ALL ES
29	Mrs O Parish Tamarisk Burthallan Lane ST IVES TR26 3AA	01736 797201 enquiries@tamarisk-bb.co.uk www.tamarisk-bb.co.uk	508 406 Easter-Oct	500 mts £30.00 D CP LSP 2D
29	Mr R Motley The Tinners Arms ZENNOR St Ives TR26 3BY	01736 796927 sleep@tinnersarms.co.uk www.tinnersarms.co.uk	454 384	500 mts £45.00 O D EM PL CP LSP DW KT 2D[2] 2S
29	Mrs N Mann Trewey Farm TREWEY Zennor TR26 3DA	01736 796936	454 384 Feb-Nov	1.5 kms £30.00 D PL CP 2D 1T 1S 2F
29	Dr Thompson Boswednack Manor BOSWEDNACK Zennor TR26 3DD	01736 794183 boswednack@ravenfield.co.uk www.boswednackmanor.co.uk	442 378 Apr-Oct	1.5 km £24.00 D PL CP LSP KT 2D[2] 1T 1S 1F
29	Mr C Inkin The Gurnards Head Hotel TREEN Zennor TR26 3DE	01736 796928 enquiries@gurnardshead.co.uk www.gurnardshead.co.uk	436 377	500 mts £65.00 O D EM PL CP DW 7D 3T 2S 1F ALL ES price per room inc. breakfast, occasional KT
29	Mr E J Coak The North Inn PENDEEN TR19 7DN	01736 788417 ernestjohncoak@aol.com www.thenorthinnpendeen.co.uk	383 344	1 km £30.00 O D EM PL CP LSP DW KT 4D/T[4] Also camping; 3 rooms can be twin and/or family rooms

Sect.	Name and Address	Tel. No. Fax. No. Web / Email	Map Reference Opening Times	Distance from Path Starting Price Facilities Accommodation
29	Mrs J Hoather The Old Chapel BOSCASWELL DOWNS Pendeen Penzance TR19 7DR	01736 786006 mobile: 07789 547806 geoffgoatherd@aol.com	385 344	1 km PD £27.50 O D EM PL CP LSP DW KTPD 2D 2T
29	Mr & Mrs T Dymond The Old Count House BOSCASWELL DOWNS Pendeen TR19 7EE	01736 788058 dymondep@aol.com www.cornwallonline.co.uk	383 344 May-Oct	1 km £25.00 D CP LSP 2D
31	Mr & Mrs P Michelmore 2 Fore Street ST JUST TR19 7LL	01736 787784 wendy.michelmore@tesco.net www.stjustbandb.com	372 314	1.75 km £30.00 O D PL CP LSP 1D 1T 1F
31	Mr & Mrs A Collinson Bosavern House BOSAVERN St Just TR19 7RD	01736 788301 info@bosavern.com www.bosavern.com	370 305	1 km £33.00 O D PL CP 3D[3] 2T[1] 1S[1] 2F[2] PL by prior arrangement
31	Mr & Mrs B Harrison The Weavers SENNEN Penzance TR19 7AQ	01736 871565 As phone weaversbb@tiscali.co.uk	355 248	750 mts £35.00 O D CP LSP KT 1D[1]
32	Mr & Mrs C Bishop Sea View House The Valley PORTHCURNO TR19 6JX	01736 810638 svhouse@btinternet.com www.seaviewhouseporthcurno.com	383 227	400 mts PD £35.00 D EM PL CP LSP KT PD 2D 2T 1S ALL ES
32	Mr & Mrs F M Byott Treville The Valley PORTHCURNO TR19 6JY	01736 810167 jbyott@live.co.uk	382 229	500 mts £30.00 O D PL CP KT PD 1D £5 single supplement
32	Mrs S Wear The Wearhouse The Valley PORTHCURNO TR19 6JX	01736 810129 wearsue@aol.com	383 226	200 mts £30.00 O D CP KT 2D[2]
32	Mr & Mrs C Hatton Rose Cottage PORTHCURNO TR19 6JY	01736 810082 chris@chrisswcpa.co.uk www.porthcurno.org.uk	382 229	500 mts £26.00 O D PL CP KT PD 2D 1S Guided walks offered Land's End & Lizard
34	Mrs R Gwennap Treverven Farm ST BURYAN TR19 6DL	01736 810221 as phone rachel.gwennap@sky.com www.treververnfarm.co.uk	409 237	800 mts O D CP LSP DW 2D[2] 1T childrens' folding beds available

Sect.	Name and Address	Tel. No. Fax. No. Web / Email	Map Reference Opening Times	Distance from Path Starting Price Facilities Accommodation
34	Mrs R Hood Castallack Farm LAMORNA TR19 6NL	01736 731969 info@castallackfarm.co.uk www.castallackfarm.co.uk	451 252	1.75 km £30.00 O D PL CP LSP DW KT 2D 1T ALL ES Single supplement
34	Mr M Male Lowenna Raginnis Hill MOUSEHOLE TR19 6SL	01736 731077 mm4lowenna@aol.com www.mousehole-lowenna.co.uk	469 262	On path £32.50 O D PL 1D 1T 1F ALL ES PL by prior arrangement
34	Mrs E Reynolds Renovelle 6 The Parade MOUSEHOLE TR19 6PN	01736 731258	469 264 Easter-Oct	on path £25.00 D PL CP 2D[1] 1S
34	Mrs D Waters White Gates Cliff Lane MOUSEHOLE TR19 6PU	01736 731691	471 267 Easter-Oct	on path £32.50 D CP LSP KT 2D[1] 1T 1F[1]
34	Mr & Mrs J Leggatt Cornerways 5 Leskinnick Street PENZANCE TR18 2HA	01736 364645 As Phone enquires@cornerways-penzance.co.uk www.penzance.co.uk/cornerways	475 308	800 mts £30.00 O EM PL KT 1D 1T 2S ALL ES laundrette next door
34	Ms E Taylor Honeydew Guesthouse 3 Leskinnick Street PENZANCE TR18 2HA	01736 364206 475 306 mobile: 07866 527948 emmaj.taylor1@homecall.co.uk www.bedbreakfastcornwall.com		800 mts £28.00 O DW 1D 1T 1S 1F ALL ES
34	Mr & Mrs Cavanagh-Wilson Warwick House 17 Regent Terrace PENZANCE TR18 4DW	01736 363881 as phone enquiry@warwickhousepenzance.co.uk www.warwickhousepenzance.co.uk	475 298	50 mts £40.00 O D PL CP LSP KT 3D 2T 2S ALL ES single supplement, wi-fi DVD library
35	Mr & Mrs D Hopkins St Michaels Fore Street MARAZION TR17 0AD	01736 711348 info@stmichaels-bedandbreakfast.co.uk www.stmichaels-bedandbreakfast.co.uk	520 306	1 km £35.00 O D PL CP KT 4D 1T 1F ALL ES
35	Miss L Whitford Rosario The Square MARAZION TR17 0BH	01736 711998	517 306	On path £35.00 O D PL CP DW KT 2D 1T 1S ALL ES
36	Mrs M Foy Mzima Penlee Close PRAA SANDS TR20 9SR	01736 763856 marianfoy@prussia-cove-holiday.com	581 288	800 mtrs PD £23.00 O D PL CP KT PD 1T 1F

Sect.	Name and Address	Tel. No. Fax. No. Web / Email	Map Reference Opening Times	Distance from Path Starting Price Facilities Accommodation
36	Mrs V Hocking Dingley Dell Pengersick Lane PRAA SANDS Near Penzance TR20 9SL	01736 763527 valhocking@uwclub.net www.dingleydell.eu	582 284	650 mts £30.00 O D CP 2D/F 1T ALL ES
37	Mr F P Hallam Seefar Peverell Terrace PORTHLEVEN TR13 9DZ	01326 573778 enquiries@seefar.co.uk www.seefar.co.uk	630 255 Easter-Oct	200 mts £30.00 D PL DW KT 1D[1] 1T[1] 1S
37	Miss S Kelynack & Mr R Perkins An Mordros Hotel Peverell Terrace PORTHLEVEN TR13 9DZ	01326 562236 info@anmordroshotel.com www.anmordroshotel.com	630 255	100 mts £31.00 D PL KT 6D 1T ALL ES single supplement
37	Mr & Mrs R Williams Rosemorran B&B 14 The Crescent PORTHLEVEN TR13 9LU	01326 574855 penny@rosemorran14.wanadoo.co.uk www.rosemorranbandb.co.uk	630 262	400 mts £60.00 price per room O CP LSP KT 1D 2T ALL ES
38	Mr & Mrs T Payne Lyndale Cottage Guest House 4 Greenbank Meneage Road HELSTON TR13 8JA	01326 561082 enquiries@lyndalecottage.co.uk www.lyndalecottage.co.uk	662 269	3.5 km £33.00 O CP 3D 2T 1S ALL ES Single supplement
38	Mrs L Elliott De Vere Lodge Cove Road MULLION TR12 7EX	01326 240047 deverelodge@aol.com www.cornwallonline.com	672 182	600 mts £30.00 O D PL CP KT 1D[1]
38	Mrs J Tyler-Street Trenance Farmhouse MULLION TR12 7HB	01326 240639 As Phone info@trenancefarmholidays.co.uk www.trenancefarmholidays.co.uk	673 185 Apr-Sept	800 mts £32.00 D PL CP LSP KT 2D 1T ALL ES single supplement
38	Mrs J Valender The Old Vicarage Nansmellyon Road MULLION TR12 7DQ	01326 240898 bandbmullion@hotmail.com www.cornwall-online.co.uk/mullionoldvicarage	677 190	1 km £35.00 O D CP KT 4D[3] 2T[2] 2F[2]
38	Mr and M P Savage The Mounts Bay Guest House Churchtown MULLION TR12 7HN	01326 241761 jan@mountsbayguesthouse.wanadoo.co.uk www.mountsbayguesthouse.co.uk	678 192	1 km PD £30.00 O D EM KT PD 4D 2T 1S 1F ALL ES

Sect.	Name and Address	Tel. No. Fax. No. Web / Email	Map Reference Opening Times	Distance from Path Starting Price Facilities Accommodation
39	Mrs A Bennett Stormfield THE LIZARD TR12 7NZ	01326 290806 alison.b60@btinternet.com www.cornwall-online.co.uk	703 126	400 mts £30.00 O D PL CP LSP KT PD 1T 1F PL by prior arrangement
39	Mr & Mrs A Pratt The Caerthillian THE LIZARD TR12 7NQ	01326 290019 caerthillian@hotmail.com www.thecaerthillian.co.uk	703 125	500 mts £32.50 O D PL CP DW KT 3D[3] 1T[1] 1S
40	Mrs J Baird Porthbeer Chynhalls Point COVERACK TR12 6SB	01326 280680 jane@porthbeer.co.uk www.porthbeer.co.uk	782 176	100 mts PD £35.00 O D PL CP LSP KT PD 2D 1T 1F ALL ES
40	Mrs A Rogers Fernleigh Chymbloth Way COVERACK TR12 6TB	01326 280626 sudan-ann03@hotmail.co.uk www.fernleighcoverack.co.uk	781 183	50 mts £32.00 O D EM PL CP LSP DW KT PD 2D 1T ALL ES
40	Mr & Mrs W Sanger Tregoning Lea LADDENVEAN St Keverne Helston TR12 6QE	01326 280947 waltersanger@aol.com	788 214	1.5 km PD £25.00 O D PL CP LSP DW KT PD 1D[1] 1T 1S EM by prior arrangement
41	Ms A Strickland Gallen-Treath Guest House PORTHALLOW St Keverne Near Helston TR12 6PL	01326 280400 as phone gallentreath@btclick.com www.gallen-treath.com	797 232	450 mts PD £32.00 O D EM PL CP DW KT PD 2D[2] 1T[1] 1S 1F[1] EM by arrangement, single & DW supplement
41	Mrs E Whale Porthvean GILLAN TR12 6HL	01326 231204	792 252	on path £20.00 O D PL CP LSP DW KT 1T[1] facilities to prepare own EM
41	Mrs J Phelps Karenza Tregildry Lane GILLAN TR12 6HG	01326 231712 phelps950@btinternet.com www.cornwall-online.com	783 249	400 mts £37.00 O EM PL CP KT PD 2D 1S 1F ALL ES PL, PD & KT by prior arrangement
41	Mrs L Jenkin Landrivick Farm MANACCAN Helston TR12 6HX	01326 231686	750 245	2 km £40.00 O D PL CP LSP 2T 1S
41	Mr & Mrs J Moore Landre MANACCAN TR12 6JH	01326 231556 wendy@johnandwendymoore.co.uk	764 251	500 mts £60.00 O D CP 1D[1] price based on 2 sharing

Sect.	Name and Address	Tel. No. Fax. No. Web / Email	Map Reference Opening Times	Distance from Path Starting Price Facilities Accommodation
41	Mrs P Royall POINT Helford Nr Helston TR12 6JY	01326 231666 pamroyall@btinternet.com www.helfordcottages.co.uk	768 263	on path £37.00 O D 1T[1]
42	Mrs C Spike Carwinion Vean Grove Hill MAWNAN SMITH TR11 5ER	01326 250513 christinespike@fsmail.net www.carwinionvean.co.uk	777 283	1.6 km £29.50 O D PL CP LSP DW 1D[1] 1T[1] 1F DW by prior arrangement only
42	Mrs S P Annan Chynoweth Carwinion Lane MAWNAN SMITH TR11 5JB	01326 250534 sally@chynoweth.org www.chynoweth.helfordriver.net	781 283	800 mts PD £30.00 O D CP LSP KT PD 1D 1T ALL ES single supplement
42	Mrs C Lake Gold Martin Carlidnack Road MAWNAN SMITH Falmouth TR11 5HA	01326 250666 gold_martin@hotmail.com www.goldmartin.co.uk	779 291	1.6 km PD £32.00 O D PL CP KT PD 2D[2] 1T[1] 1S single only let with dbl room
42	Mr & Mrs G Williams Trevarn Carwinion Road MAWNAN SMITH TR11 5JD	01326 251245 as phone mobile: 07877 580321 enquiries@trevarn.co.uk www.trevarn.co.uk	777 284	800 mts £30.00 O D PL CP LSP KT PD 1D 1T 1S ALL ES
42	Mr P Lower Gyllyngvase House Hotel Gyllyngvase Road FALMOUTH TR11 4GH	01326 312956 01326 316166 info@gyllyngvase.co.uk www.gyllyngvase.co.uk	810 318	50 mts £30.00 O D EM PL CP KT 7D[7] 2T[2] 3S 1F[1]
42	Mr Niall & Nikki Macdougall The Rosemary 22 Gyllyngvase Terrace FALMOUTH TR11 4DL	01326 314669 stay@therosemary.co.uk www.therosemary.co.uk	810 318 Feb-Nov	100 mts £35.00 EM PL CP DW KT 3D 2T 2F ALL ES pre-booking in high season difficult
42	Ms J Goodchild Falmouth Lodge Backpackers 9 Gyllyngvase Terrace FALMOUTH TR11 4DL	01326 319996 judi@falmouthlodge.co.uk www.falmouthbackpackers.co.uk	811 319	150 mts £19.00 O D CP LSP 1D[1] 2T 1S 2DORMS price includes simple breakfast
42	Mr & Mrs R Picken The Lerryn Hotel De Pass Road FALMOUTH TR11 4BJ	01326 312489 0870 3001729 lerrynhotel@btconnect.com www.thelerrynhotel.co.uk	813 319	20 mts £46.00 O EM PL CP LSP DW KT 8D 8T 4S ALL ES
42	Mr & Mrs S Davie Dolvean House 50 Melvill Road FALMOUTH TR11 4DQ	01326 313658 01326 313995 reservations@dolvean.co.uk www.dolvean.co.uk	809 319	300 mts £36.00 O D PL CP DW KT PD 6D 2T 2S ALL ES

Sect.	Name and Address	Tel. No. Fax. No. Web / Email	Map Reference Opening Times	Distance from Path Starting Price Facilities Accommodation
42	Ms T Rangecroft Anchor House 17 Harbour Terrace FALMOUTH TR11 2AN	01326 317006 tinarange@btinternet.com www.anchorhousebandbfalmouth.co.uk	805 330	150 mts £28.00 O D EM PL CP LSP KT PD 1D 1S KT,PL & EM by prior arrangement
42	Mrs D A Kevern Lynford 20 Avenue Road FALMOUTH TR11 4AZ	01326 314258	811 320	200 mts £27.50 D PL CP DW 2D[2] 2S 1F[1]
43	Mrs K Moseley Braganza Grove Hill ST MAWES TR2 5BJ	01326 270281 as phone breganzak@googlemail.com mobile 07899 967367	846 331 25 Mar-Oct	300 mts £45.00 D CP 4D/T[3] 1S KT can be arranged
43	Mrs M Bysouth Lower Meadow Newton Road ST MAWES TR2 5BS	01326 270036	845 334 May-Sept	500 mts £30.00 D CP LSP DW 1D[1]
44	Mrs D Weale Glenlorcan 9 Tregassick Road Gerrans PORTSCATHO TR2 5ED	01872 580343 diane@glenlorcan.wanadoo.co.uk www.visitus.co.uk	873 351 Mar-Oct	400 mts £28.00 D CP PD 1D 2T ALL ES £5 single supplement
45	Mr & Mrs M Rawling Treverbyn House Pendower Road VERYAN TR2 5QL	01872 501201 info@treverbyn.co.uk www.treverbyn.co.uk	914 393	2 km PD £32.00 O D PL CP KT PD 1D 1T 1S ALL ES free local PD, distances charged
45	Mrs S Treneary Jago Cottage Trewartha VERYAN TR2 5QJ	01872 501491 jago@roseland.me.uk www.roseland.me.uk	925 396	400 mts £30.00 O D EM PL CP LSP DW KT PD 1D 1T 1S ALL ES
45	Mr & Mrs K Righton Broom Parc Camels PORTLOE TR2 5PJ	01872 501803 01872 501109 lindsayrighton@ukonline.co.uk www.broomparc.co.uk	930 390 mid Feb-Oct	On Path £45.00 D PL CP LSP DW KT 1D 2T[2]
45	Mrs B Leach Carradale PORTLOE TR2 5RB	01872 501508 barbara495@btinternet.com www.theaa.com	935 394	300 mts £32.50 O D PL CP LSP KT PD 2D 1T ALL ES
45	Mr M Swannell The Ship Inn PORTLOE TR2 5RA	01872 501356 theshipinnportloe@googlemail.com www.theshipinnportloe.co.uk	936 393	150 mts £35.00 O PL EM CP LSP KT 1D 1T 1F ALL ES single supplement

Sect.	Name and Address	Tel. No. Fax. No. Web / Email	Map Reference Opening Times	Distance from Path Starting Price Facilities Accommodation
45	Mr & Mrs I Lydall Field Cottage Treviskey PORTLOE TR2 5PN	01872 501355 ianlydall@verbenacornwall.fsnet.co.uk	936 402	1 km £50.00 O D CP LSP PD 1D[1]
47	Mr & Mrs P Calcraft Grenville 1 Quilver Close GORRAN HAVEN PL26 6JT	01726 843243	011 414	300 mts £25.00 O D EM PL CP LSP KT PD 1D 1T EM by prior arrangement
47	Mrs W Bennett 20 Perhaver Park GORRAN HAVEN PL26 6NZ	01726 843777 wendyann.bennett@virgin.net	012 417	250 mts £25.00 O D PL CP LSP KT PD 1D 1S
47	Mr & Mrs D Taggart Harbours Reach GORRAN HAVEN PL26 6JG	01726 842445 admin@harboursreach.com www.harboursreach.com	011 415 Easter-Oct	50 mts £30.00 D PL CP LSP KT 2D[2] 1T
47	Mrs S Pike Tregillan Trewollock Lane GORRAN HAVEN PL26 6NT	01726 842452 tregillanapartment@tiscali.co.uk	008 418	500 mts £25.00 O D PL CP LSP DW KT PD 1D[1] 1T
48	Ms J Conneely Mandalay Guest House School Hill MEVAGISSEY PL26 6TQ	01726 842435 jillconneely@yahoo.com	014 452 Mar-Oct	400 mts £28.00 D PL CP DW KT PD 5D 1T 1S 2F ALL ES
48	Mrs C J Avent Wild Air Polkirt Hill MEVAGISSEY PL26 6UX	01726 843302 clareavent@aol.com www.wildair.co.uk	016 444	On path £37.50 O D PL CP KT PD 3D[2] KT & PL by prior arrangement only
48	Mrs F Thomas Kervernel 35 Cliff Street MEVAGISSEY PL26 6QJ	01726 844656 franormthomas@btinternet.com www.lightsoft.co.uk/cornwall	015 448	10 mts £25.00 O D PL KT PD 2T[1]
48	Mr & Mrs I Soper Honeycombe House 61 Polkirt Hill MEVAGISSEY PL26 6UR	01726 843750 enquiries@honeycombehouse.co.uk www.honeycombehouse.co.uk	015 446 mid Jan-mid Dec	10 mts £31.00 D KT 3D[3] 1T[1] 1S
48	Mrs S Cannone Bacchus Trevarth MEVAGISSEY PL26 6RX	01726 843473 susiecannone@yahoo.co.uk www.bacchus-cornwall.co.uk	011 450	600 mts £55.00 price per room O D CP 2D 2T ALL ES

Sect.	Name and Address	Tel. No. Fax. No. Web / Email	Map Reference Opening Times	Distance from Path Starting Price Facilities Accommodation
48	Mrs D Young Tregoney House 19 Tregoney Hill MEVAGISSEY PL26 6RD	01726 842760 as phone Mobile: 07815 936336 dianne.young@hotmail.co.uk www.tregoneyhouse.co.uk	014 448	20 mts £27.50 O D PL DW KT 1D 1T 1F ALL ES
48	Mr J Gladwin Trevalsa Court Hotel School Hill MEVAGISSEY PL26 6TH	01726 842468 stay@trevalsa-hotel.co.uk www.trevalsa-hotel.co.uk	015 453	on path £75.00 D PL EM CP DW 8D 3D/T 2S ALL ES DW by prior arrangement
49	Mr & Mrs R Callis Ardenconnel 179 Charlestown Road CHARLESTOWN PL25 3NN	01726 75469 ardenconnel@tiscali.co.uk	036 520	400 mts £27.50 O D PL CP LSP KT 1S 2F[1]
49	Mrs J Galloway Locksley Church Road CHARLESTOWN PL25 3NS	01726 72613 gallowayj265@aol.com	036 521	500 mts PD £27.50 O D PL CP LSP KT PD 1D/S/F[1] £2 single supplement
50	Mrs K Allen Tremorvah Porthpean Beach Road PORTHPEAN PL26 6AU	01726 66889 01726 66548 kate_allen@btconnect.com	031 510 Mar-Nov	300 mts £25.00 D CP KT PD 3D[1] 2T
50	Mrs S Clyne Boslowen 96 Par Green PAR PL24 2AG	01726 813720 enquiries@boslowen.co.uk www.boslowen.co.uk	079 536	10 mts £30.00 O D CP LSP KT 2D 2T 1S ALL ES
50	Mrs G Butler 84 Par Green PAR PL24 2AG	01726 813442 gillybee@pargreen.freeserve.co.uk www.walkers-pitstop.com mobile: 07969 378052	079 536	10 mts £20.00 O D CP DW KT 2T 1S Also self catering non-cooked breakfast
50	Mrs C Scrafton Reynards Rest The Mount PAR PL24 2BZ	01726 815770 carol@reynardsrest.co.uk www.reynardsrest.co.uk	071 532	600 mts PD £30.00 O D PL CP LSP KT PD 1D[1] 1T
50	Mrs M H Ball Polbrean House Woodland Avenue TYWARDREATH Par PL24 2PL	01726 812530 polbreanbandb@btinternet.com www.visitcornwall.co.uk	082 543	2 km £30.00 O D PL CP LSP KT 2D 1F ALL ES

Sect.	Name and Address	Tel. No. Fax. No. Web / Email	Map Reference Opening Times	Distance from Path Starting Price Facilities Accommodation
51	Mr S Hardinge & Mrs Davis Trevanion Guest House 70 Lostwithiel Street FOWEY PL23 1BQ	01726 832602 alisteve@trevanionguesthouse.co.uk www.trevanionguesthouse.co.uk	124 518	500 mts PD £25.00 O D EM PL CP LSP DW KT PD 3D[3] 2T[2] 1S 2F[2] EM, PD & LSP by prior arrangement £35 single price
51	Mrs S Hoddinott Trekelyn 3 Hanson Drive FOWEY PL23 1ET	01726 833375	120 514	200 mts £30.00 O D CP 1D 1T
51	Mrs P Milbank Mazirah 51 Polvillion Road FOWEY PL23 1HG	01726 833339	120 516 Apr-Nov	1 km £27.00 D PL CP 1D[1]
51	Safe Harbour Hotel 58 Lostwithiel Street FOWEY PL23 1BQ	01726 833379 info@cornwall-safeharbour.co.uk www.cornwall-safeharbour.co.uk	124 517	50 mts £40.00 O EM CP DW 5D 1T 2S 1F ALL ES
52	Mrs B Alexander Hormond House 55 Fore Street POLRUAN PL23 1PH	01726 870853 bella@chrisbella.demon.co.uk www.hormondhouse.com	126 508	250 mts £25.00 O D PL DW KT 2D/T[2] PL by prior arrangement
52	Mrs P Moore Chyavallon Landaviddy Lane POLPERRO PL13 2RT	01503 272788 chyavallon@btinternet.com www.chyavallonpolperro.co.uk	205 510	300 mts £30.00 O D PL CP 1D 1T ALL ES single supplement PL by prior arrangement
52	Mr S Shephard The House on Props Talland Street POLPERRO PL13 2RE	01503 272310 stephenshephard@btinternet.com www.houseonprops.co.uk	208 509 Mar- Nov	on path £35.00 D EM PL LSP DW KT 2D 1T ALL ES Single supplement £5
52	Mr & Mrs C Pidcock Penryn House The Coombes POLPERRO PL13 2RQ	01503 272157 01503 273055 enquiries@penrynhouse.co.uk www.penrynhouse.co.uk	205 511	500 mts £35.00 O D PL CP DW 8D 2T 1S 2F ALL ES
52	Mrs S Boyson Barlandue Polperro Road POLPERRO PL13 2JE	01503 272143 sueboyson@btinternet.com www.barlandue.co.uk	213 525	1 km £30.00 O D PL CP DW 1D 1T
53	Mr & Mrs P Barlow Schooner Point 1 Trelawney Terrace WEST LOOE PL13 2AG	01503 262670 enquiries@schoonerpoint.co.uk www.schoonerpoint.co.uk	252 536	150 mts £25.00 O D PL CP 2D 1T 1S ALL ES

Sect.	Name and Address	Tel. No. Fax. No. Web / Email	Map Reference Opening Times	Distance from Path Starting Price Facilities Accommodation
53	Mr E Mawby Marwinthy Guest House East Cliff EAST LOOE PL13 1DE	01503 264382 eddiemawby@lineone.net www.marwinthy.co.uk	256 533 Mar-Dec	On Path £24.00 D DW 2D[2] 1T 1F Single supplement varies
53	Mr & Mrs D Burton Deganwy Hotel Station Road EAST LOOE PL13 1HL	01503 262984 enquiries@deganwyhotel.co.uk www.deganwyhotel.co.uk	254 536 Mar-Oct	50 mts £31.00 D PL CP LSP KT 8D[6] 3T[3] 2S[2] 2F[2]
53	Mr S Tapal Bridgeside Guesthouse Fore Street EAST LOOE PL13 1HH	01503 263113	254 535	on path PD £25.00 O D PL CP LSP DW KT PD 6D[6] 5T[4] 2S[1] 3F[3]
53	Mrs S Broad Treliddon Farmhouse DOWNDERRY PL11 3DP	01503 250288 www.treliddon-farms.co.uk	324 551	1 km PD £25.00 O D CP LSP DW KT PD 3D[2] 1S
54	Mr M Harris Fraggle Rock 21 Whitsand Bay View PORTWRINKLE PL11 3DB	01503 230387 enquiries@fragglerockbb.co.uk www.fragglerockbb.co.uk	356 539	75 mts £30.00 O D PL CP LSP KT 1D 1T 1F ALL ES single supplement
54	Mr & Mrs J Pape Polhawn Cottage POLHAWN COVE Whitsand Bay PL10 1LL	01752 822657 polhawn@btinternet.com www.polhawncovecottage.co.uk	213 937	5 mts £27.50 O D PL CP KT PD 2D[2] 1T Single supplement
55	Mrs P Knowles 4 The Old Schoolhouse Garrett Street CAWSAND PL10 1PD	01752 822403 penelopeknowles@gmail.com www.oldschoolhouse-cawsand.co.uk	434 503 Feb-Nov	On path £40.00 D PL KT PD 1D 1T 1F ALL ES PL by prior arrangement
55	Ms A Heasman Cliff House KINGSAND PL10 1NJ	01752 823110 01752 822595 chkingsand@aol.com www.cliffhouse-kingsand.co.uk	434 506	20 mts price on application O D EM PL CP KT PD 3D 3T ALL ES Also self-catering
55	Mrs J King Coombe House B&B Coombe Farm Fourlanesend KINGSAND PL10 1LR	01752 823925 info@coombehouse-cawsand.co.uk www.coombehouse-cawsand.co.uk	429 512	500 mts £35.00 O D CP LSP 2D[1] 1T 1F[1]
55	Mrs B Graham Weir Cottage Lower Anderton Road MILLBROOK PL10 1HP	01752 822050 binna.graham@virgin.net www.weircottage.co.uk	438 523 3 Jan-20 Dec	1.5 km PD £30.00 D EM PL CP LSP DW PD 1D EM & DW by prior arrangement

Sect.	Name and Address	Tel. No. Fax. No. Web / Email	Map Reference Opening Times	Distance from Path Starting Price Facilities Accommodation
56	Mr & Mrs J Moulds Berkeley's of St James 4 St James Place East PLYMOUTH PL1 3AS	01752 221654 As Phone enquiry@onthehoe.co.uk www.onthehoe.co.uk	474 541	on path £30.00 O D CP 1D/T/F 2D 1S ALL ES single supplement
56	Mr & Mrs D Whitfield Squires Guesthouse 7 St James Place East PLYMOUTH PL1 3AS	01752 261459 As Phone info@squiresguesthouse.com www.squiresguesthouse.com	474 541	on path £26.00 O D 4D[4] 1T[1] 2S
56	Mrs A Anderson Sea Breezes 28 Grand Parade PLYMOUTH PL1 3DJ	01752 667205 As Phone info@plymouth-bedandbreakfast.co.uk www.plymouth-bedandbreakfast.co.uk	478 537	on path £35.00 O D PL KT 3D 3T 2F ALL ES
56	Mrs J Riordan Rusty Anchor 30 Grand Parade PLYMOUTH PL1 3DJ	01752 663924 enquiries@therustyanchor-plymouth.co.uk www.therustyanchor-plymouth.co.uk	473 534	on path £30.00 O D PL CP DW KT 2D[2] 4T[2] 5S[2] 2F[2]
56	Mrs C M Hawton Edgcumbe Guest House 50 Pier Street West Hoe PLYMOUTH PL1 3BT	01752 660675 01752 666510 enquiries@edgcumbeguesthouse.co.uk www.edgcumbeguesthouse.co.uk	473 537	20 mts £25.00 O PL CP DW 5D 3T 3S 2F ALL ES £10 single supplement
56	Mr L Wrench The Riviera 8 Elliott Street The Hoe PLYMOUTH PL1 2PP	01752 667379 01752 623318 riviera-hoe@btconnect.com www.riviera-hoe.co.uk	474 540 mid Jan-mid Dec	200 mts £27.50 D PL LSP KT 5D[5] 1T[1] 5S[2]
56	Mr & Mrs D Radford Rainbow Lodge 29 Atheneum Street The Hoe PLYMOUTH PL1 2RQ	01752 229699 info@rainbowlodgeplymouth.co.uk www.rainbowlodgeplymouth.co.uk	474 541	100 mts £30.00 O D PL CP LSP KT PD 5D[5] 3D/T[2] 1S 1F[2]
56	Mrs J Tooze Coombe House The Quay ORESTON Plymstock PL9 7NE	01752 482660 jet-28@hotmail.co.uk	500 534	on path £30.00 O PL CP KT PD 2D 2T £5 single supplement
57	Mrs G Shelford Heybrook Bay Guest House Beach Road HEYBROOK BAY Nr Wembury PL9 0BS	01752 862345	496 488 Apr-Nov	On path £26.00 CP LSP 3D 3T £3 single supplement
57	Mr & Mrs V Walsh The Mussel Inn DOWN THOMAS Plymouth PL9 0AQ	01752 862238 walshvictor@hotmail.com www.musselinn.co.uk	504 501	500 mts £25.00 O EM PL CP 3D 1T

Sect.	Name and Address	Tel. No. / Fax. No. / Web / Email	Map Reference / Opening Times	Distance from Path / Starting Price / Facilities / Accommodation
57	Mrs M R Denby Knoll Cottage 104 Church Road WEMBURY PL9 0LA	01752 862036 as phone Mobile: 07849 476543 davidpdenby88@tiscali.co.uk	523 489	500 mts £25.00 O D EM PL CP LSP KT 1D[1] 1T[1] 1S
57	Miss C Bedford Sea Change 43 Hawthorn Drive WEMBURY Plymouth PL9 0BE	01752 862463 Mobile: 07821 629427 helenclairebedford@yahoo.co.uk www.seachangewembury.yolasite.com	525 489	1 km £36.00 O D PL CP LSP KT 1D 1S ALL ES
57	Mr & Mrs J Pitcher 1 Barton Close WEMBURY Plymouth PL9 0LF	01752 862151	527 494	1 km PD £25.00 O D PL CP KT PD 1T[1] £5 single supplement
57	Mr & Mrs B Baxter Beckdale Guesthouse 19 Riverside Walk YEALMPTON Plymouth PL8 2LU	01752 881504 info@beckdaleguesthouse.com www.beckdaleguesthouse.com	581 516	3.5 km PD £29.00 O D PL CP KT PD 2D 1T 1S 1F ALL ES PL by prior arrangement, single supplement
58	Mrs J Cross Wood Cottage Bridgend NEWTON FERRERS PL8 1AW	01752 872372 j.cross@homecall.co.uk	555 482	1 km £25.00 O D PL CP DW KT PD 2D 1T/F[1]
58	Mrs S Spooner Rogers Cellars Passage NOSS MAYO PL8 1EU	01752 872771 suespoonerrogers@btinternet.com	534 475	on path £35.00 O D EM PL CP LSP KT PD 1T 1F ALL ES EM by prior arrangement, local PD free, distances charged
58	Mrs J Barnett Revelstoke Coombe Hannaford Road NOSS MAYO PL8 1EJ	01752 872663 mrandmrsbarnett@fsmail.net	546 469	850 mts £35.00 O D PL CP LSP KT PD 3D[1] 1T[1]
58	Mrs J Rogers Worswell Barton NOSS MAYO PL8 1HB	01752 872977 jackierogers1hb@btinternet.com www.worswellbarton.co.uk	537 470	800 mts £35.00 O D PL CP LSP 2D 1T
58	Mrs J Stockman Bugle Rocks The Old School BATTISBOROUGH Holbeton PL8 1JX	01752 830422 01752 830558 stay@buglerock.co.uk www.buglerocks.co.uk	601 473 Mar-Oct	3km access by Mothecombe only £35.00 D PL CP 3D 1T 1F ALL ES single supplement

Sect.	Name and Address	Tel. No. Fax. No. Web / Email	Map Reference Opening Times	Distance from Path Starting Price Facilities Accommodation
58	Mrs L Wallis Windlestraw Penquit ERMINGTON PL21 0LU	01752 698384	646 544	2 km PD £32.00 O D EM PL CP LSP PD KT 1T 1S Will PD Yealm Erme Avon EM by prior arrangement
58	Mr G Smith The Dolphin Inn KINGSTON TQ7 4QE	01548 810314 as phone info@dolphininn.eclipse.co.uk www.dolphin-inn.co.uk	635 478	2km £34.00 O D EM PL CP LSP DW KT PD 2D 1T ALL ES £42.50 single DW & PD by prior arrangement
58	Mrs E Dodds Ayrmer House RINGMORE Nr Kingsbridge TQ7 4HL	01548 810391 isabelladodds@aol.com www.ayrmerhouse.org	651 459	1 km £35.00 O D PL CP LSP KT 2D[2] 1T
58	Mrs K Purdy Ringmore Vean RINGMORE TQ7 4HL	01548 810382 Mobile: 07968 718901 enquiries@ringmorevean.co.uk www.ringmorevean.co.uk	651 459	900 mts £32.50 O D EM CP LSP KT 1D[1] EM by prior arrangement
58	Mr & Mrs M A Farrell Warren Cottage Marine Drive BIGBURY-ON-SEA TQ7 4AS	01548 810210 as phone michaelfarrell1@mypostoffice.co.uk	650 440	On path £25.00 O D EM PL CP LSP DW KT 1T 1S
58	Kim Pritchard & Tony Roberts Summer Winds Marine Drive BIGBURY-ON-SEA TQ7 4AS	01548 810669 pritchard212@btinternet.com	651 443	On path £60.00 price per room O D PL KT 2D 1F ALL ES single supplement
58	Mrs V Walker The Milking Parlour 9 Combe Farm Barns BIGBURY TQ7 4NH	01548 830958 mobile 07745 481894 valerie@themilkingparlour.co.uk	676 487	3 km PD £30.00 O D EM PL CP LSP KT PD 1D/T[1] 1D/T EM by prior arrangement local PD, distances charged
58	Mrs V Alexander Aune Cross Lodge BANTHAM TQ7 3AD	01548 561182	679 443	750 mts £25.00 O D EM PL CP LSP DW 1D[1] 1T EM & PL by arrangement
58	Mrs E Meldrum Meadow Cottage WEST BUCKLAND Kingsbridge TQ7 3AF	01548 560759	681 438	1 km inland from Bantham ferry £27.00 O D PL CP 1T 1S

Sect.	Name and Address	Tel. No. Fax. No. Web / Email	Map Reference Opening Times	Distance from Path Starting Price Facilities Accommodation
58	Mrs E Hanson Rafters Holwell Farm SOUTH HUISH TQ7 3EQ	01548 560460 raftersdevon@yahoo.co.uk www.raftersdevon.co.uk	695 415	2 km £32.50 O D CP DW 2D 1T ALL ES
59	Mrs L Dixon Smiley Lodge 9 Weymouth Park HOPE COVE TQ7 3HD	01548 561946 enquiries@smileylodge.co.uk www.smileylodge.co.uk	680 403	350 mts £35.00 O D PL CP LSP DW KT 2D[1] DW by prior arrangement; KT to Salcombe only
59	Miss S Ireland Tanfield B&B HOPE COVE Kingsbridge TQ7 3HJ	01548 561555 01548 561455 info@hopecove.com www.hopecove.com	675 401 Feb-Dec	On path £25.00 D EM PL LSP DW 5D 2T 1S ALL ES book in at Cottage Hote
59	Miss S Ireland The Cottage Hotel HOPE COVE Kingsbridge TQ7 3HJ	01548 561555 01548 561455 info@hopecove.com www.hopecove.com ·	675 401 Feb-Dec	25 mts £25.00 D EM PL CP LSP DW 26D/T[24] 3S[2] 5F[5]
59	Mr P Brown The Sunbay Hotel INNER HOPE COVE Kingsbridge TQ7 3HH	01548 561371 sunbayhotel@btconnect.com www.sunbayhotel-hopecove.co.uk	676 400 mid Feb-Jan	10 mts £45.00 D EM PL CP DW 11D 3T 2F ALL ES
59	Mr K Makepeace Soar Mill Cove Hotel Soar Mill Cove MALBOROUGH Near Salcombe TQ7 3DS	01548 561566 01548 561223 info@soarmillcove.co.uk www.soarmillcove.co.uk	705 377 Feb-Nov	500 mts £69.00 D EM PL CP LSP DW KT PD 15D/T 6F ALL ES
60	Mr & Mrs R Petty-Brown Rocarno Grenville Road SALCOMBE TQ8 8BJ	01548 842732 rocarno@aol.com www.rocarno.co.uk	736 389	500 mts £27.50 O D PL CP KT 1D 1T ALL ES
60	Mr & Mrs R Vaughan Trennels Herbert Road SALCOMBE TQ8 8HR	01548 842500 trennels@btinternet.com	737 388 Apr-Oct	400 mts £30.00 PL CP LSP 2D 1T ALL ES
60	Mrs P Snelson Waverley Devon Road SALCOMBE TQ8 8HL	01548 842633 paulinesnelson@tiscali.co.uk www.waverleybandb.co.uk	738 388 Mar-Nov	500 mts £30.00 D PL CP KT 2D 3T 1S ALL ES £10 single supplement
60	Mrs E M Weymouth Motherhill Farm Main Road SALCOMBE TQ8 8NB	01548 842552 as phone djweymouth@tiscali.co.uk	730 393 May-Sept	1.5 km £22.00 D CP LSP 1D 1T 1S

Sect.	Name and Address	Tel. No. Fax. No. Web / Email	Map Reference Opening Times	Distance from Path Starting Price Facilities Accommodation
60	Ms A Woodhatch Rainbow's End 11 Platt Close SALCOMBE TQ8 8NZ	01548 843654 annwoodhatch@tiscali.co.uk	730 393	1.5 km £25.00 O D CP LSP KT PD 1D/F 1T ALL ES Single supplement £5-£8 according to season
60	Mrs S Davies Castle Combe Sandhills Road SALCOMBE TQ8 8JP	01548 843361 as phone sueandjohndavies@talktalk.net	731 382	25 mts £38.00 O D PL CP LSP KT 1D 1T[1]
60	Mr & Mrs R Moore Ringstead Coronation Road SALCOMBE TQ8 8EA	01548 842006 rogerhmoore@gmail.com	736 391 Apr-Oct	800 mts £35.00 D CP KT 1D[1] 1T
61	Mr & Mrs R Agar Ashleigh House Ashleigh Road KINGSBRIDGE TQ7 1HB	01548 852893 as phone reception@ashleigh-house.co.uk www.ashleigh-house.co.uk	731 439	6 km £30.00 O D PL CP LSP DW KT 5D 1T 2F ALL ES £10 single supplement
61	Mrs J Foss Down Farm START POINT Kingsbridge TQ7 2NQ	01548 511234 downfarm@btinternet.com www.downfarm.co.uk	806 377	600 mts £30.00 O D EM PL CP LSP KT 1D 1T 1F ALL ES
61	Mrs J Sainthill Lamacraft House START POINT Kingsbridge TQ7 2NG	01548 511291 www.lamacrafthouse.co.uk	813 385	500 mts £30.00 O D PL CP LSP KT 2D[1] 1T 1S
61	Mr & Mrs N Heath The Cricket Inn BEESANDS TQ7 2EN	01548 580215 www.thecricketinn.co.uk	819 402	on path £30.00 O EM PL CP 4D 1F ALL ES
61	Mrs V Johnston Valseph The Green BEESANDS TQ7 2EJ	01548 580650 joseph.johnston@virgin.net www.beesands-bedandbreakfast.co.uk	819 406 Mar-Nov	on path £30.00 CP LSP 1D[1]
61	Ms C Ley Linger Lodge TORCROSS TQ7 2TJ	01548 580599 ley@lingerlodge.co.uk www.lingerlodge.co.uk	822 421	400 mts £38.00 O D CP LSP 3D [3]

Sect.	Name and Address	Tel. No. Fax. No. Web / Email	Map Reference Opening Times	Distance from Path Starting Price Facilities Accommodation
61	Mrs S Webber Kiln House B&B Kiln Lane STOKENHAM TQ7 2SQ	01548 581106 stay@slaptonsands.co.uk www.slaptonsands.co.uk	805 430	2 km PD £30.00 O D PL CP LSP DW KT PD 1T 1F ALL ES
62	Mrs V A Mercer Old Walls SLAPTON Nr Kingsbridge TQ7 2QN	01548 580516	823 449	500mts £30.00 O D PL DW KT PD 1D[1] 1T 1S 1F
62	Mr & Mrs R Gloyn Thorn Park SLAPTON TQ7 2RD	01548 521389 robert@gloyn.eclipse.co.uk	809 475	3.2 km £27.50 O D EM PL CP LSP DW KT PD 1D[1] 1S EM, DW & PD by prior arrangement
62	Mrs J Makepeace Skerries STRETE Nr Dartmouth TQ6 0RH	01803 770775 01803 770950 enquiries@skerriesbandb.co.uk www.skerriesbandb.co.uk	842 470 Mar-Oct	on path £37.50 D PL CP KT 3D[3] No single July-Sept
62	Mr & Mrs C Tonkin Fairholme Bay View Estate STOKE FLEMING Dartmouth TQ6 0QX	01803 770356 As Phone stay@fairholmedartmouth.co.uk www.fairholmedartmouth.co.uk	863 488	100 mts £30.00 O D CP 2D 1T ALL ES £35 single occupancy
62	Mr M Jones Springs Warfleet DARTMOUTH TQ6 9BZ	01803 833514 Mobile: 07773 237685 hellomike@talktalk.net	880 504	100 mts £35.00 O CP 1D 1T[1]
62	Mrs J Wright Camelot 61 Victoria Road DARTMOUTH TQ6 9RX	01803 833805 jjwright@talktalk.net	875 514	500 mts £25.00 O D 2D[1] 1T[1] D room offered as single in low season
62	Miss J Robinson The Maitland 28 Victoria Road DARTMOUTH TQ6 9SA	01803 835854 enquiries@themaitland.co.uk www.themaitland.co.uk	875 513	500 mts £25.00 O D PL CP KT PD 3D[2]
62	Mr & Mrs M Cairns-Sharp Valley House B&B 46 Victoria Road DARTMOUTH TQ6 9DZ	01803 834045 enquiries@valleyhousedartmouth.com www.valleyhousedartmouth.com	872 512	400 mts £30.00 O D PL CP KT 2D 1T ALL ES single supplement

Sect.	Name and Address	Tel. No. Fax. No. Web / Email	Map Reference Opening Times	Distance from Path Starting Price Facilities Accommodation
62	Mr J Hammond & Ms S White Hill View House 76 Victoria Road DARTMOUTH TQ6 9DZ	01803 839372 as phone enquiries@hillviewdartmouth.co.uk www.hillviewdartmouth.co.uk	872 512	1 km £28.50 O CP 3D 2T ALL ES Single supplement starts at £10
62	Mrs C B Roberts Brook House 6 Market Street DARTMOUTH TQ6 9QE	01803 832920	876 514	40 mts £25.00 O D PL CP DW KT PD 1D 1D/T/F ALL ES Single supplement
62	Mr & Mrs A Depledge The Crows Nest 5A Lower Street DARTMOUTH TQ6 9AJ	01803 834323 mobile: 07920 053580 info@crowsnestdartmouth.co.uk www.crowsnestdartmouth.co.uk	878 511	50 mts £25.00 O CP KT 1D/T/S/F single supplement
63	Mrs H Jones Fir Mount House Higher Contour Road KINGSWEAR TQ6 0DE	01803 752943 info@mannafromdevon.com www.mannafromdevon.com	887 512	500 mts £40.00 D PL CP LSP KT 2D[1] 2T 2S[1] 1F
63	Mrs C Haddock Coleton Barton Farm Brownstone Road KINGSWEAR TQ6 0EQ	01803 752795 01803 752241 coletonbartonfarm@emailfarm.co.uk	905 512	250 mts £30.00 O D EM PL CP LSP DW 1D[1] 1T Prior booking essential
63	Mr & Mrs G Sowerby Raddicombe Lodge Kingswear Road HILLHEAD Brixham TQ5 0EX	01803 882125 stay@raddicombelodge.co.uk www.raddicombelodge.co.uk	904 538	2 kms PD £25.00 O D EM PL CP DW KT PD 4D 2T 1S 2F ALL ES EM & LSP by prior arrangement
63	Mr & Mrs B Hammersley Anchorage Guest House 170 New Road BRIXHAM TQ5 8DA	01803 852960 enquiries@brixham-anchorage.co.uk www.brixham-anchorage.co.uk	916 555	1.5 km £27.00 O PL CP KT 4D 2T 1S 1F ALL ES
63	Mr & Mrs K Colby Melville Hotel 45 New Road BRIXHAM TQ5 8NL	01803 852033 melvillehotel@brixham45.fsnet.co.uk www.themelville.co.uk	920 559	500 mts £25.00 O D PL CP 8D 2T 2S 2F ALL ES
63	Mr & Mrs D Satchwill Sampford House 57/59 King Street BRIXHAM TQ5 9TH	01803 857761 sampfordhouse@yahoo.co.uk www.sampfordhouse.com	927 562	40 mts £27.00 O D CP DW KT 4D 1T 1F ALL ES DW by prior arrangement

Sect.	Name and Address	Tel. No. Fax. No. Web / Email	Map Reference Opening Times	Distance from Path Starting Price Facilities Accommodation
63	Mrs L McRae Nods Fold Mudstone Lane BRIXHAM TQ5 9EQ	01803 856138 as phone nodsfold@googlemail.com	931 555	200 mts PD £24.00 O D PL CP LSP KT PD 1D[1]
63	Mrs C Hemus Homeleigh 49 New Road BRIXHAM TQ5 8NL	01803 850781 carol@hemus3926.fsnet.co.uk www.homeleigh-brixham.co.uk	920 559	400 mts £30.00 O D PL CP 2D 1S
63	Mrs J Moore Devon Cottage Higher Furzeham Road BRIXHAM TQ5 8QZ	01803 857501 brixhamroofing@onetel.com	922 567 Mar-Nov	250 mts £25.00 D PL CP LSP KT PD 2D[1]
63	Mrs L Goodwill Midhurst B&B 132 New Road BRIXHAM TQ5 8DA	01803 857331 www.midhurstbnb.co.uk	925 555	400 mts £28.00 O D PL CP 2D[2] 1T[1] 1S PL by prior arrangement
64	Mr & Mrs P Webb Benbows Guesthouse 1 Alta Vista Road Roundham PAIGNTON TQ4 6DB	01803 558128 benbowshotel@btinternet.com www.benbowshotel.co.uk	894 599	100 mts £21.00 O D EM PL CP DW 5D[2] 2T[1] 1S 2F[1] EM & DW by prior arrangement
64	Mrs F Bamford-Dwane The No Smoking Clifton at Paignton 9/10 Kernou Road PAIGNTON TQ4 6BA	01803 556545 as phone freda@cliftonhotelpaignton.co.uk www.cliftonhotelpaignton.co.uk	891 607 Apr-Oct	100 mts £31.00 D EM PL 3D[3] 5T[5] 4S[2] 2F[2]
65	Mr G Adamson & Miss S Coombes The Haute Epine 36 Bampfylde Road TORQUAY TQ2 5AR	01803 296359 gerryhauteepine@tiscali.co.uk www.haute-epineguesthouse.co.uk	907 642	740 mts £20.00 O D EM PL 5D[4] 2T[2] 1S[1] 3F[3]
65	Mr & Mrs D Blenkinsopp Aveland House Aveland Road BABBACOMBE Torquay TQ1 3PT	01803 326622 01803 328940 avelandhouse@aol.com www.avelandhouse.co.uk	921 652	800 mts £32.00 O D EM PL CP LSP KT 4D 2T 2S 2F ALL ES
65	Mrs S Brewer Coastguard Cottage 84 Babbacombe Downs Road BABBACOMBE Torquay TQ1 3LU	01803 311634 Mobile: 07780 661381	927 653	50 mts £25.00 O D PL 1D 1S 1F ALL ES
65	Mr & Mrs R McCoustra The Babbacombe Palms Hotel 2 York Road BABBACOMBE Torquay TQ1 3SG	01803 327087 reception@babbacombepalms.com www.babbacombepalms.com	922 655	300 mts £25.00 O D PL CP DW KT 5D 1T 1S 2F ALL ES

Sect.	Name and Address	Tel. No. Fax. No. Web / Email	Map Reference Opening Times	Distance from Path Starting Price Facilities Accommodation
65	Mrs N Moore Buckingham Lodge Falkland Road TORQUAY TQ2 5JP	01803 293538 01803 290343 stay@buckinghamlodge.co.uk www.buckinghamlodge.co.uk	906 640	1 km £35.00 O D EM PL CP LSP KT 4D 3T 1S 1F ALL ES single supplement in dbl room
65	Ms J Beckett West Wing Ringmore Lodge Salty Lane SHALDON TQ14 0AP	01626 872754 ringmorelodge@hotmail.co.uk www.stayindevon.co.uk	927 722	1.1 km £33.00 O D PL CP KT 1D 1F ALL ES
65	Ms K Drummond Teign Crest The Strand SHALDON TQ14 0DL	01626 873212 katrina@teigncrest.co.uk www.teigncrest.co.uk	934 723	on path £35.00 O D CP KT 1D 1T 1F ALL ES single room on request
65	Mr P Hockings Brunswick House 5 Brunswick Street TEIGNMOUTH TQ14 8AE	01626 774102 info@brunswick-house.com www.brunswick-house.com	941 727	50 mts £27.00 O D PL DW 4D 3T 1S 1F ALL ES DW by arrangement, single supplement
65	Mrs D Loach Coombe Bank Guest House Landscore Road TEIGNMOUTH TQ14 9JL	01626 772369 01626 774159 dianne.loach@btopenworld.com www.coombebankhotel.net	935 732	750 mts £23.50 O D PL CP LSP KT PD 4D[4] 2T[2] 2S[1] 1F[1]
65	Mr & Mrs J Allan Thomas Luny House Teign Street TEIGNMOUTH TQ14 8EG	01626 772976 alisonandjohn@thomas-luny-house.co.uk www.thomas-luny-house.co.uk	939 729	500 mts £49.00 O D CP 2D 2T ALL ES
65	Mrs J Purbrick The Stables 8 Windward Lane HOLCOMBE EX7 0JQ	01626 865363 mike.jackie12@btinternet.com	958 748	100 mts £25.00 O D CP LSP PD 1D/F 1S ALL ES
66	Mrs A Ferris The Blenheim 1 Marine Parade DAWLISH EX7 9DJ	01626 862372 blenheimholidays@btconnect.com www.theblenheim.uk.net	962 765	10 mts £29.00 O D CP DW 3D 3T 1S ALL ES Variable single supplement throughout season
66	Mrs A Timmins Hadleigh House Exeter Road DAWLISH EX7 0BT	01626 864580 anna@attheseaside.co.uk www.attheseaside.co.uk	757 543	On Path £35.00 O D EM PL CP LSP DW 2D 1T

Sect.	Name and Address	Tel. No. Fax. No. Web / Email	Map Reference Opening Times	Distance from Path Starting Price Facilities Accommodation
66	Mr C Maddison & Mr K Chambers The Croft Guest House Cockwood Harbour STARCROSS EX6 8QY	01626 890282 croftcockwood@aol.com www.thecroftcockwood.com	975 808	On Path £35.00 O D PL CP DW 5D 3T ALL ES Single supplement, bird observatory
66	Mr & Mrs G Dawe 24 Highfield Clyst Road TOPSHAM EX3 0DA	01392 874563 geoffdawe50@hotmail.com	965 892	1km PD £25.00 O D PL CP KT PD 1D 1S PD Topsham
66	Mrs C Logan Carberry Lodge 2 Carberry Avenue EXMOUTH EX8 3EH	01395 263869 chris@carberrylodge.co.uk www.carberrylodge.co.uk	002 823	1.8 km PD £33.00 O D PL CP KT PD 1D 1T 1S ALL ES
66	Mrs M Grant Anchoring B&B 106 St Andrew's Road EXMOUTH EX8 1AT	01395 268849 anchoring106@yahoo.co.uk www.anchoringbandb.com	995 806	100 mts £30.00 O D PL KT PD 1D[1] 1T[1] 1S 1F[1]
66	Mrs R Jessen Quentence Farm Salterton Road EXMOUTH EX8 5BW	01395 442733 palleandrose@hotmail.co.uk www.selfcatering-devon.co.uk	038 820	1 km £27.00 O D PL CP LSP DW KT PD 1D[1] 1T[1] 1S 1F[1]
67	Mrs S Freeman 10 Knowle Village BUDLEIGH SALTERTON EX9 6AL	01395 445807	050 825	1.5 km PD £25.00 O D PL CP LSP DW KT PD 1D 1T[1] 1S
67	Mrs H J Simmons Chapter House 6 Westbourne Terrace BUDLEIGH SALTERTON EX9 6BR	01395 444100 janesimmons1952@hotmail.com	059 818	10 mts £30.00 O D KT PD 2D 1T 1S 1F ALL ES
67	Mrs J Duckworth Brambles 2 Moorlands Road BUDLEIGH SALTERTON EX9 6AG	01395 444336 julia@bramblesinbudleigh.co.uk www.bramblesinbudleigh.co.uk	050 822	1 km PD £35.00 O D PL CP PD 2D[1]
67	Mrs H Shiels Hansard House Hotel 3 Northview Road BUDLEIGH SALTERTON EX9 6BY	01395 442773 01395 442475 enquiries@hansardhotel.co.uk www.handsardhousehotel.co.uk	058 818	200 mts PD £45.00 O D PL CP LSP DW KT PD 3D 6T 2S 1F ALL ES KT by prior arrangement
67	Mrs H Morrish Appletree Cottage 23 Victoria Place BUDLEIGH SALTERTON EX9 6JP	01395 445433 hilary@appletreecottagebudleigh.co.uk www.appletreecottagebudleigh.co.uk	061 818	150 mts £25.00 O D PL CP KT 3T[1]

Sect.	Name and Address	Tel. No. Fax. No. Web / Email	Map Reference Opening Times	Distance from Path Starting Price Facilities Accommodation
68	Mrs E Tancock Lower Pinn Farm Peak Hill SIDMOUTH EX10 0NN	01395 513733 liz@lowerpinnfarm.co.uk www.lowerpinnfarm.co.uk	101 868	500 mts £29.00 O D CP LSP DW 1D 1T 1F ALL ES
68	Mrs L Lever Larkstone House 22 Connaught Road SIDMOUTH EX10 8TT	01395 514345	125 878	500 mts £28.00 O D CP DW KT 1D 1S 1F[1]
68	Mr D Leach Newland Guest House Temple Street SIDMOUTH EX10 9BA	01395 514155 mobile: 07855 953739 sheshe@fsmail.net	126 881	500 mts PD £23.00 O D PL CP LSP DW KT PD 2D[2] 2T[1] 1S[1] 1F[1]
68	Mr & Mrs D Haslam Bramley Lodge Guest House Vicarage Road SIDMOUTH EX10 8UQ	01395 515710 haslam@bramleylodge.fsnet.co.uk	127 880 Feb-Nov	650 mts £30.00 D EM CP DW KT 2D[2] 1T[1] 2S[1] 1F[1] EM & DW must be pre-booked
68	Mrs L Vincent The Longhouse Salcombe Hill Road SIDMOUTH EX10 0NY	01395 577973 pvcia@aol.com www.holidaysinsidmouth.co.uk	139 879	600 mts £35.00 O D PL CP LSP KT 2D[2] single supplement
68	Mr & Mrs P Beesley Salcombe Close House Sid Lane SIDMOUTH EX10 9AW	01395 579067 thebeesleybunch@aol.com www.salcombeclosehouse.com	131 885	1 km O D CP PD 2D/T[2]
69	Mr & Mrs C Slaney The Masons Arms BRANSCOMBE EX12 3DJ	01297 680300 01297 680500 reception@masonsarms.co.uk www.masonsarms.co.uk	204 889	400 mts £40.00 O D EM PL CP DW 15D 5T 1F ALL ES single supplement
69	Mr S Gooch Belmont House Clapps Lane BEER EX12 3EN	01297 24415 simongooch12345@aol.com www.belmonthousebedandbreakfast.co.uk	228 892	200 mts £30.00 O D PL CP LSP KT PD 5D 1T ALL ES single supplement
69	Mr & Mrs M White Durham House Fore Street BEER EX12 3JL	01297 20449 durhamhouse@waitrose.com www.durhamhouse.org	227 894	300 mts £28.00 O D PL CP 6D[5] 1T[1] 1F[1] Seasonal CP
69	Mrs H Cartwright The Bay Tree 11 Seafield Road SEATON EX12 2QS	01297 246110 seafield11@tiscali.co.uk www.baytreeguesthouse.co.uk	242 900	250 mts O D PL CP KT 2D[2] 2T[1] 1S 2F[2]

Sect.	Name and Address	Tel. No. Fax. No. Web / Email	Map Reference Opening Times	Distance from Path Starting Price Facilities Accommodation
69	Mrs E D Jordan Lyndhurst Manor Road SEATON EX12 2AQ	01297 23490	244 902	800 mts £26.00 O CP DW 1D 1T 1S
69	Mr & Mrs B Rosewarne Sea Glimpses Burrow Road SEATON EX12 2NF	01297 22664 as phone Mobile 07929 436547 liz@seaglimpses.fsnet.co.uk	250 899	20 mts £35.00 O D CP KT 2D 1T
69	Mrs G Sedgwick Holmleigh House Sea Hill SEATON EX12 2QT	01297 625671 gaynorjones_8@hotmail.co.uk www.holmleighhouse.co.uk	243 900	70 mts £38.00 O D KT 1D/T[1] 1D 1F[1]
70	Mrs P Trezise Stepps House Stepps Lane AXMOUTH EX12 4AR	01297 20679 as phone pattrezise@btinternet.com	260 909 Mar-Oct	500 mts PD £35.00 D PL CP LSP KT PD 1D 1T 1F single supplement
70	Mr & Mrs J MacClements Cobb Arms The Marine Parade LYME REGIS DT7 3JF	01297 443242 cobbarms@lymeregis.com www.cobbarms@lymeregis.com	338 917	10 mts £40.00 O D EM PL DW 3F[3] single supplement
70	Mr & Mrs S Percival Berrydown Highcliff Road LYME REGIS DT7 3EW	01297 444448 shpercival@aol.com	333 920	500 mts £35.00 O D PL CP KT 1D 1T ALL ES KT by prior arrangement
70	Mr & Mrs F Rogers Thatch Uplyme Road LYME REGIS DT7 3LP	01297 442212 thatchbb@btinternet.com www.thatchatlymeregis.co.uk	335 924	3 kms PD £30.00 O D PL CP LSP DW KT PD 1D[1] 1T[1] 1S
70	Mr R Hamon The Nag's Head Silver Street LYME REGIS DT7 3HS	01297 442312 debhamon@aol.com www.nagsheadlymeregis.co.uk	338 922	400 mts £30.00 O D PL DW KT 3D 1T 1S 1F ALL ES possible CP & LSP
70	Mr & Mrs P Howes Albany Guest House Charmouth Road LYME REGIS DT7 3DP	01297 443066 albany@lymeregis.com www.lymeregis.com/albany	344 924	On Path £35.00 O D CP 2D 2T 1S 1F ALL ES
72	Ms C Roberts The Cabin Duck Street CHIDEOCK Bridport DT6 6JR	01297 489573 cathy@cathyroberts.fslife.co.uk www.cabinchideock.com	421 927	1 km £30.00 O D PL CP LSP KT PD 1D 1S ALL ES £5 single supplement

Sect.	Name and Address	Tel. No. Fax. No. Web / Email	Map Reference Opening Times	Distance from Path Starting Price Facilities Accommodation
72	Mr J Taylor Brook Cottage Mill Lane CHIDEOCK Bridport DT6 6JS	01297 489528 jim@chideock.co.uk	423 926	400 mts £35.00 (£41 with full breakfast) O D PL CP 1D 1T 1S ALL ES PL by prior arrangement
72	Mr & Mrs D Scott Warren House CHIDEOCK Bridport DT6 6JW	01297 489996 kathy@warren-house.com www.warren-house.com	419 928	1 km PD £27.50 O D PL CP LSP KT PD 2D 1T 1F ALL ES
72	Mr & Mrs M Kelson Rose Cottage Main Street CHIDEOCK Bridport DT6 6JQ	01297 489994 as phone enquiries@rosecottage-chideock.co.uk www.rosecottage-chideock.co.uk	423 927	1 km £32.50 O D CP KT 1D 1T ALL ES KT by prior arrangement
72	Mrs P Bale Highway Farm West Road BRIDPORT DT6 6AE	01308 424321 as phone bale@highwayfarm.co.uk www.highwayfarm.co.uk	443 928	1.5 km £40.00 O D EM PL CP LSP 1D 1T 1F ALL ES on bus route, self catering also available
72	Mrs G French Eype's Mouth Country Hotel EYPE Bridport DT6 6AL	01308 423300 01308 420033 info@eypesmouthhotel.co.uk www.eypesmouthhotel.co.uk	448 914	400 mts £60.00 O D EM PL CP LSP DW KT PD 12D 3T 2S 1F ALL ES
72	Mr A Hardy Britmead House West Bay Road BRIDPORT DT6 4EG	01308 422941 britmead@talk21.com www.britmeadhouse.co.uk	465 912	500 mts PD £32.00 O D CP DW KT PD 4D 2T 2F ALL ES single supplement
72	Mrs A Munro Southfield Marsh Gate Burton Road BRIDPORT DT6 4JB	01308 458910 angela@southfield-westbay.co.uk www.southfield-westbay.co.uk	467 914	750 mts £40.00 O D PL CP LSP KT 1D 1T 2F ALL ES also self catering
72	Mrs G R Bramah 143 Victoria Grove BRIDPORT DT6 3AG	01308 456617 ramblerrose.bramah@virgin.net	467 934	3km PD £22.00 O D CP LSP KT PD 1T
72	Mrs V A Moore Eggardon View 261 St Andrews Road BRIDPORT DT6 3DU	01308 459001 valamoore@hotmail.com www.roundaboutbritain.co.uk	477 942 Mar-Dec	4 km PD £26.00 D PL CP LSP KT PD 2T[1] 1S

Sect.	Name and Address	Tel. No. Fax. No. Web / Email	Map Reference Opening Times	Distance from Path Starting Price Facilities Accommodation
72	Mrs S Marks Beachcroft B&B 23 Forty Foot Way WEST BAY Bridport DT6 4HD	01308 423604 sue_marks@sky.com www.beachcroftbedandbreakfast.co.uk	461 905 Feb-Dec	100 mts £30.00 D PL CP KT 3D 1T ALL ES PL by prior arrangement
73	Mrs L Comley Bridge Cottage Guest Rooms 87 High Street BURTON BRADSTOCK DT6 4RA	01308 897222 lizcomley@aol.com www.bridgecottagebedandbreakfast.co.uk	487 893	300 mts £30.00 O D PL CP DW KT 2D 1T 1F ALL ES
73	Mr A Overhill The Anchor Inn High Street BURTON BRADSTOCK DT6 4QF	01308 897228 andrewoverhill@hotmail.com www.dorset-seafood-restaurant.co.uk	487 896	1 km £35.00 O D EM CP 1F[1] single supplement
73	Mrs N Millard Blegberry Swyre Road WEST BEXINGTON DT2 9DD	01308 897774 01308 898300 normamillard@aol.com	532 872	400 mts PD £25.00 O D CP LSP KT PD 1D 1F Super views of Lyme Bay PD by prior arrangement
73	Mrs E M Edwards Sea Fret Coast Road PUNCKNOWLE DT2 9DQ	01308 897435 enquiries@seafret.co.uk www.seafret.co.uk	537 874	1 km PD £30.00 O D PL CP LSP DW KT PD 1D 1T ALL ES 100 mts from inland alternative route section 80
73	Mrs S Collier Offley Looke Lane PUNCKNOWLE DT2 9BD	01308 897044 www.offleybb.com	537 887	400 mts £45.00 price per room O CP LSP DW 1D[1] 1T 1S
73	Mrs I Donnelly Cowards Lake Farmhouse 13 West Street ABBOTSBURY DT3 4JT	01305 871421 cowards-lake@btconnect.com	573 853	800 mts £65.00 price per room O D CP LSP DW KT PD 1D 1T ALL ES
73	Mr & Mrs J Cooke Abbey House Church Street ABBOTSBURY DT3 4JJ	01305 871330 info@theabbeyhouse.co.uk www.theabbeyhouse.co.uk	577 852	50 mts £70.00 price per room O CP 3D[2] 2F[2]
73	Mrs L Streets Abbotsbury Tea Rooms 26 Rodden Row ABBOTSBURY DT3 4JL	01305 871143 as phone atr@uwclub.net www.abbotsbury-tearooms.co.uk	578 852	600 mts £35.00 O D PL DW KT 3D[3] 1S £5 single supplement

Sect.	Name and Address	Tel. No. Fax. No. Web / Email	Map Reference Opening Times	Distance from Path Starting Price Facilities Accommodation
73	Mrs P Crockett 21 Rodden Row ABBOTSBURY DT3 4JL	01305 871465 Mobile 07925 350023	579 855	750 mts £25.00 O D 1D 1T
73	Mr & Mrs N Melville Wheelwrights 14 Rodden Row ABBOTSBURY DT3 4JL	01305 871800 suenigel@wheelwrights.co.uk www.wheelwrights.co.uk	577 853	150 mts £35.00 O CP 1D/T[1] single charge £50
73	Mrs C Rawlings 8 West Street ABBOTSBURY DT3 4JT	01305 871882 as phone clarerawlings@sky.com	573 853	1.5 km £25.00 O D EM DW KT 1D 1T
73	Mrs A Martin The Old Fountain 36 Front Street PORTESHAM DT3 4ET	01305 871278 as phone martann981@aol.com	603 860	2 km PD £27.50 O D PL CP KT PD 1D 1T
73	Mr J Parker The Lugger Inn West Street CHICKERELL DT3 4DY	01305 766611 john@theluggerinn.co.uk www.theluggerinn.co.uk	642 806	1 km £30.00 O D EM PL CP LSP KT 7D 2T 5F ALL ES single supplement
73	Mr & Mrs R Hounsell Brambles B&B Seaview Farm Fleet Lane CHICKERELL DT3 4DF	01305 786824	646 795	600 mts £25.00 O D PL CP LSP KT 1D 1S 1F[1]
74	Mr & Mrs J Ramsden Pump Cottage Friar Waddon Road UPWEY DT3 4EW	01305 816002 mobile: 07891 917872 ronjamsden@hotmail.com www.pumpcottagebedandbreakfast.com	652 857	500 mts PD £27.50 O D EM PL CP LSP DW KT PD 2D[1] 1T[1] EM & PL by arrangement, on inland route
75	Mrs M Reay Raven's Worth 8 Wakeham PORTLAND DT5 1HN	01305 820576 mr@wakeham.f9.co.uk www.wakeham.f9.co.uk	694 716	1 km £45.00 O 1D[1] 1T 1F
76	Mrs D Quick Harbour Lights Guest House 20 Buxton Road WEYMOUTH DT4 9PJ	01305 783273 as phone harbourlights@btconnect.com www.harbourlights-weymouth.co.uk	672 779 Mar-Dec	500 mts £30.00 D CP 5D[5] 2T[2] 2S 2F[2]
76	Ms S Arnold Greenwood Guest House 1 Holland Road WEYMOUTH DT4 0AL	01305 775626 enquiries@greenwoodguesthouse.co.uk www.greenwoodguesthouse.co.uk	673 793	1 km PD £28.00 O D PL CP DW KT PD 3D[1] 2T[1] 1F [1] PL & DW by prior arrangement

Sect.	Name and Address	Tel. No. Fax. No. Web / Email	Map Reference Opening Times	Distance from Path Starting Price Facilities Accommodation
76	Mrs O Nurrish Glenthorne Castle Cove 15 Old Castle Road WEYMOUTH DT4 8QB	01305 777281 info@glenthorne-holidays.co.uk www.glenthorne-holidays.co.uk	675 776	on path £45.00 O D CP LSP DW 2D 3T 3S 2F ALL ES
76	Mr M Clark Oaklands Edwardian Guesthouse 1 Glendinning Avenue WEYMOUTH DT4 7QF	01305 767081 stay@oaklands-guesthouse.co.uk www.oaklands-guesthouse.co.uk	678 800	500 mts £30.00 O D EM PL CP LSP 6D[5] 2T[2] 1F[1]
76	Mr Penman Horizon Guest House 16 Brunswick Terrace WEYMOUTH DT4 7RW	01305 784916 info@horizonguesthouse.co.uk www.horizonguesthouse.co.uk	682 799	On path £30.00 O 2D 2T 1S 1F ALL ES
76	Mrs S Leach Sunnyside B&B 15 Brunswick Terrace WEYMOUTH DT4 7SA	01305 786358 as phone sunnysideweymouth@hotmail.co.uk www.sunnysideweymouth.com	682 799	10 mts £25.00 O D DW 1D 1T 3F[3]
76	Mr & Mrs J Green Tara Guesthouse 10 Market Street WEYMOUTH DT4 8DD	01305 766235 lesley_john@btinternet.com www.thetara.co.uk	681 787	1.5 km £26.00 O 3D 1T 2S ALL ES
76	Mr & Mrs Horvath 1 Old Coastguard Cottages OSMINGTON MILLS DT3 6HQ	01305 832663	736 817	20 mts £32.50 O PL CP LSP KT 1D 1S ALL ES
76	Mr & Mrs B Burrill Graybank Main Road WEST LULWORTH BH20 5RL	01929 400256 valandbarrysagarmatha@btinternet.com	822 802 Feb-Nov	500 mts £35.00 D PL CP KT 4D[1] 1T 1S 1F
76	Mrs J Laing Tewkesbury Cottage 28 Main Road WEST LULWORTH BH20 5RL	01929 400561	823 806	700 mts £45.00 O D CP DW 2D[1] 1T
76	Mrs M Caudell Deer Leap 2 Lytchett Lane BOVINGTON BH20 6PA	01929 463355 maggie_caudell@yahoo.co.uk www.deerleap.org.uk	842 880	8 km PD £35.00 single supplement O D CP LSP DW KT PD 1D 1T ALL ES PL by prior arrangement
78	Mrs G Hole Bradle Farm CHURCH KNOWLE Kimmeridge BH20 5NU	01929 480712 01929 481144 info@bradlefarmhouse.co.uk www.bradlefarmhouse.co.uk	930 806	4 km PD £35.00 single supplement O D EM PL CP KT PD 2D 1T ALL ES EM at cafe owned by farm

Sect.	Name and Address	Tel. No. Fax. No. Web / Email	Map Reference Opening Times	Distance from Path Starting Price Facilities Accommodation
78	Mrs S Mitchell Alford House 120 East Street CORFE CASTLE Wareham BH20 5EH	01929 480156 info@alfordhouse.com www.alfordhouse.com	963 816	2 km PD £35.00 single supplement O D PL CP DW KT PD 2D 1D/T ALL ES DW by prior arrangement, local PD
78	Mr D Ensor Chiltern Lodge 8 Newfoundland Close WORTH MATRAVERS BH19 3LX	01929 439337 976 778 mobile: 07906 508125 densor@btopenworld.com www.chilternlodge.co.uk	976 778	1.5 km PD £28.00 O D EM PL CP KT PD 1D 1T
78	Mrs A Styles Langton Manor Farmhouse LANGTON MATRAVERS BH19 3EU	01929 421247 alexstyles999@aol.com www.gocoastal.co.uk	003 789	2 km PD £35.00 O D PL CP KT PD 1F[1]
79	Mr & Mrs D Fegan The Limes SWANAGE BH19 2AE	01929 422664 info@limeshotel.net www.limeshotel.net	033 783	250 mts £36.00 O D PL CP LSP DW KT 2D[2] 4T[4] 4S[1] 3F[3] PL & LSP (low season) by prior arrangement only
79	Mr & Mrs A Preston Sunny Bay House 17 Cluny Crescent SWANAGE BH19 2BP	01929 422650 gill@sunnybay.co.uk www.sunnybay.co.uk	031 784	1 km £25.00 O D CP 1D[1] 1T[1] 1S 1F[1]
79	Mrs K Gibson 93 Kings Road West SWANAGE BH19 1HN	01929 427255 harmonyhouse-swanage@hotmail.com	022 789	800 mts PD £27.50 O D PL KT PD 2D[2] 1T 1S
79	Mr & Mrs M S Cooper Sunny South 118 Kings Road West SWANAGE BH19 1HS	01929 422665 sunnysouth@btinternet.com www.sunnysouth.btinternet.co.uk	023 789	812 mts £25.00 O D PL CP 2D[1] 1D/T[1] PL by prior arrangement
79	Miss L Wall Footsteps 38 Quarry Close SWANAGE BH19 2QY	01929 421441 lou@shojjy.orangehome.co.uk www.swanagefootsteps.com	025 788	1.5 km PD £18.00 no cooked breakfast O D PL CP DW KT PD 1D 1T ALL ES PL by prior arrangement PD more than 5 miles charged
79	Mr & Mrs D Bishop The Old Post Office 4 Ballard Estate SWANAGE BH19 1QZ	01929 422041 david@outwardbound.plus.com www.oldpostofficeswanage.co.uk	032 802	on path £30.00 O D CP LSP KT PD 1D 1T[1]

79	Mr & Mrs M Anderson Danesfort Hotel 3 Highcliffe Road SWANAGE BH19 1LW	01929 424224 031 798 reception@danesforthotel.co.uk www.danesforthotel.co.uk	25 mts £31.00 O D EM PL 3D 2T 1S 2F ALL ES
79	Mrs C Rose Shell Bay Cottage Glebe Estate STUDLAND BH19 3AS	01929 450249 037 817 as phone shellbayrose@btinternet.com www.shellbaycottage.com	500 mts £45.00 O D CP LSP KT PD 1D/T 1F KT & PD by prior arrangement
79	Mrs North The Laurels 60 Britannia Road POOLE BH14 8BB	07837 737368 033 913 info@thelaurelsbandb.com www.thelaurelsbandb.com	3.5 km £38.00 O D CP 3D/T/S/F[2]
79	Mrs S Fox Foxes 13 Sandbanks Road POOLE BH14 8AG	01202 269633 030 914 0871 6613689 sue.fox@foxesbandb.co.uk www.foxesbandb.co.uk	5.5 km £40.00 O D PL CP 2D[2] single supplement

CAMPSITES

A list of campsites has been prepared in path order.

The following letter code is used;

T	=	Toilets	S	=	Showers
G	=	Grocery Shop	CP	=	Car Parking
LSP	=	Long Stay Parking	LY	=	Laundry
O	=	Open All Year	DW	=	Dogs Welcome
KT	=	Kit Transfer	PD	=	Pick Up/Drop

KT - Kit Transfer. A service being offered by some of our accommodation providers is to transfer your kit to your next accommodation. This could prove useful to you. Naturally a fee may be levied for this service.
PD - Pick Up/Drop. This code appears following the distance from the path and denotes a facility whereby your host is prepared to collect and return you to the coast path within reasonable distance. No fee should be charged for this service.
Distance from Path. Please remember these are only approximate and may not be accurate.

The part of the address in CAPITALS is an aid to location; it does not signify the postal town. The extreme left-hand column refers to the appropriate section in the 'Trail Description'; we feel it may help you to find addresses quickly. The amount quoted gives an **indication of the starting rate** per night, and may well rise. If working on a tight budget, it is best to ask first.

Individuals - but we stress **not parties** - usually find no problem in obtaining leave to camp away from official camp sites if they request permission to do so. In fact, our correspondence has many examples of extra kindnesses extended by farmers and others to campers. We would, however, very much emphasize the requesting of permission first. It would be so easy for the thoughtlessness of a few to undo the good relationships of many others built up over some years.

This list is thin in many areas. Suggestions for inclusions in future lists will always be welcome. Information of any new sites should be addressed to the Administrator.

Sect.	Name and Address	Tel. No. Fax. No. Web / Email	Map Ref. Distance from Path	Facilities Starting Price Opening Times
1	Minehead&Exmoor Caravan & Camping Park Porlock Road MINEHEAD TA24 8SW	01643 703074 www.mineheadandexmoorcamping.co.uk	952 458 800 mts	O T S LY G CP LSP DW £5.00 Please telephone for low season availability
1	Holiday Site Manager Camping & Caravan Club Site Hill Road, North Hill MINEHEAD TA24 5LB	01643 704138 www.campingandcaravanningclub.co.uk/minehead	958 471 550 mts	T S LY CP DW £4.50 reservations tel. 0845 1307633 non-members welcome
1	Mr P R Weaver Sparkhayes Farm Camp Site Sparkhayes Lane PORLOCK TA24 8NE	01643 862470 www.porlock.co.uk/camping	886 469 on path	O T S LY G CP LSPDWKT £6.00 Apr to Oct Price per person, on bus route

Sect. Name and Address	Tel. No. Fax. No. Web / Email	Map Ref. Distance from Path	Facilities Starting Price Opening Times
3 Mr & Mrs M Fletcher Newberry Farm Touring Camping Site Woodlands COMBE MARTIN EX34 0AT	01271 882334 01271 882880 relax@newberryvalleypark.co.uk www.newberryvalleypark.co.uk	574 470 500 mts	T S LY G DW £10.00 Easter - End Oct
3 Mr & Mrs A Hill Mill Park Campsite Mill Lane BERRYNARBOR EX34 9SH	01271 882647 millparkdevon@btconnect.com www.millpark.co.uk	558 470 500 mts	T S LY G DW £6.50 one-night only in low season
4 Mrs S Barten Little Meadow Camping Site Lydford Farm WATERMOUTH EX34 9SJ	01271 866862 info@littlemeadow.co.uk www.littlemeadow.co.uk	554 479 100 mts	T S LY G CP LSP DW £4.00
6 Mrs H Lethbridge Damage Barton MORTEHOE EX34 7EJ	01271 870502 info@damagebarton.co.uk www.damagebarton.co.uk	476 457 2 km	T S LY G CP DW £6.00
10 Mr & Mrs R Croslegh Steart Farm Touring Park HORNS CROSS Bideford EX39 5DW	01237 431836 as phone steartenquiries@btconnect.com www.steartfarmtouringpark.co.uk	356 229 1 km	T S LY CP LSP DW £4.00 Easter-30 Sept
11 Mr & Mrs S Hilsdon Hartland Camping Barn Mettaford Farm HARTLAND EX39 6AL	01237 441249 hartlandcampingbarn@hotmail.com www.hartlandcampingbarn.co.uk	279 245 2.5 km	T S LY CP LSP £12.00
12 Mr P Haggarty Upper Lynstone Caravan & Camping Park BUDE EX23 0LP	01288 352017 01288 359034 reception@upperlynstone.co.uk www.upperlynstone.co.uk	204 052 100 mts	T S LY G CP DW £10.50
13 Mr B Heard Lower Pennycrocker Farm BOSCASTLE PL35 0BY	01840 250257 01840 250613 holidays@pennycrocker.fsnet.co.uk www.pennycrocker.com	124 925 500 mts	T S CP LSP DW £5.00
17 Mrs R Harris South Winds Camping & Caravan Park POLZEATH PL27 6QU	01208 863267 01208 862080 info@southwindscampsite.co.uk www.polzeathcamping.co.uk	948 790 2 km	T S LY CP LSP DW Mar to Sept DW on lead at all times

Sect.	Name and Address	Tel. No. Fax. No. Web / Email	Map Ref. Distance from Path	Facilities Starting Price Opening Times
17	Mr R Harris Tristram Caravan & Camping Park POLZEATH PL27 6UG	01208 862215 01208 862080 info@tristramcampsite.co.uk www.polzeathcamping.co.uk	948 790 On path	T S LY G CP LSP DW Mar to Nov DW on lead
18	Mr S Zeal Dennis Cove Camping Ltd Dennis Lane PADSTOW PL28 8DR	01841 532349 denniscove@freeuk.com www.denniscove.co.uk	920 745 500 mts	T S LY CP DW £6.40 Apr - Sept Price for 2 campers
20	Mrs J Raymont Trevean Caravan & Camping Park ST MERRYN PL28 8PR	01841 520772 as phone trevean.info@virgin.net	874 724 1.5 km	T S LY G CP LSP DW £8.00
20	Mrs C Pawley Carnevas Farm Holiday Park PORTHCOTHAN BAY PL28 8PN	01841 520230 as phone carnevascampsite@aol.com www.carnevasholidaypark.co.uk	862 728 800 mts	T S LY G DW £10.00 1 Apr to 31 Oct Price based on 2 people
20	Mr & Mrs J Nederpel Old Macdonald's Farm PORTHCOTHAN BAY PL28 8LW	01841 540829 enquiries@oldmacdonalds.co.uk www.oldmacdonalds.co.uk	867 877 1 km	O T S CP LSP DW £10.00 Also B&B
21	Mrs L Lightfoot Magic Cove Touring Park MAWGAN PORTH TR8 4BZ	01637 860263 magic@magiccove.co.uk www.magiccove.co.uk	850 679 300 mts	T S LY DW £4.00 G 250 mts from site
21	Mr & Mrs S Tavener Sun Haven Valley Holiday Park MAWGAN PORTH TR8 4BQ	01637 860373 sunhaven@sunhavenvalley.com www.sunhavenvalley.com	861 667 1 km	T S LY G CP DW £10.00 Discount for Association members on production of guide book
24	Ms J. Sawle Beacon Cottage Farm Touring Park Beacon Drive ST AGNES TR5 0NU	01872 552347 beaconcottagefarm@lineone.net www.beaconcottagefarmholidays.co.uk	705 505 400 mts	T S LY G CP LSP DW £6.00 Apr to Oct Mobile 07879 413862
24	Mrs P Williams Presingoll Farm Caravan & Camping Park ST AGNES TR5 0PB	01872 552333 as phone pam@presingollfarm.fsbusiness.co.uk www.presingollfarm.co.uk	720 495 1.6 km	T S LY CP LSP DW KT £6.50
28	Miss K Sharps Ayr Holiday Park ST IVES TR26 1EJ	01736 795855 01736 798797 kerry@ayrholidaypark.co.uk www.ayrholidaypark.co.uk	511 405 350 mts	O T S LY CP LSP DW £11.00

Sect.	Name and Address	Tel. No. Fax. No. Web / Email	Map Ref. Distance from Path	Facilities Starting Price Opening Times
30	Mr E J Coak The North Inn PENDEEN Penzance TR19 7DN	01736 788417 ernestjohncoak@aol.com www.thenorthinnpendeen.co.uk	383 344 1 km	O T S CP LSP DW KT £4.00 B&B also, nearby shop
30	Mr & Mrs G Stokes Trevaylor Caravan & Camping Park BOTALLACK Penzance TR19 7PU	01736 787016 trevalor@cornishcamping.co.uk www.cornishcamping.co.uk	370 328 500 mts	T S LY G CP DW £7.00 Apr to Oct
30	Mr & Mrs A Collinson Secret Garden Caravan & Camping Park Bosavern House ST JUST IN PENWITH TR19 7RD	01736 788301 mail@bosavern.com www.secretbosavern.com	371 305 1 km	T S LY CP £14.00 Also B&B
33	Mrs H Gwennap Treverven Campsite Treverven Farm ST LOYE St Buryan TR19 6DG	01736 810200 as phone www.drycor.co.uk/camping/treverven	419 245 800 mts	T S LY G CP LSP DW £7.00
37	Mrs L Matthews Tamarisk RINSEY CROFT Helston TR13 9TW	01736 761937 ladylindy-lou@hotmail.co.uk	602 279 1 km	T S CP LSP £4.00
39	Mr & Mrs R H Lyne Henry's Campsite Caerthillian Farm THE LIZARD TR12 7NX	01326 290596 www.henryscampsite.co.uk	701 125 500 mts PD	O T S LY G CP LSP DW KT PD £7.00 Open all year
45	Mr & Mrs P Walker Treloan Coastal Farm PORTSCATHO TR2 5EF	01872 580989 info@treloancoastalholidays.co.uk www.coastalfarmholidays.co.uk	874 348 300 mts PD	O T S LY CP LSP DW KT £5.00 grocery shop nearby
45	The Holiday Site Manager Veryan Camping & Caravanning Club Site Tretheake VERYAN TR2 5PP	01872 501658 www.campingandcaravanningclub.co.uk/veryan	934 414 1 km	T S LY CP DW £5.70 Reservations 0845 1307633 Non-members welcome
47	Mr J Whetter Trelispen Caravan & Camping Park GORRAN HAVEN PL26 6NT	01726 843501 as phone trelispen@care4free.net www.trelispen.co.uk	005 421 1 km	T S LY CP DW £10.00

Sect.	Name and Address	Tel. No. Fax. No. Web / Email	Map Ref. Distance from Path	Facilities Starting Price Opening Times
52	Mr & Mrs K Cox Polruan Camping & Caravanning POLRUAN PL23 1QH	01726 870263 as phone polholiday@aol.com www.polruanholidays.co.uk	132 507 250 mts	T S LY G CP DW £5.00
52	Ms S Erskine Highertown Farm Campsite LANSALLOS PL13 2PX	01208 265211 highertownfarmcampsite@nationaltrust.org www.nationaltrust.org.uk	173 516 800 mts	T S LY DW £10.00 mobile 07980 600851
52	Mrs J Williams Great Kellow Caravan & Campsite POLPERRO PL13 2QL	01503 272387 as phone kellow.farm@virgin.net www.bestofsecornwall.co.uk	200 521 500 mts	T S CP LSP DW £5.00
53	Mr D Byers Polborder House Caravan & Campsite Bucklawren Road ST MARTIN Looe PL13 1NZ	01503 240265 reception@peaceful-polborder.co.uk www.peaceful-polborder.co.uk	283 555 2 km	OT S LY G CP LSP DW £10.00 £10 per couple, DW by prior arragement
53	Mr S R Cox Camping Caradon Park Trelawne LOOE PL13 2NA	01503 272388 01503 272858 enquiries@campingcaradon.co.uk www.campingcaradon.co.uk	542 218 2.4 km	O T S LY G DW £10.00 Nov-Mar booking essential
58	Mr J Tucker Mount Folly Farm BIGBURY ON SEA TQ7 4AR	01548 810267 as phone chris.cathy@goosemoose.com www.bigburyholidays.co.uk	661 447 on path	O T S CP LSP DW £5.00 Open All Year
60	Mrs S M Squire Higher Rew Camping Park MALBOROUGH Kingsbridge TQ7 3DW	01548 842681 01548 843681 enquiries@higherrew.co.uk www.higherrew.co.uk	714 382 1.5 km	T S LY G CP DW £6.00 Easter-end Oct
62	Holiday Site Manager Camping & Caravanning Club Middle Grounds SLAPTON TQ7 1QW	01548 580538 www.campingandcaravanningclub.co.uk/ slaptonsands	825 450 400 mts	T S LY CP DW £5.70 Reservations Tel: 0845 130 7633 non-members welcome
65	Mrs A Mann Long Meadow Farm Combe Road Ringmore SHALDON TQ14 0EX	01626 872732 01626 872323 anne@longmeadowfarm.co.uk www.longmeadowfarm.co.uk	922 721 2 kms	T S CP LSP DW £10.00 Also self catering

Sect.	Name and Address	Tel. No. Fax. No. Web / Email	Map Ref. Distance from Path	Facilities Starting Price Opening Times
66	Mr A Bulpin Leadstone Camping Warren Road DAWLISH EX7 0NG	01626 864411 post@leadstonecamping.co.uk www.leadstonecamping.co.uk	974 782 800 mts	T S LY G CP DW £6.50
67	The National Trust Prattshayes Farmhouse Maer Lane EXMOUTH EX8 5DB	01395 276626 as phone	025 807 1.5 km	T S G CP DW £4.00
68	Mr A Franks Oakdown Caravan Park WESTON Sidmouth EX10 0PT	01297 680387 01297 680541 enquiries@oakdown.co.uk www.oakdown.co.uk	167 902 2 km	T S LY G CP DW £12.70 Apr to Oct
69	Mr N Hook Salcombe Regis Caravan & Camping Park SALCOMBE REGIS EX10 0JH	01395 514303 01395 514314 contact@salcombe-regis.co.uk www.salcombe-regis.co.uk	151 892 1.5 km	T S LY G CP DW £11.00 15 Apr - 28 Oct
71	Mr R Loosmore Manor Farm Holiday Centre CHARMOUTH DT6 6QL	01297 560226 enq@manorfarmholidaycentre.co.uk www.manorfarmholidaycentre.co.uk	368 937 500 mts	O T S LY G CP LSP DW £12.00 Open All Year £19 high season price
72	Mr M J Cox Golden Cap Holiday Park Seatown CHIDEOCK DT6 6JX	01308 422139 01308 425672 holidays@wdlh.co.uk www.wdlh.co.uk	425 919 200 mts	T S LY G DW £13.70
72	Mr & Mrs M Cox Highlands End Holiday Park EYPE Bridport DT6 6AR	01308 422139 01308 425672 holidays@wdlh.co.uk www.wdlh.co.uk	453 916 100 mts	T S LY G DW £10.50 Mar to Nov
73	Mr R Condliffe Freshwater Beach Holiday Park BURTON BRADSTOCK Nr Bridport DT6 4PT	01308 897317 01308 897336 enquiries@freshwaterbeach.co.uk www.freshwaterbeach.co.uk	898 479 on path	T S LY G CP 17 Mar - 12 Nov
76	Durdle Door Holiday Park C/O Lulworth Castle Estate Office EAST LULWORTH Wareham BH20 5QS	01929 400200 01929 400260 durdle.door@lulworth.com www.lulworth.com	811 811 800 mts	T S LY G CP DW £10.00 Also static caravans

Sect.	Name and Address	Tel. No. Fax. No. Web / Email	Map Ref. Distance from Path	Facilities Starting Price Opening Times
78	Mrs L Lawrence Swanage Coastal Park Priestway SWANAGE BH19 2RS	01590 648331 01590 645610 holidays@shorefield.co.uk www.shorefield.co.uk	019 785 1 km	T S LY CP DW £9.50 Also self-catering
78	Mr & Mrs J Wootton Toms Field Campsite & Shop Toms Field Road SWANAGE BH19 3HN	01929 427110 As Phone tomsfield@hotmail.com www.tomsfieldcamping.co.uk	995 785 1.5 km	T S LY G CP LSP DW £6.00 Mid Mar to Oct Walkers barn also available open all year
78	Mrs J M Scadden Ulwell Cottage Caravan Park ULWELL Swanage BH19 3DG	01929 422823 01929 421500 enq@ulwellcottagepark.co.uk www.ulwellcottagepark.co.uk	022 807 3 km	T S LY G CP DW £6.50 1 Mar - 7 Jan

YOUTH HOSTELS

There is an amazing variety of Youth Hostels along the South West Coast Path, 21 in total and all offering comfortable, friendly accommodation. Prices start from £8.95 (U18) £11.95 (Adult) per night, including bed linen, the use of self-catering kitchens, drying rooms and cycle sheds. The YHA is a membership organisation, however non-members are welcome to join on arrival at the hostel. Membership enables you to take advantage of more than 4000 Youth Hostels world wide, and discounts at with online and high street retailers and local tourist attractions. YHA annual membership costs are currently: Under 26 - £9.95, individual - £15.95 and family (2 adults & children) - £22.95. The meals are excellent value, at around £4.65 for breakfast, Packed Lunches £4.50 to £5.50 and Evening Meals are also available.

Book directly with the Youth Hostel of your choice or for further assistance, please contact YHA Customer Services, Tel: 01629 592700, or why not visit their website at www.yha.org.uk

YHA, Trevelyan House, Dimple Road, Matlock, Derbyshire, DE4 3YH.
E-mail: customerservices@org.uk.

YOUTH HOSTELS

Minehead					
Alcombe Combe	MINEHEAD	TA24 6EW	Phone:0870 770 5968	Grid Ref: 973 442	
Elmscott					
Hartland	HARTLAND	EX39 6ES	Phone:01237 441276	Grid Ref: 231 217	Self Catering Only
Boscastle					
Palace Stables	BOSCASTLE	PL35 0HD	Phone:0845 371 9006	Grid Ref:098 913	
Tintagel					
Dunderhole Point	TINTAGEL	PL34 0DW	Phone:0870 770 6068	Grid Ref: 047 881	Self Catering Only
Treyarnon Bay					
Tregonnan Treyarnon	PADSTOW	PL28 8JR	Phone:0870 770 6076	Grid Ref: 859 741	
Perranporth					
Droskyn Point	PERRANPORTH	TR6 0GS	Phone:0870 770 5994	Grid Ref: 752 544	Self Catering Only
Portreath Bunkhouse	PORTREATH	TR16 4QX	Phone:01209 842244	Grid Ref: 669 444	
Land's End					
Letcha Vean	ST JUST	TR19 7NT	Phone:0870 770 5906	Grid Ref: 364 305	
Penzance					
Castle Horneck, Alverton	PENZANCE	TR20 8TF	Phone:0870 770 5992	Grid Ref: 457 302	
Lizard Lighthouse					
The Lizard	HELSTON	TR12 7NT	Phone: 0870 770 6120	Grid Ref: 051 495	Self Catering Only
Coverack					
Park Behan, School Hill	HELSTON	TR12 6SA	Phone:0870 770 5780	Grid Ref: 782 184	
Boswinger	GORRAN	PL26 6LL	Phone:0870 770 5712	Grid Ref: 991 411	Breakfast Only
Golant					
Penquite House, Golant	FOWEY	PL23 1LA	Phone:0870 770 5832	Grid Ref: 116 556	
Salcombe					
Sharpitor	SALCOMBE	TQ8 8LW	Phone:0870 770 6016	Grid Ref: 728 374	
River Dart					
Maypool House, Galmpton	BRIXHAM	TQ5 0ET	Phone:0870 770 5962	Grid Ref: 877 546	
Exeter					
47 Countess Wear Road	EXETER	EX2 6LR	Phone:0870 770 5826	Grid Ref: 941 897	
Beer					
Bovey Combe, Townsend	SEATON	EX12 3LL	Phone:0870 770 5690	Grid Ref: 223 896	
Litton Cheney					
Litton Cheney	DORCHESTER	DT2 9AT	Phone:0870 770 5922	Grid Ref: 548 900	Self Catering Only
Lulworth Cove					
School Lane	WEST LULWORTH	BH20 5SA	Phone:0870 770 5940	Grid Ref: 832 806	
Portland					
Hardy House, Castletown	PORTLAND	DT5 1BJ	Phone:0870 770 6000	Grid Ref: 685 741	Self Catering Only
Swanage					
Cluny Crescent	SWANAGE	BH19 2BS	Phone:0870 770 6058	Grid Ref: 031 785	

TOURIST INFORMATION CENTRES

MINEHEAD	17 Friday Street		TA24 5UB	Phone: 01643 702624	Fax: 01643 707166
LYNTON	Town Hall	Lee Road	EX35 6BT	Phone: 01598 752225	Fax: 01598 752755
COMBE MARTIN	Sea Cottage	Cross Street	EX34 0DH	Phone: 01271 883319	Fax: 01271 883319
ILFRACOMBE	The Landmark	The Sea Front	EX34 9BX	Phone: 01271 863001	Fax: 01271 862586
WOOLACOMBE	The Esplanade		EX34 7DL	Phone: 01271 870553	
BRAUNTON	The Bakehouse Centre	Caen Street	EX33 1AA	Phone: 01271 816400	Fax: 01271 816947
BARNSTAPLE	36 Boutport Street		EX31 1RX	Phone: 01271 375000	Fax: 01271 374037
BIDEFORD	Victoria Park	The Quay	EX39 2QQ	Phone: 01237 477676	Fax: 01237 421853
BUDE	Visitor Centre	The Crescent	EX23 8LE	Phone: 01288 354240	Fax: 01288 355769
PADSTOW	Red Brick Building	North Quay	PL28 8AF	Phone: 01841 533449	Fax: 01841 532356
PENZANCE	Station Road		TR18 2NF	Phone: 01736 362207	
FALMOUTH	11 Market Strand	Prince of Wales Pier	TR11 3DF	Phone: 01326 312300	Fax: 01326 313457
FOWEY	5 South Street		PL23 1AR	Phone: 01726 833616	Fax: 01726 833616
ST IVES	The Guildhall	Street an Pol	TR26 2DS	Phone: 01736 796297	Fax: 01736 798309
MEVAGISSEY	St. George's Square	Mevagissey	PL26 6UB	Phone: 01726 844857	Fax: 01726 844 857
LOOE	The Guildhall	Fore Street	PL13 1AA	Phone: 01503 262072	Fax: 01503 265426
PLYMOUTH	Plymouth Mayflower	3-5 The Barbican	PL1 2LR	Phone: 01752 306330	Fax: 01752 257955
IVYBRIDGE	The Watermark		PL21 0SZ	Phone: 01752 897035	
SALCOMBE	Council Hall	Market Street	TQ8 8DE	Phone: 01548 843927	Fax: 01548 842736
DARTMOUTH	The Engine House	Mayors Avenue	TQ6 9YY	Phone: 01803 834224	Fax: 01803 835631
KINGSBRIDGE	The Quay		TQ7 1HS	Phone: 01548 853195	Fax: 01548 854185
BRIXHAM	The Old Market House	The Quay	TQ5 8TB	Phone: 01803 852861	Fax: 01803 852939
TORQUAY	Vaughan Parade		TQ2 5JG	Phone: 01803 297428	Fax: 01803 214885
PAIGNTON	The Esplanade		TQ4 6ED	Phone: 01803 558383	Fax: 01803 551959
TEIGNMOUTH	The Den	Sea Front	TQ14 8BE	Phone: 01626 215666	Fax: 01626 778333
DAWLISH	The Lawn		EX7 9EL	Phone: 01626 215665	Fax: 01626 865985
EXMOUTH	Alexandra Terrace		EX8 1NZ	Phone: 01395 222299	Fax: 01395 269911
BUDLEIGH SALTERTON	Fore Street		EX9 6NG	Phone: 01395 445275	Fax: 01395 442208
SIDMOUTH	Ham Lane		EX10 8XR	Phone: 01395 516441	Fax: 01395 519333
SEATON	The Underfleet		EX12 2TB	Phone: 01297 21660	Fax: 01297 21689
LYME REGIS	Guildhall Cottage	Church Street	DT7 3BS	Phone: 01297 442138	Fax: 01297 443773
BRIDPORT	47 South Street		DT6 3NY	Phone: 01308 424901	Fax: 01308 421060
WEYMOUTH	King's Statue	The Esplanade	DT4 7AN	Phone: 01305 785747	Fax: 01305 788092
SWANAGE	The White House	Shore Road	BH19 1LB	Phone: 01929 422885	Fax: 01929 423423
WAREHAM	Trinity Church	South Street	BH20 4LU	Phone: 01929 552740	Fax: 01929 554491
POOLE	Tourism Centre	The Quay	BH15 1BW	Phone: 01202 253253	Fax: 01202 684531

SOUTH WEST COAST PATH ASSOCIATION - HISTORY

We are sometimes asked what we have achieved and have set out below some of the things in which we have been involved in one way or another. We do as well send a steady flow of reports on path deficiencies, both as regards maintenance and the route of the path to the local authorities and the Natural England and the South West Coast Path Team.

1973   Official Formation in May.
Attendance Cornish Opening at Newquay.
First Information Sheets produced.

1974   Attendance at South Devon and Dorset Opening in September at Beer.
Registration as a Charity.
First Description issued.

1975   Mark Richard's book 'Walking the North Cornwall Coastal Path' published - a work in which we may fairly say we played a part.
Clematon Hill, Bigbury, small new section of Coast Path agreed at SWWA's instigation.
Attendance at Opening of so-called Exmoor Coastal Path.
Bideford Public Enquiry - successful opposition to Golf Course on the Coastal Path at Abbotsham.
Hartland Point   Success in getting path south from Hartland Point over Blagdon and Upright Cliffs.
Lulworth walk the new Range Coast Path.

1976   First Footpath Guide issued.
Thurlestone Diversion opposed.
North Cliffs Improvements between Portreath and Hayle secured, thanks to National Trust.
Kingswear Public Enquiry with R.A. on the section Kellys Cove to Man Sands.
Watermouth Consulted by Devon County Council.
Abbotsbury Consulted by Dorset County Council.

1977   Publications of Letts Guides in three volumes. The first satisfactory books to whole path.
Attendance at Coverack Youth Hostel official opening.
Evidence presented to Lord Porchester's Exmoor Study.
Badges produced.
Evidence given to Devon County Council for Taw/Torridge Estuary Survey.

1978   First Printed Footpath guide.
Westward Ho! Attendance at Somerset/North Devon Opening.
Dean Quarry, St Keverne, Cornwall Opposition to diversion.
Pentewan Lack of Path submitted to Local Ombudsman.
Hartland New path seaward of Radar Station obtained, thanks to South West Way Association.

1979   Evidence given at Public Enquiries at Abbotsbury and Lulworth Cove.
Submission to Mr Himsworth for his report on Areas of Outstanding Natural Beauty.
First printed News Letters and Descriptions, and the first illustrated description.
Pine Haven to Port Quin gap submitted to Local Ombudsman.

1980   Result of 1976 Public Enquiry at Kingswear published.
Discussion about Dean Quarry route, St Keverne, Cornwall.
Dialogues with Countryside Commission about path deficiencies.
Alternative coastal path open Glenthorne Estate, Somerset and we submit proposals for rerouting in Exmoor National Park.
St Loy, Cornwall Special report submitted.
Widmouth Head Attendance at Public Enquiry.
Opinions expressed to Department of Environment on draft 'Wildlife and Countryside Bill'.

1981   **Kingswear** Attendance at second Public Enquiry.
Countryside Commission decide that path wardenship will be greatly extended.
Duckpool, North Cornwall Bridge provided.
Path improvements at Watermouth; Braunton to Barnstaple; Dean Quarry; Clematon Hill; Bigbury; Mothecombe and Maidencombe.

1982   Wardenship of coastal path in Cornwall completed.
Further openings at: Cleave Farm in North Cornwall, Pentewan and Mount Edgcumbe in South Cornwall, Higher Brownstone Farm, Kingswear and a short section west of Berry

Head in South Devon.
Agreement was also reached for a high tide route at Mothecombe in South Devon.

1983   Opening of the Widmouth Head section in North Devon and a second long section in South Devon between Kingswear and Man Sands.
Crackington Haven, North Cornwall Major improvements to the path on the western side.

1984   **New Section** A new section of the path opened on the east bank of the mouth of the River Dart close to Kingswear and giving access to Mill Bay Cove and a splendid stretch of coastal walking.
Trebarwith Strand to Backways Cove in North Cornwall A coastal route opened.

1985   **Culbone - Foreland Point** The alternative Coast Path at the Glenthorne Estate was waymarked as the official route.
Pinehaven - Port Quin (North Cornwall) The new path was opened and is a vast improvement.

1986   **Minehead to Porlock Weir** New alternative path between North Hill and Hurlstone Point signposted and waymarked.
Black Head, Cornwall Now purchased by the National Trust thus allowing a coastal route.

1987   **Barnstaple/Bideford/Northam** The new route completed along the railway lines and open.
Bude Attendance at Public Enquiry to prevent development adjacent to footpath.
Chynhalls Point Coast Path moved to seaward of hotel.
Branscombe Attendance at Public Enquiry to urge true coast path instead of inland route. Preferred route adopted.
Bidna/Northam Owing to breach in sea wall an acceptable diversion is negotiated.

1988   **Woody Bay to Trentishoe** Devon County Council adopts our recommended, nearer the coast route as the official Coast Path.

1989   **Culbone** On site exploration with Countryside Commission and Exmoor National Park Authority to discover an acceptable alternative to the long unnecessary Culbone diversion.
Chynhalls Cliff On site exploration for a more coastal trail.
Fire Beacon Point/Pentargon Cornwall County Council installs new path.
Wembury Attend public meeting at Down Thomas to successfully oppose erection of locked gates across Coast Path by Royal Navy.
Strete Gate/Warren Cove Attend public meeting and give evidence to support proposals by Countryside Commission and Devon County Council for an improved and more true Coast Path.

1990   **Membership** Now over 1000.

1991   **Buckator** At our request Cornwall County Council re-route official path around the headland.
Worthy/Culbone On site explorations for a preferable diversion to that proposed by Exmoor National Park Authority.
Strete Gate/Warren Cove Continuing our strong argument with Devon County Council for a Coast Path.
Lyme Regis Continued pleas to Dorset County Council to reinstate the Coast Path along the golf course.
We estimate the Coast Path to be about 613 miles (982 km) long.

1992   **Watcombe and Maidencombe** Our recommended route put in by Devon County Council.
Worthygate Wood Our suggested path installed by National Trust.
Commenced discussions with Countryside Commission to examine sections of coast suitable for 'Set Aside' under the new european agricultural rules.

1993   **Foreland Point** Successful opposition to an application to close path on west side.
Buck's Mills Success with our request for a Coast Path avoiding the holiday complex.
Port Quin Our suggested path is installed by National Trust.
Write and produce the `trail description' in this book the 'Other Way Round' for those walking Poole to Minehead.

1994   Invited by the Countryside Commission to become a member of the South West Coast Path Steering Group to review the management of our Coast Path.

1995 Membership reaches 2000

Culbone section re-opened by Exmoor National Park.

Strete Gate/Warren Point - continuous pressure causes Devon County Council to explore again for a route that will provide an acceptable Coast Path.

Continuing involvement in the 'Coast Path Project'.

Association details on the Internet. See Web address on page 2.

1996 Path descriptions for the whole SWW written and printed.

Continuing involvement in the Coast Path Project and production of the strategy document.

Lyme Regis - Golf Course Route reinstated by Dorset County Council.

Strete Gate/Warren Point - Devon County Council decides to install our preferred route but rejected by Countryside Commission.

1997 **Red River at Gwithian** A new footbridge put in by Cornwall County Council.

The SWCP Project published its strategy for the future management of the Coast Path.

The Association becomes a member of the SWCP Management Group.

1998 Our Silver Jubilee Year (25 years old). Application made, jointly with Ramblers' Association to Minister for the Environment requesting he use his powers to create a Coast Path between Strete Gate and Warren Point. Application refused.

Mount Batten Point, Plymouth opened as a Coast Path.

Jennycliff Plymouth City Council installs an off-road Coast Path.

South West Way Association launches its Silver Jubilee Appeal to raise funds towards markers at each end of the Coast Path.

South West Way Association produces a Development Plan for the next three years.

1999 Name changed to South West Coast Path Association.

Continued involvement with celebratory markers at each end of the Coast Path.

A history of the Coast Path written by Philip Carter and published.

2000 Global Positioning reveals the length of the Coast Path (1014 km - 630 miles) from Minehead to Poole - it is Britain's only National Trail to exceed 1000 km.

Strete Gate / Warren Point - South West Coast Path Team undertakes a complete review of this section.

St German's Beacon - progress made in realising an acceptable Coast Path.

Crock Pits - Exmoor National Park installs a coastal route sought by us for many years.

Revised Path Descriptions now produced in-house.

2001 Eight Winter Cliff Falls Disrupt Line of Dorset Coast Path.

Celebratory marker installed at Minehead.

Whole Coast Path closed for 3 months due to Foot and Mouth Crisis.

11 August - Whole Coast Path walked on one day by Association members to celebrate the re-opening of the Coast Path.

Countryside Agency Board accept the review by the South West Coast Path Team that recommends vital Coast Path realignments between Strete Gate and Stoke Fleming.

2002 Celebratory marker installed at South Haven Point, Poole Harbour.

St German's Beacon - True coastal route installed between Downderry & Portwrinkle due to work done by Chris monk and his County Council team.

2003 **South West Coast Path Association** is 30 years of age.

Easter Saturday - Association arranges 'Walk the whole path in one day' to celebrate the 25th anniversary of the official inclusion of the Somerset and North Devon sections into the South West Coast Path. The 70 sections all had walkers, 668 took part.

3000th Member – Rebecca Emery aged 13 years of Penzance

Youngest Yet – we receive news that Sarah Britton and Anna Radford, both aged 11, have completed the whole Coast Path.

Chynhalls Cliff – South West Coast Path Association's desired realignment is installed by Cornwall County Council.

Strete Gate to Warren Point – Countryside Agency accepts and agrees to fund the negotiated realignment.

Isle of Portland – Countryside Agency accepts the route around the Island.

Tregantle Cliff – South West Coast Path Association's desired realignment throughout the rifle ranges is installed by the MoD as a permissive path. As a result of this improvement, we award the MoD our Annual Award.

2004 **Strete Gate to Warren Point** – on site works on Coast Path realignment starts.
Membership reaches 3500.
Annual award presented to National Trust's Countryside Manager, Brian Muelaner, and his volunteers for their work at Lansallos.

2005 **Strete to Stoke Fleming** – realigned Coast Path opened.
Wembury Point – South West Coast Path Association donates £1000 to National Trust fundraising to buy this land.
4000th Member – Chairman Bryan Cath and Sir Ian Amory make presentations to Frank Hawley of Cromford, Derbyshire.
Association Logo – new logo created by Malt Design adopted by South West Coast Path Association.
South West Coast Path History – Association writes and produces history of Coast Path and the Association.

2006 After 33 years in members' homes, our Administration department moves to new office accommodation at Lee Mill, Devon.
Our first Association calendar is produced.
Cain's Folly – Coast Path reinstated after 6 years of an unsatisfactory diversion.

2007 **Minehead - Porlock Marsh - Thatcher Point** – Association's requested realignments installed.
Watermouth – Major funding pledged by South West Coast Path Association for Coast Path realignment off road.
Porthallow – Design and artists chosen for the halfway marker.
DEFRA – South West Coast Path Association responds to proposals from DEFRA relating to coastal access.

2008 A questionaire about the Coast Path and the Association sent to all members. 68 % responded.
Association On-Line Shop opened.
5000th Member - Chairman Bryan Cath and Ian Liddle-Grainger MP made a presentation to Jill Fletcher, of Portishead, at the Minehead Coast Path marker.

2009 Honorary Secretary, Eric Wallis, listed in New Year's Honours, to receive MBE for his voluntary service to this registered charity.
Porthallow Halfway marker unveiled in May by Andrew George MP.

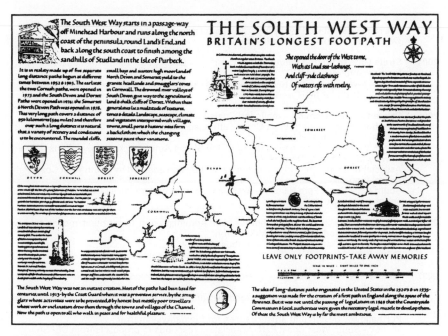

A CALLIGRAPHIC MAP OF THE SOUTH WEST COAST PATH

This quality produced calligraphic map of the South West Coast Path, Britain's longest footpath was designed, illustrated and written by James Skinner of Gloucester. He is a keen rambler and member of a number of walking organisations including the South West Coast Path Association and the Ramblers' Association.

The printed calligraphic map has been written entirely by hand complemented by fine pen and ink drawings illustrating many of the sights to be found whilst walking the path.

The **COLOUR** indicating the relief of the peninsular was achieved through using professional quality colour pencils. James has been interested in calligraphy since the mid 1980s when he attended a local summer school. In 1991 he completed a full-time professional course in Calligraphy and Book-binding at Digby Stuart College, London. This calligraphic map would make a superb gift, or an ideal memento for anyone having walked part or all of the path.

For every map ordered a donation will be made to the South West Coast Path Association - please mention this Guide when applying.

Overall size (approximately) 560 mm deep x 760 mm wide or 22 inches x 30 inches
Image size: 464 mm deep x 675 mm wide or 18.5 inches x 26.5 inches

ALL PRICES ARE INCLUSIVE OF POSTAGE AND PACKING

Calligraphic Map UK £10.95 EUROPE €18 USA $25

Other overseas countries excluding Europe and USA £14.50
(PAYABLE BY STERLING DRAFT DRAWN ON A LONDON BANK)
Please contact James Skinner at 49, Appleton Way, Hucclecote, Gloucester, GL3 3RP.

T: 01452 611614 E: jamesskinnercalligrapher@hotmail.com

View map at www.jamesskinnercalligrapher.co.uk

OFFA'S DYKE PATH - A MONUMENTAL TRAIL

Walkers on the Offa's Dyke Path glimpse the sea only twice as they progress from Sedbury Cliffs on the Severn estuary to Prestatyn on Liverpool Bay, or vice versa. In between their first and last day, however, they pass through a very varied landscape as they follow the approximate historic border of England and Wales. Unspoilt moorland, rolling hills and farmland are crossed by the path between the tourist areas of the Wye Valley and the North Wales coast. Across the plains of Gwent, over the Black Mountains, the river valleys of Radnor, the Severn and Dee valleys, the limestone hills round Llangollen and the Clwyddian ridges; the list of varied attractions is long. For nearly half the route, the Offa's Dyke ancient monument is a silent companion, sometimes almost eroded away, but at others an impressive 6.5 yards (6 m) from ditch to the bank top as the earthwork rolls across the hills of the Clun area. Many ancient hill-forts, castles and abbeys lie on or near the route whose 177 miles (285 km) can be covered in a week, although most visitors will prefer a longer period in which to absorb its varied attractions.

Offa's Dyke Association was formed in 1969 as a pressure group to press for the establishment of the trail. When the route was officially opened in 1971, the Association continued its voluntary work by providing information services to walkers in the form of 'strip maps', route notes, guide books and its 'Where to Stay' accommodation and camping booklet. Pressure group activities continued to ensure the maintenance of the route, as its system of volunteers watched over lengths of the path.

Since 1982 the trail has been maintained by a professional service for which the Association lobbied. This has developed into the 'Offa's Dyke Management Service' financed by the Countryside Council for Wales and the Countryside Agency through Powys and Shropshire County Councils. ODA helps this body, with whom it shares premises at the recently opened Offa's Dyke Centre at Knighton, whilst also continuing to support walkers, run the Knighton TIC, and provide educational services based on the Offa's Dyke Interpretive Exhibition.

For details of membership and services offered, contact Offa's Dyke Association, West Street, Knighton, Powys, LD7 1EN. Tel: 01547 528753. E-mail oda@offasdyke.demon.co.uk Website: www.offasdyke.demon.co.uk

Next Year's Updated Annual Guide

South West Coast Path Association Membership 2011

You may be one of those who have either bought this book from us or at a book shop. You can guarantee receipt of next year's updated, revised edition next March by joining the Association.

We, all volunteers, will update every section of this book, now in your hands, ready for a mail-out to members at the end of February 2011.

Membership rates are: Single UK £12.50; Joint UK £14.00; Non UK £19.00; Single Life £190.00; Joint Life £210.00.

Membership Application Form

I wish to join the South West Coast Path Association for the year 2011:

Name(s) ....

Address ....

....Post Code ....

Telephone: .... e-mail ....

Payment Details:

Payment made by:

☐ Cheque ☐ Amex ☐ Visa/Mastercard ☐ Maestro

Valid from _____ / _____ Expiry _____ / _____ Issue No. _____

Insert card Number _____

Last 3 digits on the reverse of the card _____

Gift Aid

Under the Gift Aid Scheme the Association can reclaim the income tax paid on any donation or membership subscription received, provided you are a UK tax payer. If you would like to help us in this way then please indicate below and sign. All that we ask is if you cease to pay income tax in the future, please let us know.

I am a UK tax payer and would like the South West Coast Path Association to reclaim the tax paid on any subscriptions or donations I make to them.

Please sign here: Date:

Signature(s)

Please send completed form to: Liz Wallis, Administrator, South West Coast Path Association, Bowker House, Lee Mill Bridge, Ivybridge PL21 9EF. Tel: 01752 896237 Fax: 01752 893654

INTRODUCTION TO THE SOUTH WEST COAST PATH ASSOCIATION

Whilst walking the path, or on any other occasion, should you meet someone interested in this book, the Association, or the Coast Path, do not worry if no one has a pencil and paper - just tear off one of these:

The South West Coast Path Association was formed 37 years ago to promote the interest of users of our Coast Path. We continue to press the authorities to maintain it properly and to complete the path. An annually updated guide to the whole 630 miles (1014 km) of the South West Coast Path is issued to members every Spring. They also receive newsletters that provide the latest news about the state of the path.

For information about membership and how to obtain this annual guide, contact:

SWCPA, Bowker House, Lee Mill Bridge, Ivybridge, PL21 9EF

T: 01752 896237   **F:** 01752 893654
E: info@swcp.org.uk   **W:** www.southwestcoastpath.org.uk

The South West Coast Path Association was formed 37 years ago to promote the interest of users of our Coast Path. We continue to press the authorities to maintain it properly and to complete the path. An annually updated guide to the whole 630 miles (1014 km) of the South West Coast Path is issued to members every Spring. They also receive newsletters that provide the latest news about the state of the path.

For information about membership and how to obtain this annual guide, contact:

SWCPA, Bowker House, Lee Mill Bridge, Ivybridge, PL21 9EF

T: 01752 896237   **F:** 01752 893654
E: info@swcp.org.uk   **W:** www.southwestcoastpath.org.uk

The South West Coast Path Association was formed 37 years ago to promote the interest of users of our Coast Path. We continue to press the authorities to maintain it properly and to complete the path. An annually updated guide to the whole 630 miles (1014 km) of the South West Coast Path is issued to members every Spring. They also receive newsletters that provide the latest news about the state of the path.

For information about membership and how to obtain this annual guide, contact:

SWCPA, Bowker House, Lee Mill Bridge, Ivybridge, PL21 9EF

T: 01752 896237   **F:** 01752 893654
E: info@swcp.org.uk   **W:** www.southwestcoastpath.org.uk

The South West Coast Path Association was formed 37 years ago to promote the interest of users of our Coast Path. We continue to press the authorities to maintain it properly and to complete the path. An annually updated guide to the whole 630 miles (1014 km) of the South West Coast Path is issued to members every Spring. They also receive newsletters that provide the latest news about the state of the path.

For information about membership and how to obtain this annual guide, contact:

SWCPA, Bowker House, Lee Mill Bridge, Ivybridge, PL21 9EF

T: 01752 896237   **F:** 01752 893654
E: info@swcp.org.uk   **W:** www.southwestcoastpath.org.uk